T0196201

PLAYING GOD

Intuitive Reflections and Discourse on Life

BROWN OGWUMA

iUniverse, Inc.
New York   Bloomington

PLAYING GOD

Intuitive Reflections and Discourse on Life

Copyright © 2010 by Brown Ogwuma

All rights reserved. No part of this book may be used or reproduced by any means, graphic, electronic, or mechanical, including photocopying, recording, taping or by any information storage retrieval system without the written permission of the publisher except in the case of brief quotations embodied in critical articles and reviews.

iUniverse books may be ordered through booksellers or by contacting:
iUniverse
1663 Liberty Drive
Bloomington, IN 47403
www.iuniverse.com
1-800-Authors (1-800-288-4677)

Because of the dynamic nature of the Internet, any Web addresses or links contained in this book may have changed since publication and may no longer be valid. The views expressed in this work are solely those of the author and do not necessarily reflect the views of the publisher, and the publisher hereby disclaims any responsibility for them.

ISBN: 978-1-4502-1853-5 (pbk)
ISBN: 978-1-4502-1854-2 (ebk)
ISBN: 978-1-4502-2090-3 (hbk)

Library of Congress Control Number: 2010904983

Printed in the United States of America
iUniverse rev. date: 6/2/10

Contents

Glossary of Terms

Word/Term	Meaning
Adanne (Ada Nne)	Ada, first daughter; Nne, mother. Together, Mother's first daughter. In Igbo culture, younger siblings and half-siblings often opt to appropriately call the first daughter Ada Nne, and sometimes before her first name.
Daa (Da).	An Igbo (Ngwa) term, prefixed to the name of an older female, to show respect; as calling that person by her first name without this prefix is culturally seen as a blatant disrespect.
Dede (Dee/De).	As in Daa above, but applies to older male.
Ọfọ-na-Ogu.	An embodiment of morality and at the core of Igbo traditional relating with Chuwkwu (the supreme deity and the behind-it-all of all manifestations). "The Igbo believe in the concept of Ọfọ and Ogu, which is like the law of <u>retributive justice</u>. It is believed that Ọfọ and Ogu will vindicate anyone that is wrongly accused of a crime as long as their "hands are clean". It is only the one who is on the side of Ogu-na-Ọfọ that can call its name in prayer. Otherwise such a person will face the wrath of Amadioha (the god of thunder and lightning)".
Pharaohdom.	Pharaoh-like Kingdom. To operate, function, and carry on, mostly ruthlessly, unreflectively, and remorsefully, in the mold of the Ancient Egyptian Kingdom of the Pharaohs.
Pharaohites.	The loyal, devoted, and die-hard believers and operatives of the Pharaohdom.

Preface

There is hardly such a thing as equal opportunity in life, irrespective of allusions to such. Although efforts by human societies and governments to promote equal opportunity in employment/jobs or in other spheres of human endeavor are noteworthy, attaining that state will remain elusive. On the human level, for as long as something in humans causes them to judge and discriminate; life chances and opportunities will continue to favor and disfavor individuals and groups differently.

The reflections presented in this discourse, *Playing God*, would interest all people of inquisitive mind and those struggling with reconciling the puzzles in life, therefore seeking knowledge; particularly adults and others for whom conventions, the everyday, and the "obvious" are no longer what they seem and claim to be. From my fellow Igbo of the ethnic group of Southeastern Nigeria, where Christianity successfully demagogued and displaced the traditional religion, to the rest of Nigeria and Africa where this also obtains, *Playing God* will captivate the reader. Beyond that region of the world to the United States where I have now spent about half of my life and elsewhere, this will be the case also, for the inquisitive mind.

Whether through tradition, religion, culture, or other convention, one has been taught and has learned to "pull oneself up by the bootstraps" or to self-blame when not able to do so. It does not matter whether or not one had feet, let alone boots, when one started out in life. If this first orientation to life is rooted in organized religion; one has learned, even as a baby/child, that s/he has committed some sin against "God's" dictates. The implication is that one chose to belong to Satan's network. One further learned that his/her making that "choice" contributed to making "God's" perfect world the horror it has become. Cursed and condemned by God for the rest of his/her life, therefore, one is punished to suffer till his/her death.

It is not that difficult to imagine the potentially crippling damage resulting from immersing children, given that they are in their formative years, in such a spiritual sea of guilt and the shame they bear as a result could cause. For this to be the fate of even one person at any point in his/her life is one expense too many in the name of the god. One such example is Matthew J. Murray, aged twenty-four, the gunman in the deadly shootings in the Youth with a Mission (YWAM) group in Arvada and the New Life Church in Colorado Springs, both in the state of Colorado, United States, on Sunday, December 9, 2007. Ordinarily, Murray's deep Christian upbringing would suggest that he is a "child of God." That, however, may have been the root of his problem, at least going by his understanding. Here's some background information on Murray:

> Murray was homeschooled in a deeply religious Christian household, and he attended, but did not complete, a missionary training program at the YWAM Arvada facility in 2002. Early on in the investigation, law enforcement officials stated that Murray had been sending "hate mail" to the program and that he "hated Christians," the religion in which he had been raised. Before the second shooting, Murray left several violent and threatening messages on several religious Web sites, espousing his hatred for Christianity and his intentions on killing as many Christians as possible. One message read: *"I'm coming for EVERYONE soon and I WILL be armed to the ... teeth and I WILL shoot to kill. ... God, I can't wait till I can kill you people. Feel no remorse, no sense of shame, I don't care if I live or die in the shoot-out. All I want to do is kill and injure as many of you ... as I can especially Christians who are to blame for most of the problems in the world."* … One psychologist even offered her services after reading his poem called "Crying all alone in pain in the nightmare of Christianity."

The urge would be to dismiss all this as an isolated case of a lunatic with nothing to do with his Christian background and experience. But if information from a patient in the cause of his/her diagnosis and treatment is solicited and considered, the information from Matthew Murray himself regarding his problem must be looked at seriously and analyzed for a better understanding of his circumstances. Dismissing it should not be an option.

From the early religious initiation into the worthless sinner formulation emerges this modus operandi: *To God all good things are credited; to Satan all bad things are attributed and blamed.* Therefore I say to you, the reader, if you have operated in this mind-set and have, or have periodically had, some questions around bearing this burden of having a role, through a sin you supposedly committed just because you were born, and the self-blame that goes with it, read on. You may find and/or resolve that there is another, informed way, through an analytical look at facts, to approach life and its overwhelming unknowns. One thing that you could do is, given that life has been credited to an omniscient and omnipotent "God," resolve to purge yourself of that burden of guilt and blame "God" instead for not living up to "his" omniscient and omnipotent qualities, and feel no guilt about putting the blame where it rightfully belongs. You may also understand how and why I have asserted that *playing God* to help improve the life they have to live is what humans, including you, have had to do. Simply put, humans have stepped in to try filling the void that "God's" imperfection and failure created.

On that imperfection, I do not realistically expect humans to eradicate the uneven playing field that "God" himself put in place—lopsided fortunes that are rooted in variable factors that are both visible and invisible. Specifically, race, complexion, skin pigmentation, height, size, looks, region and geography of the world, control and power, innate and constitutional endowments, and genetic inheritance, for instance, all play into opportunities and life chances.

I am appreciative of the life I have had so far. Anyone who knows my life's history, and not just my family name, would understand why I do appreciate what I have in life. I have been so blessed that I have been able to make lemonade from the lemon that life dealt me in my early to middle teenage years with the loss of my father. Born to my parents, the eleventh of the twenty-two children of my father and the second of my mother's five, in Nigeria, I'm an Igbo by origin and grew up in my rural and agrarian community and environment.

Knowing the way life is and unfolds differently for individuals, it could be, or could have been, worse. *Playing God*, therefore, is not an exercise in venting or complaints about failings or misfortunes in my personal life. Far from it, this is just a discourse based on intuitive promptings that stem from the complexities and convoluted nature of life. These reflections, sentimental as they may be, are indeed factually based. I will be discussing concrete and actual life situations—mine and those of other people. Typical discussions on the phenomena and course of life approach the subjects mainly on an abstract level, dealing with words, semantics, and concepts. This discourse will take a practical dimension.

Until I reached this level of maturity in life, I would have taken all the credit for having done well despite my earlier not-so-good fortune. But seeing and knowing life the way I now do, I could assert that certain innate aspects of me in particular, as well as parental heritage, factored into my success. So I consider myself blessed and fortunate. While I find myself this blessed, there are some other people who may have been in similar, better, or worse situations than I was who were or are not able to fair as well or better. Admittedly, people do make bad choices. However, bad choices cannot always explain circumstances, achievements, success, or failures. It should be clear that some factors behind life's outcomes are beyond the control of the individual. Take ill health and the illness of diabetes for instance; how and why would anyone choose to have his or her pancreas not produce enough insulin to regulate the sugar into which the food he or she eats is converted so that he or she would become diabetic and have some limbs amputated, become blind in some cases, or even die?

The fact is that in life, chaos, and stress, and tragedy are the norm and not the exception. Making this observation here reminds me of a discussion I had with Simon, an African from Tanzania, who was a colleague as we both worked for Night Hawk Restaurant, South Congress Avenue, Austin, Texas, back in the early 1980s. Simon had talked about a man back in his community in Tanzania, who was always drunk. This man is said to be so routinely drunk that should one found him sober, which was rare, that one would be shocked to the point of questioning one's sight or perception, and would unavoidably ask: *What's wrong*? If the Adam of some religions comes to anyone's mind here as the cause for the agony and mortality of humans, I'll bring Adam into some limited focus in the course of this discourse.

Having come of age chronologically and biologically, I'm excited that I have also come of age mentally. The fact of my coming of age mentally is evident in my engaging in a discourse of this nature. The level of conviction I or anyone so inspired to feel is such that it could not be hidden or disguised. This has meant that much as I try to tone things down around my wife, Ngozi Beatrice, who joined me here in the United States some years ago from Nigeria, recently found to be a very religious nation, it is difficult for me to hold back enough. So, she gets to hear me philosophize about life, and she is getting used to it, I might add, for she is more "understanding" of me now. As the deeply embedded official corruption has left the majority of Nigerians so crippled and trapped in poverty, they have done just about everything to wrap themselves in religious faith for hope and to numb the harsh reality, even as they are also fleeced and further plundered by the con artists of religion. Therefore, in the Nigerian environment of recent years, being religious automatically connotes or translates to being good and doing right. The labels of "born-again" and "Christian mothers, fathers, brothers, and sisters" automatically connote goodness and doing right; making those labels what matter. Then, there is my young adult son, Uba, who has shown strong traits for independent thinking. While it took me much longer than his current age to emancipate mentally to where I am now, Uba appears to be doing so much sooner. As one who now has little or no respect for ideologues and closed minds and the indoctrination and brainwashing that programmed and sealed them, I am very satisfied that my son is opting not to cede his mind to the control of others, but to engage it and be the master of it. He questions life and the authenticity of religion.

As I reminisce about my life, I have decided to capture in writing the dialogues, many of them rhetorical, that I have engaged in while doing so. *Playing God* is my way of capturing this mental exercise as broadly as makes sense to me at this time in my life. My sense is that the great thinkers of earlier or ancient times who blazed similar trails were conformists in the early stages of their lives. They had to be because everyone starts out and grows up only knowing and dealing with the everyday societal norm. Then along the way, something in their life experiences and about the nature of life itself caused them to explore and espouse ideas and ideals beyond the ordinary, many of which eventually were embraced and grew to be the norm over time. It is along this line that some of the famous quotes of the modern times arose. One is this by Robert Francis Kennedy, a brother of the former president of the United States, John Fitzgerald Kennedy, in his time as a United States Senator and the attorney general: "There are those that look at things the way they are, and ask, why? I dream things that never were; and ask why not?"

Similar trends are captured also in the reggae music lyrics of Jimmy Cliff, like the one saying that too many people are suffering and too many people are sad. That too few people have everything, while too many people have nothing. He goes on to wish for a remaking of the world with love and happiness, and putting one's conscience to the test.

In essence, this is about what could have been or what was not but is prompted by what is. The what is has shaped all manner of things in life, including, of course, human behaviors and the endemic competitions on different levels—intrapersonal and interpersonal, intracommunal and intercommunal, intranational and international, intracontinental and intercontinental, intraregional and interregional, and intraworld. On one level of the competition is the inherent that comes naturally with being a living organism that needs to continue living, as one must compete with others, and even with self, for the scarce resources one needs to survive and live. On the other is the learned—driven and fueled by human excesses. In the latter category, and on its different levels, it has gone beyond what is reasonable for surviving, thriving, and succeeding, to competition for the sake of competing. Some border on personality issues, even on the non-personal levels of nations and regions. This could be seen in the paranoia that characterizes the way some nations operate. In their imagination or perception, something or someone is always after them, or they have gotten used to being number one and the most powerful, or on the top echelon, that power and top-notch status drive them. They cannot imagine life without the sense of who they are, and they'd rather not live to be outstaged in the spotlight and would do just about anything—including bombing others to blazes—to hold on to their highly coveted position and spot.

A few words about vernacular—the use of a few sentences, phrases, and words of my native Igbo language in this discourse—some convention in published written work in English is to be wary of those. My understanding of that wariness is the desire to not alienate one's audience/readers. Believing, as I do, that my audience or an audience for a work of this nature would understand that some anecdotes would feature here and my personal life experience is bound to include my culture of origin, I believe some thoughts would best be captured for me when expressed in the words and context of the culture. Also, in every one of those injections, an English translation follows immediately. Therefore, those should not, and would not, work to disengage the reader.

With the introduction that follows next, this is how I have laid out this discourse:

Chapter 1, "Rhetorical Dialogues," describes the mental exercise that I engage in as I look at and try to reconcile what actually obtains in life with what I have been taught to accept as real about life. That there is no reconciling of the two, except in perpetuation of the make-believe realities, is what triggers those mental engagements. If the reader frees his/her mind of prejudices, s/he should find that the contemporary and legendary events used to challenge dogma suddenly have better meaning and yield appreciable insight. Chapter 2, "Life," beginning by describing some abstract things about life, cites actual life experiences of some individuals and humanity in general. This opens up the crediting of life to one almighty God to examination. This is because that notion could hardly hold up in the light of the irreducible facts laid out in this chapter.

Chapter 3 takes a look at the purpose of life vis-à-vis a purpose in life and challenges one (the reader) to look ahead, while one lives, and truly identify what one's life would mean in the end, considering all one had to contend with to get to live while one could. Chapter 4 focuses on morality and its source—human or God—especially in the light of the contentious nature of life and surviving in it, given also the many who are victimized by fellow humans and by nature. Chapter 5 looks into and dissects religion. Particular focus is on the claim of proponents of religion that they know for sure that a God almighty is the source of life and the case made that religion is a socially and culturally constructed reality, a fact that is wished away, ignored, and overlooked. Chapter 6, "Conflict," assesses the place and role of conflict—imbedded in nature or wrought by humans for a number of excuses—in the lives of individuals and those of a community and nations. The reader should be able to come to see that but for human excesses, life could and would be less draining, if humans were able to focus on things they share in common and let go of others that divide them. Chapter 7 takes a look at intraworld relations and politics and what they have contributed to making the world more contentious, with the powerful wanting more power in a world that has become more of a global society, due to and despite human advancements in science and technology. The next, chapter 8, "The Future Is Now," is a realization, through my personal life experience from earlier years, that having played God, pulling myself up by my bootstraps for a good part of my life, I needed to live life in the now, which was the future, before I died. And I suggest that everyone does so. The last chapter, chapter 9, "Death," symbolically ends this discourse, just like it ends life. It looks into some of the ways death occurs, considers what could be described as getting a second chance at life after coming so close to death—near-death experiences (NDEs)—and some of things death has been blamed on (causes of death). Considering that death is a natural end of life, I termed those causes "blames."

In documenting this discourse, I put some emphasis on highlighting some concepts, ideas, and topics by putting them in subheadings and/or in bold print. I have also cast some charts in one or two tables in the main text. Doing this, I am hoping not to have points that might excite the reader buried or hidden in a sea of text but to have them jump out at the reader, grabbing his/her attention, and probably help make his/her reading fun.

Introduction

To state or even imply that people play God would most probably conjure some negative reactions or feelings in many people, particularly religious adherents and the political "conservative" rear fringe. Seen through these prisms, one's opinions and actions would be judged as a foolish and perilous encroachment on what is considered the exclusive domain of the one and only almighty God. In the context to be discussed here, "God" is defined as the source of life and all manifestations; the behind-it-all, and could be interchanged with "nature." To religion, however, and Christianity, in particular; God is definitely and certainly known to be encapsulated in a human form, and a male. He is also perfect, omnipotent, omniscient, omnipresent, immortal, kind, merciful, compassionate, just, fair, forgiving, and in control of all heavenly and earthly transactions. By implication, he is conscious and conscientious. For the ability to be in control of all heavenly and earthly transactions stems from his being conscious and omnipresent, while his qualities of justice and fairness stem from his being conscientious. From these above distinctions, there is a marked difference in the meanings of "God" from the two perspectives—religion and this discourse.

To illustrate the point of "playing God;" consider again that the concept of God, as it applies to this discourse, is the source of life and all manifestations. Beyond manifestations, however, life needed sustaining and prolonging—the way humans see it, at least. And from what humans assume and the way they have carried on, albeit stemming mostly from religious faith, God so loves the life he gave that he is also desirous of sustaining and prolonging it. For this purpose, of sustaining and prolonging life, the realities/manifestations of air, water, sunshine, and edible objects (food) in their manifested forms, did not prove adequate. Humans, admittedly with their natural endowments, stepped in to do more to enhance what has been manifested to achieve sustenance and prolongation of life. What humans have done through the ages, and still do, to accomplish a good degree of sustenance and prolongation of the life that God riginated, therefore, I see as playing God—again, a role inherently human.

Positively implicit in the above is the fact that humans have done a great deal for humanity. These inherent survival deeds include playing critical roles in relieving what ails fellow humans. Sometimes, this comes by way of compassion and empathy in incidents and events of prolonged suffering, some of which come in the form of terminal diseases. For the care, compassion, and empathy they show, individuals are sometimes better positioned and disposed to decide that a loved one's life may no longer be worth the agony, especially when the prognosis points to no remission of the ailment, but an obvious termination of life. Making such determinations and others that include aborting fetuses that have been determined to be deformed or diseased have routinely drawn the condemnation of "playing God" from the religious zealot and the conservative rear fringe. Mostly, this is the side of playing God—the foolish and perilous encroaching on the exclusive domain of the religion's almighty God—that gets attention. It does not matter that without humans playing God on the side of complementing what God has started and left off at a point; many a life would be lost prematurely. Any decision by anyone to end any life, irrespective of its state or quality, is judged negatively and condemned. Whether or not playing God is a concept that should be understood and treated as above is what needs to be reviewed vis-à-vis the perspective and context of this discourse. In presenting the other concept of "playing God," this discourse is clear that humans play an inherent role in sustaining life and that there is nothing wrong in this.

My intent or goal here is not to persuade anyone to adopt my point of view. I do not believe it takes persuasion to get to this position, as discussed here. Getting here unfolded for me in the journey of my life. On some level, I don't know whether or how I would have fully come to this position had I not lived what is now a big chunk of my life in the United States. With her global interest/domineering role in the world and the ability, through technology, to saturate and beam (like floodlight to make clearer visually) the world, the United States has given me what I consider a vantage mountaintop view of the world, allowing me to get a solid perspective on life. Getting to this position does not and did not happen overnight. The unfolding would only occur at some point in the life journeys of individuals so disposed. Not everyone can replace religion as his or her major tool for coping with life, and organized religion knows it can count on that *ad infinitum,* probably.

I want to point out here that I intentionally will repeat some words or thoughts in this discourse. Among those to be repeated is what I term the ascribed qualities of God: *perfect, omnipotent, omniscient, omnipresent, immortal, kind, merciful, compassionate, just, fair, forgiving;, and in control of all heavenly and earthly transactions.* This is for emphasis and also to help illustrate contrasts, contradictions, and obvious paradoxes. As I so repeat, I'll try to be careful not to be redundant. Hopefully, the reader will find them not to be redundant, or tautological, like I did not.

My hope, overall, is that the reader is challenged, excited, and entertained, and that s/he has fun with this discourse.

Chapter 1

Rhetorical Dialogues

The rhetorical dialogue is a process that I have personally engaged in as I reflect on life, its mysteries, miracles, conflicts, intrigues, glories, and abounding tragedies. I will be describing here the mental activities that intuitively kick in for me and prompt me to take a second, third, fourth, and even more look over time at the many and differing factors of practical everyday living experiences. This is more so because the reality of this experience obviously runs counter to the tenets that were inculcated early in my life that form the foundation on which I fall back and the lens through which I look, to attempt making sense of the living experience. Suffice it to say that taking things at face value is not illuminating, as things are not always what they seem and looks could be deceiving.

As these dialogues are real, they will be expressed here the same way they hold, like it is, or like I see them—mostly unfiltered and real—observing little or no political correctness rules. Like exercises of its nature, they are honest, in that they come naturally. Not sharing or communicating them the same way compromises them and really reduces them to typical, everyday exchanges and concepts, that no matter how successful as a documented and acclaimed work are but conspiracies to achieve selfish ends. What I am doing here with a discourse of this theme fits into an exception, as the norm with people in life is to gravitate or be drawn to ideas or concepts that give them formulas to feel they can achieve. This explains the huge religious congregation audiences or those of other presentations on physical and emotional health, which are so consumed by what they hear that they are glued and fixed on the presenter with profound attention. In contrast, this discourse cuts to the chase of distortions of what ultimately prevails in life. Not very many people are ready to hear this or are likely to ever be ready to face it before it comes through.

These reflections on life grew over time and became routine, deeper, and wider, I believe, with experience and maturity. Rhetoric is fitting of this process because rhetoric is not just oratorical and public speech, it is also persuasion. These dialogues, the discourse within, have steered me to the theory that humans indeed do "play God" in many positive ways. That these "interactions" are within and in a thinking-through processes make them dialogues. For a man, me, who in the journey of life, has reached the half-century point and beyond, it definitely took considerable coping and adaptive mechanisms to make it this far; although, relatively speaking, fifty-plus years could also be considered young. To underscore this point, Bob Hope, the famous American comedian, once used this one-liner when talking about the older George Burns, a fellow comedian, who was also famous and also near or above one hundred years old then, "George Burns is one man who could still say to me, 'Come here, boy!'" And like the boy he was (as they are both now dead) to George Burns, Bob Hope skipped and hopped his way to George Burns.

The mechanisms humans employ to cope in the arduous life journey span the gamut of the physical and concrete through the religious, the spiritual, the mental health (practical), and others. Over time, there has been a paradigm shift for me in the emphasis on which one of these models for coping serves my needs better. Born to my Igbo parents of Southeastern Nigeria way after Christianity was exported to Nigeria from the Western world, successfully demagouging and displacing the religion of my foreparents, I was inevitably born into and immersed in Christianity. Naturally, therefore, the Christian religion and its model was the way to identify with, relate to, and cope with life for the most part of my life thus far. The shift in emphasis to the practical (mental health) came for me in the past few years.

As a living and thinking being, the more I became contented with this shift in my psychic coping, the more I realized that it was a matter of time before this shift took hold. After all, the biblical stories are but culturally based fictional stories of the Jewish/Hebrew people of the Middle East and are littered with fictional characters and legends just like those of other cultures, including those of my heritage.

Belief, Faith, the Mind, and Psychology
While relying on my Christian tenets to understand life and the world does not make sense to me any longer, I recognize that numerous other followers of that faith still find it meeting their

needs for answers and coping. Given the subjective nature of faith and beliefs, this is not a surprise. Objectivity and universality are not attributes of belief, because belief and faith are functions of the mind, and the human mind is vulnerable and susceptible to influence. So, for as long as anyone remains sold on concepts and perspectives, that person continues to see and hear as he or she is predisposed. With this predisposition, that person would swear by the familiar perception.

Seeing in the Mirror What One Wishes for, Expects, or Is Looking to See

I am reminded here of a statement that my wife credits to her younger sister, Nkechi. This is on the issue of people who look odd in their attire and seem not to care about it, which makes one wonder whether or not that individual ever looked in the mirror. Nkechi is said to remark that one sees in the mirror what one wishes for and expects to see, *a self-fulfilling prophecy* actually, as what the mirror actually reflects and projects never registers. With the mind so boxed in and stowed away, all the individual does is say: "My mind is made up; the facts only stress and confuse me." Reality, then, becomes a subjective function of the mind, as perceived in one's mind; for perception is reality, as reality is also perception.

Because of its aspects of vulnerability and susceptibility, the human mind is constantly targeted, bombarded, and influenced for different purposes. The battle for the mind is pitched from different and diverse sources: business, through commercials and ads, to market and sell products; governments and politicians for support of points of view and for votes; religions and other groups spinning for identification with their faith and the values they represent.

While the Christian vows his God is the only real deal and superior to those of other religions, the Hindu, the Muslim, the Buddhist, the Animist, and people of other faiths, do just fine with their faith and beliefs. I would be remiss here if I didn't mention that Ọfọ-na-Ogu, the traditional/cultural belief of my Igbo heritage, meets my spiritual needs.

Just consider the fact that some people cannot stand the sight or imagine the killing of animals—for food, clothing, or other purposes; yet others kill in a heartbeat, for their religious faith, their country, or to prevail in some personal altercation. Those familiar with the Jonestown massacre in the Caribbean Island of Guyana in 1978 could understand that aspect of mind control. In that tragedy, it was learned that about 913 of the 1,100 followers and members of the Reverend Jim Jones had committed suicide in "the

People's Temple" commune in conformity with their faith and belief. A similar incident happened at Rancho Santa Fe in California in March 1997, where thirty-nine members of the Heaven's Gate Christian group took their own lives, believing they were entering heaven.

Imagine also how nations glorify soldiers for going out to kill and die, which I admit is a heck of a task. But soldiers and soldiering are created by nations as the answer to threats—real, imagined, or whimsically concocted and provoked by politicians pursuing political philosophies and agendas in the name of patriotism. To the discerning mind, soldiers are created by a regimen of psychological and physical conditioning and programming that achieves depersonalization of hideous murderous acts and demonization of those who disagree with the leading politicians of nations. For those going out and destroying as programmed to, the psychological mix of brainwashing includes awarding medals and memorializing the dead and living soldier through the erection of monuments and performance of annual rituals. Flaunt before young/upcoming and impressionable people the prospect of being immortalized heroes and patriots, dead or alive, and that of employment and/or a career, mechanical killers who readily accept what they're fed as real and the truth are created. Yes, they are branded heroes. The fact is that they are zeroes for the most part—fungible, used, and discarded.

Granted that all humans are always under one form of influence or another, it also takes the mature, rounded, and grounded person to do a better gatekeeping of his mind. This means that one who is well versed, anchored, and secure in his word will not always fall easily to the barrage of assaults on the mind for influence and control.

For being part of this experience called life, humans have no choice but to submit to certain influences. For instance, acquiring educational and vocational skills, getting a job, and belonging to social, economic, cultural, and other groups automatically subject one to some influence. But some beliefs and/or faiths that claim to have a lock on the real truth are ignoring that reality and the truth, in the realm that I discuss, are subjective, not universal.

Going forward, this discourse goes through the path that the rhetorical dialogues have taken, causing me to conclude that humans inevitably share with God the responsibility and credit for life. While the role of humans in life may have always seemed obvious, the point that needs emphasizing is that without this role, inherent in humans, that rises to "playing God," the life created by God would not be as known. It follows, therefore, that the concept of this discourse was inspired by the fact that I found too many paradoxes and fallacies between the practical reality of life and the biblical/

Christian answers to life and the living experience. Suffice it to say that my Christian/religious foundation and its scripts seem to fall far short and became less persuasive the more I attempted to fall back on them. I so wished, and still remotely do occasionally, that the biblical formulations and constructs held true. Frustratingly, indications are that it shows no potential to so hold. Like a child, I have wished for the magical realization of the serene concepts presented to me.

Just envisage the thoughts and feelings of a child who, after believing in Santa Claus/Father Christmas, gets to realize that he may not exist really. Imagine having the only one, all-knowing, all-able, perfect, conscious, conscientious, merciful, loving, just, and actively in-charge God, who is encapsulated in a human-like body, doing right by all his children. The lots in life of all people and everybody would have faired far better. In fact, they could have been perfect. It is in the course and process of juxtaposing this illusionary biblical construct to what really obtains and repeatedly finding the former lacking that both prompted the shift for me and, again, inspired these reflections and this discourse.

Perspectives on God
The commonalities and diversities in life do not help in this God puzzle. Instead, they complicate things further. Take humans, for instance, many things—good/ill health, emotion, etc.—are shared and affect them the same way. Conversely, experiences, inheritances, and chances at life, among other things, differ. Religion has been one, if not the major, way that most people look for clues and answers to life matters. This has meant that God is at the center of all religious faith. God being at the center of all religious faith seems to be where the agreement among different faiths ends, as they do differ in their interpretation of God's words and ways. The reality, plainly, is that there are perspectives to God. This informs the intrareligious and interreligious and denominational conflicts and polarizations to the point of doing battles that result in the killing of the mortal faithful and followers in order to protect the immortal God, apparently.

The Metaphor of an Elephant Beholden by Blind Men
One way to look at perspectives on God and even life generally is the allegory of the elephant and the blind men, who upon feeling and imagining the elephant came away with different conclusions of what it is like. One likened it to a tree after feeling the legs; another, feeling the ear, found the semblance of an umbrella; and yet another, feeling the tail, likened it to broom, etc.

5

A religious ideologue reading this may see it as crazy or call me personally crazy. My response to this is that life and its reality is nothing short of crazy, with the ideologue's spin on life and God equally crazy or *crazier.* That my imagined ideologue's thoughts here are centered on and in his defense of God goes to the crux of the craziness, for God could have unquestionably saved the world from this; yet the craziness stems from questions and uncertainties about him.

The 2004 Tsunami

A further illustration of the way people of different leanings who are looking at exactly the same issue could infer different meanings and messages is this discussion on tsunami. The U.S. Fox channel's program, *Scarborough Country*, featured a panel of three—two women, one Christian, one Atheist; and one male, a Jewish rabbi—to discuss the notorious 2004 tsunami and its savage ravaging of Southeast Asia. The Christian sermonized that the devastation was God's punishment on the world for deviating from and not abiding by his will. Ticked off by this statement, the rabbi jumped in and lambasted the Christian, calling her blasphemous, and rhetorically asked, and I paraphrase, "What type of God would punish the people of Southeast Asia, including poor women and children, for the sins of the world?" Continuing, he added, "I sure do not want to see that God."

The atheist then retorted, paraphrasing also, "What else is needed to prove that there is no God, and that if we don't take care of each other, nothing else will?"

As far as faith-based concepts go, there may always be stubborn attacks on the point of perceptions not equating reality. Because natural disasters are sometimes termed the "act of nature," or the "act of God;" the Christian in the Tsunami panel here may be embracing the "act of God" term, and using that to make her case for God's punishment of the world for not following his dictates. Alternately, the term "act of God" also lends some credence to a notion that a God that would unleash such wrath of savagery on his beloved children with heart and souls must be evil and the personification of it.

Where religion is not the root cause of devastating conflicts and wars, it has been employed and used as a divide-conquer-and-rule tool. The devastating, perennial war between the British and the Irish through the ages is one case where this applies, although both sides to this conflict are of the Christian faith, with the British being Protestant, and the Irish, Catholic. However it's diced, religion is indeed dangerous. It has been used and is still being used as a cover for ulterior motives, from the locale of those who seek dominion over others to elsewhere across the world.

It may not be common knowledge that the original conflict between the Catholics and Protestants in Ireland was a matter of social class. Below is some background information, per Wikipedia online, on this conflict/war in which religion eventually became employed as a dangerous tool.

The majority of the population in Ireland, post AD 1000, was Catholic. They never underwent the church reform that England did in the 1500s. Thus, by the 1600s, England = Anglican (Protestant), and Ireland = Catholic.

> When England began to establish plantations in Ireland and establish themselves as the ruling class, they often did it in a relatively unpleasant and domineering fashion, making themselves unpopular with their new subjects in the manner of America and India.

Hostility arose between Catholics and Protestants in this way not because the religions themselves bore marked differences, but because these denominations were attached to two very different classes. Intermarriages were frowned upon, not for spiritual reasons, but because the Protestant was marrying below their class.

This hostility between the denominations continued into the present for many of the same reasons. Protestantism represents the continued presence of England in Northern Irish affairs, while Catholicism bears the stigma of being the religion of the poor, the rebels, and the socialists intent on a free Ireland.

Still on religion-based perspectives on what different people would believe about their God, one often reads and hears in the Western media about "radical Islamists" and "Muslim fundamentalists." People so termed are said to commit horrific acts in the name of Islam and for the promise of seven virgins if they die in the pursuit of these acts considered horrific in the West. And to the West, where Christianity dominates, God promises, through Christ, the hope of heaven in the life hereafter, for those who meet the litmus test of the Ten Commandments and maybe more. While the Christian would find it ridiculous that God reserves seven virgins for anyone for the taking of life, for instance, the Muslim, conversely, would find it equally absurd that any "infidel" who intrudes on the sacred territory of an Islamic state for influence, dominance, and material control would inherit heaven from Allah—God.

Much as there is the necessity and wish for the meaning and the essence of God to be the same universally and to all people, the fact is that they are not. This fact holds because there is no one universal experience and perception in all facets of life in the consciousness of all mankind. Beginning with diverse racial and parental heritage, there is also diversity in the geographic place of birth, as well as in socialization, values, cultures, and other influences that come from the immediate environment. What obtains, therefore, are relative takes on God and nothing absolute or universal.

Playing God and Politics

Political ideologies are front and center in the arena of playing God here in the United States. Dr. Jack Kevorkian, the American physician known for assisting the hopelessly or terminally ill end their lives at their request, is one victim who had to languish in prison for years for obliging such requests. In the power play of the mostly two-winged political landscape, that the so-called social and cultural conservatives celebrated the jailing of Dr. Kevorkian needs to be stated. Whether or not a physician obliging the requests to assist in the ending of miserable lives is seen as humane, as I do, it is important to abide by the laws as long as they are in effect, even though working to change them may prove to be a tall if not impossible order politically. So, following the airing, on November 22, 1998, by CBS's *60 Minutes* news magazine, of a videotape showing Kevorkian administering a lethal injection to Thomas Youk, fifty-two, who suffered from Lou Gehrig's disease, the state of Michigan charged Dr. Kevorkian with first-degree murder, violating the assisted suicide law, and delivering a controlled substance without a license in the death of Mr. Youk. On April 13, 1999, a Michigan judge ruled on that lawsuit, convicting Dr. Kevorkian of second-degree murder and delivery of a controlled substance in the death of Youk. He, Dr. Kevorkian, was sentenced to ten to twenty-five years in prison, being eligible for parole in six years. Until then, Dr. Kevorkian had scaled many such lawsuits in different states. The incarceration of Kevorkian is an indication that such laws should be revisited with the intent to distinguish Kevorkian-like humanitarian work from a blatant ending of a fledging human life.

All said, Dr. Kevorkian's role described above, seen in the context of easing the pain of souls trapped in badly compromised bodies, was vital, necessary, and compassionate in the scheme of "playing God" that has been slated for humans.

Judging him and hurling him into jail only serves to feed into the power play and territorial posturing into which people have ditched themselves.

What this so-called conservative approach does is judge those who do not see this issue their way as tampering with life and therefore lacking morality. Ironically, though, despite their preaching of the sanctity of all life, including those compromised at the fetal and others at terminal stages, people so inclined also tend to be quick to start and wage wars and hurl those at the prime of their lives—teens and young adults—into premature death. Yet, they're blinded to this moral hypocrisy.

The politicizing of what should be a personal and private decision on whether life in a vegetative state ought to linger or end was very clear in the case of Terri Schiavo. Mrs. Schiavo was in a coma for about fifteen years and was certified clinically dead by physicians, but was kept "alive" by machine ventilation. Having exhausted all medical means through the years to revive and save her life, her husband, Michael Schiavo, decided that it was humane to end the torture and the illusion of hope by disconnecting the ventilation machine to allow his wife's body to slip out of the coma and into death.

To frustrate this decision by Mr. Schiavo, high-profile politicians of the "conservative" wing chose to exploit Mrs. Schiavo's plight to rally their base by both opposing Mr. Schiavo legally and by judging his decision as "liberal" and anti-life. Notable among those politicians was Tom Delay of Texas, a former Republican Party leader in the U.S. House of Representatives. Another was Jeb Bush, the younger brother of President George W. Bush and the governor the state of Florida, the home state of the Schiavos.

Chapter 2

Life

Life, what a torture and a waste! If this observation stuns you, read through this chapter and you may understand. A journey of, and an experience in, running scared, here is one formal definition of life found Webster's New World Dictionary of the American Language, Second College Edition:

> Life is that property of plant and animals which makes it possible for them to take in food, get energy from it, grow, adapt themselves to their surroundings, and reproduce their kind. It is the quality that distinguishes a living animal or plant from inorganic matter or dead organism.

Phenomenally, life is what all humans and lower life forms are thrust into. For humans, finding themselves so thrust, the business of living and preoccupies the entire journey of life from the beginning to the end. Inevitably, life gets to end—for individual humans so far and potentially for humanity and all lives ultimately. Through time, humans have tried to make sense of the phenomena of life, in terms of its source, meaning, purpose, and why, how, and where it ends. They have employed many media and channels to seek insight and to ease anxiety. On an organized level of some of these media of search, religion in particular, they have been told to accept what is and forget further probing for their own good and sanity. This is often advised in deference to and reverence for God, who is said to have so commanded and demanded of all his creatures, which he also commands to respect, fear, and remain ever loyal and thankful to him.

While many of the religious faithful buy and heed these commands, many others, still puzzled by the phenomena and not about to give up on their intuitively driven inquiry, still rhetorically ask and search. They also accept that their quest is but rhetorical and indefinite and still embark on this intuitive pursuit anyway. To these others, including myself, the satisfaction does not necessarily come from getting answers, for there may never be any, but from engaging in this process and logically following where it takes one. It is appropriate to point out here that apparently not all humans are capable of going beyond the tasks of everyday living to ponder on the level of the phenomena of life. Infants and children are one group to which this applies, for the reason that they have yet to develop physically and/or mentally the capacity for such. Another group are people who, although grown to adulthood physically, come unequipped to engage in such process. Also, there are individuals who never develop the mental capacity to function independently in life, irrespective of their physical size and numeric age, having been naturally stripped of that quality, as it were. These individuals do require assisted living their entire lives. While many humans come to life bountifully equipped, some others come profoundly stripped; some physically, some mentally, and some both.

The Amazement of Life
To behold life, all of life, is an amazingly awesome experience. By all of life, I mean life in basically two phases. One phase is the physical —the manifestations of space, day and night (sun and moon), shapes, forms, space; the topography of hills, mountains, rocks, valleys, water/seas/oceans; fertile/arable lands, dry/arid deserts, trees; animals of higher and lower order; and systems that are self-regenerating and sustaining. Despite the fact that "nature" did not provide an articulated, physical manual to guide these on how to self-regenerate and sustain, systematically they do. The other phase is the spiritual, the mental, intellectual, psychological—the non-physical.

The Animal as a Functional System
Focusing, for a moment, on the animal—higher (humans) and lower—and its internal functioning system, the thoughts get even more amazing. The head encases and protects the brain, the neurological (electrical) center that ignites and regulates the human system's functioning. The heart, which, like an engine, powers the system and pumps the blood (fuel) to the brain and the entire body, is encased in the thorax and rib cage. The arteries, like wires, are the conduit through which the heart pumps the blood to the brain and elsewhere in the body as needed. The nose, through

the nostrils, takes in the air, which the nose hairs filter, and lets it into the body where it is regulated by the lungs for the use and functioning of the body and for life to be sustained. As the body must be mobile to take care of the business of living; the legs, and most importantly, the motor skills, are in place to enable locomotion/ambulation. The hands, the wonderfully versatile instruments that aid the human to live life, like propellers, are also critical for locomotion through swinging. Like headlights, the eyes show the light and the way as registered in the brain, transmitted there through the optic nerves. For their part, the ears, like satellite dishes, aid in the registering of audio cues and communications through that medium as well. The tongue teams with the mouth in verbal communication. The liver helps break down the food consumed to aid digestion. To eliminate waste, the plumbing system includes the mouth, through which food is also ingested, the anus, the urethral openings, etc. This certainly is an amazing system in place that enables humans and animals to function. Apparently, humans modeled this original system, through science and technology, in the motor, automation, locomotion, and other engineered products that aid human life in the modern world.

Complementing Opposites
Inherent in the nature of life are the complementing opposites that make it continue. This is seen in pollination and cross-pollination in plants. Although animals may play a role in the process by constituting a transfer agent from one source to the other, regeneration, or the birth of a new life, is only possible when the male-female factors are present in the transferred properties.

Human Regeneration: The Complementing Male-Female Opposites
For regeneration, consider the beginning of the process for humans, for instance. At conception, the fetus starts the process of development, following impregnation. In the very early stages, gynecologists and obstetricians and others in this area of the medical field have, with the help of modern apparatuses, determined that the fetus is not distinguished as either male or female, as the budding genitalia has not so differentiated in the beginning. Depending on the interaction of the X and Y chromosomes; this changes internally, as the testes are formed in the male and the ovaries in the female. This eventually includes the forming of the entire male and female anatomies in the two complementing sexes. Also, in a way, the hormones responsible for human characteristics—the male testosterone and the female estrogen—perform their mysterious work. After birth when another process, this time of growth, begins and proceeds to the stage

of puberty; the male/female hormones continue to work their respective magic. For the male, physical and notable features include facial, chest, and pubic hair; broad chest; deep voice; bulking muscles and frame; and sprouting height. The female breasts bud, sprout, and protrude from the chest. The pubic hair appears, and menarche ensues. The hips expand, with the buttocks developing and becoming more pronounced. Overall, while the male figure generally becomes bigger and sturdier, that of the female, generally also, is relatively thinner, smaller, and "softer" and her frame shaped like the hourglass or the figure eight. In some cultures where women wear tight trousers, that their legs come close to a shape like the letter "X" is pronounced and evident. The female's features are also effeminate; especially as her socialization in her gender roles embellish these.

Out of the norm, one male not fitting the ideal male physique emerges out of so many, and, conversely, a big-framed and huge female also emerges out of many, constituting "a whole lot of woman," as my son, Uba, would say. The nature of these opposite, essentially positive and negative, but complementing features, are such that a mating of both—penile-vaginal copulation, conventionally—results in the impregnation of the female by the male and the birth, in due course, of another human. I rehash this common knowledge this much to bring commensurate context to bear on the intricacies of this systemic nature of life, even just on the minute area that I have chosen to illustrate, the things that are amazing about this phenomenon.

The Paradox
The above facts alone are enough for some to conclude the existence of a loving, almighty God, who has the intelligence and the mercy to create and give life. However, ponder the other of the two phases of "all life"—death, the end of all life. When this is not instant at birth, there are diseases; fending to survive; the tear, wear, and the breakdowns; posturing, fighting, and losing face for turf; aging, loss of glamour/vigor; and fading into the twilight. After this mental exercise of pondering, the question resulting naturally seems to be: if God is so intelligent and merciful to create and give life, as illustrated in the one phase, it must take his sadistic, crazy, or mortal side to allow the realities of this other phase or to fail to anticipate them, given his omniscient and omnipotent qualities alone. This, therefore, seems the beginning of the process of the inquiries and searches that have characterized the human life.

It is the resulting paradox of juxtaposing the two phases of "all life" that casts doubt about the form and the qualities of God as presented by religious, social, and institutional authorities. Humans desire answers, as uncertainty is unsettling. This in and of itself fuels human fascination with inquiries into and the re-examinations of life and its fabric. It is also this unsettling nature of uncertainty and the desire for a firm and settling reality that seemingly make people gravitate toward religious faith, in search of a magic wand—a cure-all—for the relief of anxiety, hence the conclusion, without the evidence to support that belief.

Here's how I sum up the argument that I must believe in "the God" and worship him:

1. That I was born into this world and life as part of humanity, with other humans who also have an individual identity
2. That I have a need to live and enjoy life while fearing and avoiding death
3. That achieving the 2 above is beyond my control and in that of "the God," which is evidenced by that fact I entered the life that I am desperate to keep living by no power of mine
4. That the only way for me to keep living and enjoying life is by being continuously beholden to "the God," begging him, and worshipping him for the rest of my life, and
5. That when I have been around enough to realize that I will die at some point despite my wishing death away and avoiding it, I'll shift into wishing to continue to live in "heaven" and would need to appease "the God" and hope he'll grant me this wish.

Because there must be a source of all manifestations, the behind-it-all; does it automatically translate to a male almighty that has skillfully and intelligently created? What is skillfully, artfully, and intelligently "created," especially by an omniscient, omnipotent, loving, compassionate, perfect and flawless almighty, should not and could not be riddled with so many flaws.

Staying locked into those conventional, irrational beliefs could have been my faith had I not been lucky to have lived this long, getting some exposure, good life experience, and some wisdom that have come with these. Among other things, this has meant that I have seen how things work out differently for different people for various reasons. For me, this has poked too many holes in what should have been an ironclad control of life for the better by the great and the almighty God. There's a good chance that had I not lived long enough to see things differently, I would have taken my childhood idea of God with me to my grave.

If I were to fit into the mold and track of my summation of the case made that I must believe in "the God" and "he" were to grant my wish and invite me to heaven, I would decline that favor on second thought. Not doing so would mean taking a big gamble. If it did happen before in that same God's perfect heaven that there was rebellion that made God flush Satan down to earth turning the also perfect earth to the dungeon of strife that it has since become, it could repeat in heaven. When it does the next time, having learned a lesson from sparing some in heaven during the first dissent, God would likely spare none next time around. It is the chance to embark on another journey mired in sin and punishment that I would not want to take.

With the options and possibilities at God's disposal, one would wonder, did it have to come to this reality as we, humans, know it? Personally, had I the luxury of just two options: the way it is now or not to be made, I would choose not to be made. In this scenario, the dialogue with God might have gone thus:

The Offer

God: Hello, Brown! I am God, the everlasting and the almighty one, the maker of all things. I have started my human creation business, and it's now your turn to be created. Would you want to be created? Just so you know, if you choose to be created, you'll have an amazing life. And for every moment of your living experience, you must be thankful to me. You must also continue to thank, praise, and remain beholden to me for the duration of your life.

I: I have heard about you, God, and it's a privilege to be speaking with you. Recall, God, that I was minding my business when you approached me with this offer. You, of all beings, should know that offers such as this should come with mutual benefit for the parties to the deal. Except for an amazing life that inures to me, all I have heard so far is my indebtedness to you—the praises and the thanks that I shall give to you. Do you mind clueing me in to what I would get from this deal of being created by you beyond an amazing life? Tell me more about the amazing life, please. Better yet, give me a written proposal spelling out what my benefits will be in this deal.

God hands me a document, which in bold print reads:

> You would have parents, siblings, and other humans and relatives to share your life and world with. You could also get to marry a woman who could be beautiful, and whose

company and relationship you will get to enjoy, and with whom you will have children.

I: One more thing, God, I heard you say earlier "… for the duration of your life." Exactly what did you mean by that?
God: Make sure you read all the information in the written proposal that I gave you.

I flip through the pages and notice fine print on the bottom of the last page—a disclaimer of sorts.

> You will need to acquire skills and education through training and learning from others who are in a position to impart such knowledge to you. You will also have to get a job to earn some income without which you may not enjoy life. Going through this process over time carries some consequences. These include bad relationships with bosses, peers, and subordinates, if you get to be elevated in your job. Personal relationships with your spouse and other family members also have the potential to be sour and painful. You will also experience stress, anxiety, worry, illnesses, and diseases. Also, at a time of my choosing, I will end your life. This means you will cease to exist—you will die—later in your life from old age, if I so choose, or much earlier, possibly when you're having it good and your family may need you desperately. With dying, being careful; doing certain things in certain ways may save you accidental death, which could result from utilizing some of the human-made implements you may use in your job to be more productive and efficient and others that help you improve the quality of your life to enjoy living.

> Accidental death may also result from your using other human-made materials that you may only be able to acquire from being successful, in order to make your life comfortable. Notable among these is an automobile and other means of rapid transportation by air, rail, and sea. Events and circumstances of catastrophic nature beyond the control of humans, maybe termed *natural disasters*, might strike. And depending on your geographic location on earth when any of these hit, you could be caught up in one. If you are, this could also mean the end of your life, or you could be left in a situation where you may lose a body part or become paralyzed. In such case, of course,

you would lose a significant part of your functioning and with it your quality of life. By the way, when you die, depending on your faith and/or belief, your body will be buried underneath the earth, burned/cremated, dumped into a river or into a forest. Depending on the mode of disposing of your body, it will rot and become manure that will feed plants and other forms of life, or constitute a meal for carnivorous animals that they too may live a while longer.

I: (Now thinking to myself: *What the ...? The devil is truly in the details, as they say. Fine print, even from God, tends to be more than the main text and tries to conceal the rip-off in deals. This God must be egomaniacal. He gets to stick around forever, and in the exclusive luxury of heaven, extorting praises and appreciations. All I get is a torturous, tentative life that he gets to waste as he pleases.*)

The Rejection
I (still): You know what, God; no. I am declining your offer. Thanks for seeking my consent though, and good luck with the next pawn and victim ... I mean the next person.

If the same offer to the next person results in acceptance and they are created, they know better than to blame anyone, even God, but themselves, when they realize what hit them. Having been created after turning down the offer, not pleased with what I was hearing, I justify following where these rhetorical dialogues take me. Given that no one had an option to opt in or out, life and its journey fit very well in the metaphor of a train stacked and stuffed with unwilling passengers, with no one getting a chance to leave until disposed to his or her grave, as the only destination of the train is the graveyard. Also, only a very few of the unwilling passengers were lucky enough to be stuffed into the graveyard-bound train with some food, water, or even some toilet paper to clean and groom for comfort; hence so many people struggle, toil, and distress in life.

To be clear, I have not concluded that the God of my childhood fantasies does not exist. Rather, I am resolving the stalemate surrounding the truth about his existence for myself that all evidence points to this being unknowable, even as his description and qualification vis-à-vis life's reality point to his existence being unrealistic, hence my leaning toward agnosticism.

Surviving and Holding on to Life

I would like to make a transition here to taking a pertinent look at the journey of life for an individual, having started with an overview of the grand scheme of life. Chances are that the nature of this discourse may take me back and forth from one level to the other. Humans have creatively come up with ways to preoccupy themselves with living life. These include finding activities, places, and people to shift their focus away from the grim realities of life as much as possible. However, as the glamour, like those of the television "reality" or the staged festivities of fiestas, jamborees, carnivals, religious crusades, gala events, etc., end, the individual retires privately to face the reality of living his/her life, littered with innumerable incidents and events the range of which is too large to capture.

For a little perspective and context, vis-à-vis life and humans as a product of a perfect God, except for the serpent, Eve, and Adam, humans are perpetually engulfed in fear of the unknown and the mostly unpredictable nature of life. The individual human is inundated with ailments from head to toe. A sampling of these in the cranium, include benign headaches to debilitating migraines, traumatic brain injury (TBI), brain attacks that result from damage to the little arterial endings in the brain, neurological diseases like Alzheimer's and others that result in slurred and lost speech, and epilepsy/convulsion. Add to these the diseases of the central nervous system, like Parkinson's. For the eyes, glaucoma lurks for those with hereditary predisposition to it, in many cases leading to blindness. In the mouth, gum diseases cause pain and difficulty chewing and eating food; people lose teeth, causing lips and jaws to collapse and compress, creating an ugly, embarrassing look, which in turn causes people some social and mental anguish.

Many are born with a cleft palate—a disfigurement of the lip(s) that exposes the teeth and leaves the mouth open to an influx of infections—subjecting the so deformed to shame, embarrassment, and social rejection. Others are born with Down's syndrome, condemning them to a disability so pronounced in the face area, affecting the eyes, lips, and tongue, stunting their brains and the functions of speech, and even limiting their life spans. In the thorax (chest) region of the body are the all-devastating heart disease, heart failure, and heart attack. The same is true for the torso/abdomen/stomach area, with liver and kidney diseases and failure. Consider also the crippling diseases of the knee and bones that potentially and do end motor, locomotion, and ambulatory ability—rheumatoid arthritis, leukemia, ALS, and others. The problems of high blood sugar and diabetes and high blood pressure and hypertension and the deadly aneurism/stroke afflict more and more people.

The World of Angels and of Spirits

In Christianity and other religions and belief systems, the world is shared with angels and other spirits. The religious faithful believes angels are physical entities that dwell in a domain of heaven above. They also believe that there are other physical spirits—some good and some bad—that both share the heavenly and earthly dwellings. That the terms *angel* and *spirit* are but metaphors for good and evil, coined in the language of man, to succinctly capture these human attributes is a fact that the religious faithful will reject and kick to eternity.

The Christian speaks of encounters with angels that bring good fortunes unto them; some other belief systems would speak of spirits—good and bad. To those that so believe, the spirits are so embedded in their lives that they play a dominant, if not every, role in their lives. Victims of aneurism/stroke in a close-to-nature community (the so-called Third World), like the one I grew up in, who may die from it may be victimized twice, while some other people living in that community would also be victimized as a result of their neighbor having suffered a stroke. Because the world of science is very much in the periphery in those societies, routine and everyday living is shrouded in the world of mystery and of the spirits.

If the victim of death by aneurism/stroke, for instance, happens to die in the farm or bush, while hunting for food or pursuing other life-sustaining objectives when that deadly catastrophe strikes, "the spirit of witchcraft" (*muo-nsi*) must have struck him, eliminating him for his witchcraft and evil acts (effectively accused of witchcraft) on his neighbors and the community. The corpse, therefore, they dare not bury; it would be discarded in the forest, where animals would devour and feast on it. If buried in defiance of the spirits, the earth deity would reject it. This rejection is determined if the grave cracks in or shows signs of some sinking, which could result from the grave sand adjusting to any hollow spots in the grave following the laying in of the coffin and the refilling of the grave. If this happens, that body is exhumed and disposed of the "right way"—casting it away in the forest. If not so treated, the consequences are said to include various forms of misfortune, including death, upon the surviving kinsfolk of the dead. If, on the other hand, the individual dies in the home, the death is blamed on other witches who have cast "the strike of spirits" (*mba-muo*) on that victim.

In this case, the enmity and the warfare that would rage among kinsfolk and neighbors from this imaginary witchcraft results in untold problems, psychological and otherwise. If one happens to be in the path of lightning and gets struck and dies, that individual is a witch, who was eliminated by "the spirit/god of thunder" (*akuku*), and that body also may not be buried.

Should one be struck dead by a tree or its branch in an open marketplace (marketplaces are typically wide-open spaces with many giant trees in place), either because of a windstorm or because the tree or the branch was dead, that victim was a witch and was eliminated accordingly by "the tree of the marketplace" (*osisi oma ahia*). In all of these, the surviving kinsfolk of the victim are subjected to rituals costing a lot of money and animals for failure to comply is said to translate to life-ending catastrophes for generations of them, including social isolation and avoidance. In the not very distant history, giving birth to twins was considered an abomination. They were cast away in the forest and their mother banished. Thanks to Western education, this no longer holds.

Although the above is but a short list of things that compound and complicate living for humans, it clearly depicts how the mind, the body, and the entirety of human life are overwhelmed. Yet, for those lucky to be reasonably spared health problems like the above or others, the major burden of life which is to find a way/means to make a living and sustain life is draining in and of itself.

The Tasking and Draining Nature of Living: Some Statistics

Speaking of the draining nature of life, even in the "modern and advanced world," one needs look no further than the stress that is attendant to everyday living and its consequences of mental and physical illnesses. The *New York Daily News* of October 25, 2007, page 8, published the results of its poll on some New Yorkers on stress. A major source of stress is identified as work, with many complaining of spending more time working, while salaries/wages stagnated. The housing costs that have escalated disproportionately in recent years, causing many families to lose their homes, are identified as another major source of stress. The level of stress does vary from time to time, depending on what it is at the time in people's lives that is pushing their pressure buttons. In the *New York Daily News* article in focus here, stress is found to have gone up across the board from 59 percent in 2006 to 77 percent in 2007, with women "more likely than men (35% compared to 28%) to say they're extremely stressed." Overall, stress was found to have escalated in the past five years, 50 percent compared to 46 percent. Here's the stress poll numbers and how it impacts the respondents: 77 percent of Americans are physically stressed; 48 percent lie awake at night, losing an average of twenty-one hours of sleep in a month; 44 percent get headaches; 36 percent feel like crying; 38 percent get upset stomachs; and 30 percent suffer muscle tension. Continuing, 53 percent are stressed from heavy workloads; 52 percent are stressed about low salaries; 51 percent are stressed about long hours on the job; and 49 percent are stressed about the lack of job opportunities.

By the way, the term *home owner*, referring to those who hold an average of a thirty-year mortgage, is a misnomer. In the thirty-year life of most home mortgages, many in this category of people could, and do, "lose" those homes to their real owner—the mortgage bankers and their banks. Speaking of losing homes, this has been exacerbated with the housing industry crisis, resulting in some killing their entire families and themselves, especially after losing their jobs. My wife and I watched on TV one case of a home repossession. In that case, the employees/agents of the home mortgage company were in the home retrieving and tossing the properties abandoned in the home into a huge truck. Apparently, the buyers, upon losing the home, had no place to put any of the property and just had to walk away with only the clothes they had on and a few others probably. It was a very new, modern, and spacious home with very modern furnishings. From children's toys to desktop and laptop computers, beds, a full wardrobe, a washer, a dryer, intact living room, dining room, and bedrooms, nothing was taken by the buyers. I remember saying to my wife that the experience could depress the buyers and even lead one to commit suicide.

Potentially, the average work life of an individual is thirty years; it could be less. With typical mortgage payments of thirty years, it takes an entire work life for those considered lucky enough to realize "the American dream" of "home ownership." With the fact that furnishing a home, including buying even a TV set, is all on credit and at a high interest, a typical home owner's life is but a vicious cycle of work and pay bills, with saving for "a rainy day" an unimaginable luxury. Any two weeks without a paycheck coming in, as one dares not miss days of work for whatever reason, the ritual of feeding the systematic bills is violated, and with this come stiff consequences that include the potential loss of the home and homelessness. Interest constitutes most of the payments in the early years of the monthly mortgage payments—up to the first ten (ten) years—adding up to from one-third to one-half, or more, of the cost of the house for the very, very few who may have paid off the home debt over a thirty-year period.

Here, our (my wife and I) mortgage statement at the end of December 2008, is evidence:

1st Mortgage

	Total	Principal	Interest	Escrow (Tax)
December	$ 2,933.56	$ 450.00	$ 1, 648.42	$ 834.74
Year-to-date	$35,202.72	$4,950.00	$22, 648.45	$7, 604.27

2ⁿᵈ Mortgage

	Total	Principal	Interest	Escrow (Tax)
December	$ 821. 21	$ 92.96	$ 728.25	
Year-to-date	$9,854.52	$1,106.52	$8,739.00	

Total Year-to-date pmt, Mortgage 1 & 2 = **$35,202.72** + **$9,854.53** = **$45,057.24**
Total Year-to-date, Less Total Loans Principal Pmt. **($45,057.24 - $6,056.52)** = **$39,000.72, Int. & Tax**
$39,000.72, Int. & Tax, less **$7604.27 (Tax Paid)** = **$31,396.45 (Interest Paid)**

Out of a total of $45,057.24 we paid in one year on our two mortgages, only $6,056.52 of it was on the loan principal, as $31,387.45 was taken for interest, and $7604.27 was property tax. One critical underlying factor that ensures this lopsidedness of the housing mirage is a mortgage payment amortization formula, with interest compounded daily, if not by the hour, that makes sure the first many years of payment is on the interest mostly. With this, the principal remains almost the same, sucking in just interest that continues to accrue in the succeeding months (or hours) over several years and decades.

What really could ever justify this? At the end of 2008, after some three and a quarter years in this house, we have paid interest in excess of $100,000.00 on mortgage loans of $436,000.00—$31,387.46 of it in 2008 alone—considering that even more of the payments do and did go to interest. Computed on a simple interest formula, $100,000.00 is 23 percent of $436,000.00. Why is this interest not enough on that principal loan amount, justifying that we continue to be plundered and distressed for thirty years? If that were to be the case—23 percent simple interest not falling far short in the greed scheme—the loan could be paid off over a shorter period, like in ten years, for instance, allowing us to not only break free from the stress but to also achieve elsewhere.

Even as the home values have so plummeted in the current housing and economic crisis, we are still making payments on the same loan on a property that would lose us about $100,000.00 (termed "underwater") if sold today for what it is said to be worth. Yet the emphasis of the government is to bail out those banks and financial institutions that have sucked in and are still sucking in interest up front calculated on the now-inflated mortgage loans and are still considered in financial distress. Nothing is said or planned for the individuals who hold these inflated mortgage obligations and continue to pay excessively on properties that could only be classified now as sinkholes. For the majority, the working class, the odds are clearly stacked in favor of renting a living, to which they are condemned for their entire lives, in favor of the minority who have a lock on owning the living—the conspirators.

So, instead of branding these pawns "home owners," why are they not appropriately called "home occupiers and revenue sources for mortgage banks"? Is it inconceivable to make it so the people could own the homes in ten or even five years? One way of making this feasible and possible is to manipulate the variables of housing costs, interest rates, mortgage loan amortization formulas, house-buying closing costs, and wages/salaries, etc. The fact of the conspiracy is that this is more improbable than impossible, as the setup is that the class of people that the system is designed to trap in the level dubbed "the middle class" is calculatedly held there to be used to hold and fuel the society and its economy.

Pursuing such objectives would be counterproductive, for it would defeat the system and benefactors. Most people with the experience of buying a home could attest to the fact that the "closing" activity seems more like scavengers gathering for a feast, with the meal, devoured to a carcass, being the home buyer—the mortgagee—never the mortgagor who puts nothing up, who must pay all the costs and fees of all the "professionals" of the home-buying and ownership conspiracy. Besides, profit must be maximized, as a major principle of capitalism, the pride and the symbol of America, dictates. That the average "middle class" person spends his/her life renting a living means that s/he owns nothing. When s/he dies, his/her children step in to fill the void. The gimmick is repeated and continues in perpetuity. Supposedly, the rules that created this reality were written by the "unseen hands" of a *laissez-faire*, free-market economy. While the symbiotic relationship between a system and the people (humans) it was created to sustain is understood, achieving some balance should never be left out of the equation or ignored. Ultimately, *the system was made for man and not man for the system.* Here, the reverse, man being made for the system and not the system for man, is at play.

The home and housing industry is one illustration of exploiting a primary human need for a wealth-building gimmick. The "home owner" pawns are propped to believe they're building wealth through "home buying and ownership," a concept that is highly exaggerated and overrated and drives the all-too-familiar slogan, "the American dream" that is associated with "home ownership." Actually, it's the housing industry of builders, mortgage bankers, and their agents who were designed to and have cashed in on the scheme.

The working class looks for a break at all places and will grab any that he gets. I was driving to work one morning behind a certain car. I spotted a sticker on its rear bumper that read: "At least it's paid for." This caused me to take a closer look at the car. It was a rather old model, beat-up and raggedy, as we say in America. It was obvious that the driver/owner wished for a newer model car; otherwise, he would not have had that sticker on it. It was also apparent that that owner was not ready to jump on the bandwagon for a newer model. Having spent a considerable chunk of his income paying off the debt/credit on that car over five to seven years, he was not about to put himself in another bind of that length. Therefore, he opted for keeping his paid-off but beat-up and raggedy car, with the potential breakdowns on the road, rather than stress himself for another seven years.

As our nation's (the United States) economy teetered on the brink and went into recession in the middle of 2007, President George W. Bush has proposed giving the economy "a booster shot," through a bill, quickly passed by the House of Representatives late in January of this year, 2008, of writing and issuing tax-rebate checks to the middle class to nudge them to pour back into the economy by returning to the market, spending on consuming products and services, therefore helping the economy rebound. A foregone conclusion in this tax-rebate program is that saving money or earning enough to do so is bad for the system. Another is that the middle-class individual is a programmed "consumer" who simply and literally opens his mouth, gulps whatever is thrown and discharged into it like a garbage-disposal chute, and predictably behaves and does as he has been conditioned to.

This makes the term "consumer" most fitting for this class. The idea behind "the booster shot" is that the consumer would scamper to spend, even though he or she is nose-deep in debt, because he or she has no reasoning ability to choose to either use that money to reduce the debt that costs him or her untold financial and other stresses or save it for the financial emergencies that are so common. Is it difficult to see from the chart and figures of our mortgage above that one good way to get people to spend to get the economy rolling again is to address the mortgage bondage permanently, having people own much more of the money they work very hard earning? Implicit also in this teaser program is that having people earn enough money on a regular basis vis-à-vis the products and their costs that are considered standard and are used to contrast the affluence of the United States with that of other nations spells doom for the economy. The United States is so used to measuring the good life and affluence by having her citizens spend way ahead of their income. Artificial first-world standards, like the idea that siblings cannot share a bed or room in many cases, are set, forcing parents who cannot afford those "luxuries" to break and crumble under the weight of debt.

Apparently, considering excessive credit deceitful, Senator Lloyd Bentsen of Texas, a U.S. vice-presidential candidate and the running mate of Walter Mondale on the Democratic ticket in 1984 had, during a debate, made this statement: "Give me the permission to write hot checks, and I'll give you the illusion of prosperity." It is the established position of the nation then that it is better that the middle class is fungible—to be sacrificed—as they could and would be replenished to continue to serve the purpose of feeding and sustaining the economy, than have them have sustained stability and some real ownership of their lives. If writing and issuing "booster-shot checks" to the middle class is good for the economy, why not have a permanent "booster-shot" program every quarter? This, of course, would be the biggest of jokes, as the "consumer" middle class would have too much money that would only make them content and relaxed, so they would become deprogrammed from working and defeat its purpose in society.

Speaking of losing homes, there are other ways this happens. One way is catastrophically through natural disasters like tornadoes, hurricanes, and the like. To put the place of shelter for humans in perspective, imagine life and living without one. It is known that even lower animals that are seen wondering about the wilderness in bushes and shrubs do have spots where they retire to at certain times in their routines. If higher animals—humans—were to have no shelter/homes, that would mean the wide, open-ended earth would be free for them to roam in all of its natural state, battling and losing to the elements—harsh, rough, scorching, and frigid weather, the season dictating—and falling prey to carnivorous and man-eating lower animals. Because humans have invented homes out of necessity and built them up to the point of equipping them with heating and cooling systems so as to insulate themselves from the harshness of the elements, it's hard to imagine life without homes. In the instances of natural catastrophe ("acts of God") hitting a community or a region of a country, causing the loss of lives and of homes on a large scale, many survivors are rendered homeless and hopeless and are overcome by fear. Many in the group of "survivors" are known to be so devastated that they still die from the stinging experience and shock and are survivors no more.

Taxation is also taxing and stressful on Americans. It is true that the good things for which the governments utilize the tax money are evident; however, that they may and do break people is not in doubt. The various forms of taxes include income, property, school, sales, car-parking, etc. It does not matter whether or not the taxed can afford it at the time it is due, and this also applies to many nuisance taxes, called tickets, on parked cars; people get to lose property to the governments. Here's a drama from the wrestling world, which depicts this stress of taxes well.

Mike Rotundo, a.k.a. Irwin R. Shyster (I.R.S.), of World Wrestling Entertainment (WWE), had dramatized exhuming from the cemetery the body of an individual who, before he died, owed taxes to the Internal Revenue Service, the feared and dreaded federal tax authority with such powers that probably no other U.S. government department enjoys. On the principle that the tax burden is never escaped, no matter what, I.R.S. had to exhume that tax debtor's body even if to drive that point home. In actuality, the property of a dead tax debtor would be impounded and seized by the IRS and sold to recoup whatever was owed in taxes. In cases where the tax debtor is living, if the seized property is said to be sold for an amount less then what was owed, the "debtor" is hounded and prosecuted further and may be imprisoned. Dead or alive, the tax burden does not disappear. As I. R. S., with the help of IRS/tax agents, exhumed the body of this dead tax payer turned debtor, he laid it on the ground and began to lambaste and chastise it: "You thought you could get away with it. You really thought you could get away with it, huh? No, you won't; oh no, you won't, and you just learned that."

Turning to the spectators, he said: "For those of you who may be thinking you would get away with not paying your taxes too; well, you've just learned you never will. It was George Washington who said that in life, two things are inevitable: taxes and death. You know what? Ol' George was right; he died, and you're still paying taxes." (This statement is actually attributed to Benjamin Franklin, and the wrestling professionals and the wrestling world may know it too.)

In whatever way life is diced, it is mired in harshness of natural and man-made proportions. There are things that ail humans that come with being human—from genes and other factors, just for being a creation of the almighty, all-knowing, and all-able, perfect God, who is also loving, caring, and merciful, and to whom thanks and praises are perpetually due.

Considering all this, why would anybody really be praising any God or anything for this life?

I can see praising anyone who helps and/or supports people through any of life's demands and challenges. Those worthy of such praise are individuals or groups of people who really do *play God* where it matters. These could be family members, friends, or organizations. Sciences have done a lot in mitigating inundating problems that plague the human life. In the medical sciences, for instance, specialization in subareas has helped hone skills by delineating areas of practice. Hence the neurologist, the cardiologist, the ophthalmologist, the dentist, the podiatrist, the pediatrician, the obstetrician and gynecologist, the endocrinologist, the family and general practitioner, etc., all target different parts of the body resulting in better health care overall. On another level, pharmaceutical research is developing and producing more effective medicines targeted at different diseases. Without the effect of this elaborate human endeavor, life with faith and God would remain mostly what it was at that level: a life span in the twenties or thirties at best, very probably.

Where one person sees a problem, another sees an opportunity; this is also true about the fears and problems of humans, stemming from the uncertainties of life and the attendant fears that God has put in place. As humans in one area positively play God, devising means and ways to improve the lot of human lives within the given constraints, others are literally "cashing in" by exploiting those uncertainties and fears. I am reminded here of a legendary tale from my native community in which a Caucasian male, in a big local market of the larger community, approached a clay-pot merchant, picked up a pot, and flipped it up; upon landing, it busted into pieces on the ground. Turning to onlookers, the man retorted that the maker of the pot would never ever go hungry and could also be rich. Next, the man approached a wooden-mortar merchant. Doing the same thing he did with the clay pot, this time, the mortar hit the floor hard and not only left an impressive dent on the floor, it practically jumped back up and in the man's face as if to say, "What? What? What do you want with me?" This led the man to retort that the maker of the wooden mortar would really go hungry and would be poor, of course.

It's no surprise, therefore, that many products, like those of the health and the insurance industries, for instance, simply hype the risk of illnesses, injury, disability, and death; the potential for damage and accidents; and the tear and wear on property to trump up business. While the insurance policyholder struggles for life to make monthly insurance premium payments, the insurance entrepreneur and mangers are getting rich from those payments with bonuses and profits to buy mansions, yachts, and jets.

Con artists, clever as ever, show up in different trades to exploit human vulnerability and gullibility, knowing that people are "weak" with things that they are desperate for. Take money, for instance; who does not want money to afford some level of comfort in life? Taking advantage of this common need for which a great number of people are desperate, some target money gimmicks at people, just to fleece them really.

It crosses my mind periodically that the medical and the pharmaceutical industries could find cures to some of the ailments/ diseases that cripple life, were cashing in not a factor. This came close to being affirmed by my pharmacist of many years on April 22, 2009. In the pharmacy to pick up some refills on medication I had called in, I inquired whether the store carried a type of glucometer being advertised lately on the TV as a talking glucometer, requiring no piercing of the fingers for blood and therefore eliminating the hurt from the finger piercing. Responding, the pharmacist said that he could give me a meter free because the manufacturers now gave them away to the pharmacies free. Continuing, he said that the one I was asking about would cost me well over a hundred dollars. "Besides," he added, "you may not have to pierce your fingers using those, but you still have to pierce elsewhere on your arm; manufacturers need to sell strips for those meters. They give the meters away knowing they'll sell the testing strips. Doing away with strips would be bad for the market."

I then processed my thought on the possibility of cures for some illnesses with him, and he unhesitatingly said that that would be true, adding again that doing so—finding cures—would be bad for the market. It would be for this theory of being in business and being rich that the auto and petroleum industry "conspiracy" endures. The auto manufacturers refused to build cars to run on many more miles per gallon—improve fuel efficiency—to ensure that the driver spends more money refueling. Also, the U.S. automakers, now devastated by the U.S./global financial and economic woes, bent on playing "smart" to cash in, have for years seen their share of the market drastically reduced by the Japanese and European (German) automobiles, as those "foreign" ones have proven to be more durable and efficient, with better resale values. While the U.S. auto industry was reeling from business decline, its captains were cashing in huge salaries and multimillion-dollar bonuses.

A few months later, I went back for a medication refill at my pharmacy. I noticed a much older man, possibly in his late eighties, if not ninety, but looking good and strong, sitting and waiting for his medication. I thought; *the quest to escape death never ceases for as long as people are breathing.* Then on another thought, I realized that it could be about the quality of life; for, again, as long as the individual is not dead yet. I there and then recalled having heard in the news a few months earlier that Mike Wallace, the legendary journalist of the CBS TV news magazine program *60 Minutes*, who was then retired, had had open-heart surgery at ninety, plus or minus. I wondered then how much life and time he could buy at that age and whether it was worth the money. Affording the cost is probably not an issue for Mike Wallace, for as accomplished as he is, he must have either the money or the health insurance coverage to pay it. I thought, again, that a value is not supposed to be put on life, although it ends up being lost. I realized that it has been my wish for my mother, now in her late eighties, to live forever.

Apparently, as God has dictated, humans are simply pawns in two main ways—for God's ego-feeding frenzy, as humans must turn to him for strength to continue struggling and sing praises to him for every hour they live; also in the hands of fellow humans who have figured out ways to take advantage of their fears. It does not help issues that humans are making too much of this life that is destined to fizzle and end for every individual. Instead of allotting some more time bracing for the reality of its inevitable end, humans spend most of their time denying it and in the process wreaking more havoc on fellow humans. To the extent that they do know and accept that life has to end, their behavior, from being preoccupied with amassing wealth (although by a small but considerable percentage of the human population) to running to God routinely to save them from dying the death that he has decreed and thanking him for every day, week, month, year, and decade they survive, they are mostly in denial and wishing away the obvious.

Praying

Like most people, I like life and enjoy living it to the point of wishing there were no dying and no debilitating aging also, especially when the going is good, all things being equal. Things are hardly equal, though, much less, all things. In tough times, I reach inwards for some strength to pull through and go on. One day at a time (and sometimes one hour at a time), as a strategy to cope and survive the daily demands of work and personal life, is one expression that I have found myself exchanging with colleagues at work lately. Things that I might do, and also do, in such times include "praying"—making a wish or wishes actually—for a positive and better turn of things.

The above being my definition of prayer, here are some others:

1. The act or practice of praying, as to God.

2. An earnest request; entreaty; supplication.
3. A humble and sincere request, as to God. An utterance, as to God, in praise, thanksgiving, confession, etc. Any set formula for praying, as to God, or wish; plea.
4. In some religions, a devotional service consisting chiefly of prayers.
5. A set form of words used in praying.
6. Something prayed for or requested.

While I started off in life praying to "the God," this ritual for me now is an innate human expression of wishes and to no God per se. To continue to pray to that God reminds me of this definition of insanity: "Doing the same thing over and over and expecting a different result." For clarification, this definition came out of human behavior training; at issue and in focus was an individual in a problematic situation, which requires some change in the behavior/actions that led or contributed to that situation to correct. To stress further that prayer is gambling at best, I paraphrase a statement by Mike Tyson, a world heavyweight boxing champion in the past, in response to a question on the reason he was still fighting. To that question, Tyson responded, "Greed; that's human nature. Kneel down and pray to God all you want and see if God will put money in your pocket." That prayer and its components of faith and belief do have the placebo effect of hope as a reward notwithstanding, praying to God is but a hit-or-miss act of throwing a dart on a board while wearing a blindfold.

"Praying" has to happen because, for animals of the human level, the survival instinct in the life environment of many unknowns has made it part of living. As for whether or not my wishes do come true; the fact that I have lived to well over fifty, with considerable good fortune, is an indication that most of my wishes have come true. My sense really is that my life is so scripted or predestined. Also, I accept that when my time is up for a misfortune or for the ultimate of them—death—it is up, and nothing I did or did not do could change that.

I'm at the point now where my attitude is "What's new?" even with news of incidents of mass murder or a human catastrophic event of great magnitude, transmitted through the television from anywhere on earth or exchanged from other sources. It is not that I have no, or have lost all, human empathy, sympathy, or feelings. It is just an acceptance of the fact that for as long as there is life, disasters and loss of lives will continue. When I come across some impressive things that humans normally appreciate and wish for—be they mansions, good cars, malls, etc. —as soon as that spontaneous human reaction that may be expressed in "Wow!" flashes through my mind, the thought that "This too is temporary," quickly follows, jolting me back to reality and pausing that fantasy. This said, the business of living must be pursued. In the wise words of my fore parents; *"Onye huru mbara ocha gbaa nkwa, I'ojighi ara ahu eruchi."* In English, this means: "Whoever comes upon a stage should dance, for there's no telling when it will be no more. So, I hope we all dance. I do believe in doing what is necessary to make this short life comfortable, but not to the point of trampling on others or to very greedily amass wealth, even if I had the skills to so amass. Maximizing profit is an objective of business, or a business principle that I learned in business school. Principles like these must and do play a part in squeezing people and turning them into pawns. It must not be okay, I guess, to optimize profit, whatever that may turn out to be; profit must be maximized, according to this business maxim and objective.

To those who have it good or better, justifying their giving thanks to a God, for what do they suppose that those who have it bad thank God? Those categories of people, including the blind, the crippled, and the bedridden, because they have yet to take their last breath, should, probably, individually or as a group, be thanking God for making them and their lives so miserable that those who are far better off would have a reason to be thanking God that they have it that good. The miserable lot would be seeing that God, "in his infinite wisdom," justifies their misery for this, and they would appreciate God for, despite their misery, they serve a purpose in God's scheme of things. Or as a segment of God's "victims," they have been used in his ego-feeding games.

The point of humans being pawns in the games of God gets clearer. As the story is told, God just got up one day and decided he would create life and humans as part of it. He made Adam perfect initially. That Adam may have food, he threw in fruits but had to leave one in the midst that he must warn Adam not to eat. Then he added Eve, a would-be weak link, into Adam's life. Lastly, to ensure that the doom would be complete, he let the serpent, a.k.a. Satan or the devil, loose in the Garden of Eden, the abode of Adam and Eve. Cleverly, the serpent understood that the easiest way to complete God's script of doom for Adam and all humanity for life was through Eve. With the fear of the dangers and hazards of life; Lucifer, the serpent/Satan in the center of it all; and death ultimately hanging over their heads, God ensures that humans would hover around him begging to be spared of the dangers of life and of death and would be thanking him for every day they did not have to encounter irreversible damage or death.

There is a kind of irony to this circus of begging, pleading, and thanking God. The biblical scriptures are clear that "all have sinned, and have come short of the glory of God," and that "the wages of sin is death;" For there is not a just man on earth who does good and does not sin." (Ecclesiastes 7:20), and the like. As if disbelieving that the "words of God never fail" and "must come to pass," humans are embroiled in the wishes and hopes of being saved. As they do this, they forget that God himself is said to have flushed Satan down to earth where he has since held sway. Since sending him down, he has also sent down to earth his only and beloved son for some afterthought rescue mission, that for all is known has failed, as he, his son Jesus Christ, also fell to the powers and control of Satan, who must have seen to it that he was killed here on earth. While all this raged on, and still does, he, God, apparently fearful of the danger to his own life too, tucks himself away in the safe realms of heaven, to where Satan supposedly cannot return. Is it not confusing that Satan is so powerful that God, who also created him and should be more powerful of course, cannot contain him?

Adam

Considering also that God himself has decreed that death and destruction are unto man, are all evils, suffering, and death from any source or cause that befall man not designed by God to accomplish his script? Or must all life-ending media, which are inherent in life and include natural disasters, like earthquakes, tornados, volcanoes, and tsunamis, still be blamed on the curse of Adam, huh? (Who the hell is Adam? Really, who the bloody hell is Adam, darn it? And what's with anyone or thing telling me that this problem-ridden life is my punishment for Adam's sins and/or mine?) It's bad enough that life is as laden with woes as it is. I must then reject the saddling of the extra weight of pleading guilty to committing sins as the reason for life's woes. No, not since I have found the will and courage to refuse to clamp down on these intuitive promptings and to push back the blame to where it rightfully belongs—on God. Otherwise, it's either that all sufferers of diabetes like myself, for instance, have chosen to have their pancreas produce less insulin and their liver to absorb less or little of the sugar into which the food they ingest converts, or Adam has brought this upon them.

Christopher Hitchens, in his book, *God Is Not Great*, points out that religion is dangerous. The Matthew Murray story is one example that proves Hitchens' point. Going by the mentality of believers, tragic incidents like that could, in the spinning ways of church sermons, be put in a different perspective. It could be spun to mean that the victims (they must still be aware since the belief is that there is life after death), their families, and fellow congregants of the church, might be grateful and thankful to God that his will was done and that the victims' place in heaven is even more secured by their exiting the earth to heaven through God's house—the place of worship—where the shooting occurred, instead of mourning their loss. In the mind of the believer, could this and all other horrific deadly incidents simply be the undesirable work of the devil? If they are, could it not mean that Satan continues to prevail over God, and unlike God, readily answers prayers to him for those who seek evil upon others, while God may vacillate and pick and choose from the prayers to him on which to give favors? If this is the case, is it not understandable why it appears that more people have chosen to seek Satan and his will and favor for whatever objective they fancy?

Constitutional Factors That Affect Individual Lives
Finding him or herself in life without the benefit of an offer to accept/ decline, as in my imaginary scenario earlier, the individual deserves a soothing and comforting life. This is because pain has been undesirable and comfort soothing, in the human experience. Despite this fact, nonetheless, it remains obvious that individuals do not have equal chances at a good quality of life. This chance is a function of constitutional and environmental factors.

Beginning with birth, the first sign of a baby's life chances is whether or not it has any physical deformities. One first clue to its systemic functioning, other than being born alive, is whether or not it cried upon being delivered. Being able to cry in reaction to the change in its environment after being delivered from the womb to the outside world is an indication that aspects of the baby's functioning are good. When the baby does not cry, midwives and nurses are known to tap it in parts likely to prompt it to cry. If that baby clears this hurdle, another test for its chances in life is whether or not it will have full neurological and mental functioning, as some traits of mental retardation are present from the get-go. Depending on the degree, neurological deficiency greatly impacts quality of life.

Other constitutional factors critical to one's health and fate in life are genetic. One generally inherits attributes of one's parental genes. Therefore, traits that cause ailments like sickle cell, hypertension, diabetes, and schizophrenia, for instance, are often passed on from one generation to another, compounding the issues of daily living for the offspring. Conversely, inheriting strong and ailment-free genes, if ever such exist, is known to result in healthier, stronger offspring that tend to be less sick, even with age, and live longer also.

Other Innate Advantages or Disadvantages

There are some other factors that are also attributable to genes but show in the external features of the individual that could work to his/her advantage or disadvantage in the human social environment. Looks/appearance, for instance, could open or close doors to different people, depending on how well or badly endowed they are. Humans are drawn to things attractive. Good-looking things—humans and objects—are prone to getting human attention. Documented research, especially in marketing and consumer behavior, has shown, at least visually, that attractive cues not only grab attention, they also trigger desire. This fact is factored-in in product designs and packaging, store layouts and product displays, etc. In fact, there are instances where people with less skill have gotten ahead in jobs over others who have more skill but are less well endowed in looks. It is not only in issues of love, relationships, and marriage that the factor of looks/ appearances gets hefty consideration. I read an article on "The Power of Cleavage," which cited instances of women scantly cladding their breasts, barely covering beyond the nipple and the areola and substantially exposing the rest, to charm their ways to desired outcomes in situations where men made the decisions on what they wanted. Granted, in this instance, the fact of the chemistry of male-female attraction is at the base. Still, it falls within the domain of physical, though female, advantage—sort of "using my female attraction to tip things to me," to paraphrase the lyrics of one of Tina Turner's 1980s hits.

An Advantage of Height—in Professional Wrestling

Until I understood that professional wrestling intrigues are scripted and fixed, at least in its later years, I used to take it seriously. The scripting and fixing of the outcomes do not take away from the athletic and other skills of the professional wrestler, though. One aspect that I still very much enjoy in professional wrestling is the commentary of the commentators and the verbal posturing and altercations of the wrestlers. Another one of such that I will use in this discourse to illustrate some points is an encounter/ match between Barry Wyndham, a star wrestler, and another wrestler, less known and of lesser skill. Predictably, the match ended in favor of Barry Wyndham, who is over six feet tall. He had won the match with one of his "signature" finishing moves, which involved hoisting his opponent high on his shoulder—legs skywards and head downward—for a minute or two. He then lowered and slammed him hard onto the canvas. In response, the commentator said: "If you are slammed by Barry Wyndham, you have come a high way, baby," meaning the impact of this slamming will be more damaging than had the reverse—of the shorter and smaller opponent picking up, hoisting, and slamming Barry Wyndham—been the case.

This commentary stuck in my memory for bringing out advantage and context in a way I may not have been used to.

Going back to my childhood and early environment, I recall being used to hearing—and this is particularly relevant in the younger years—that because one is older, one must prevail in physical altercations with one's younger peers. Losing in such altercations to one's younger peer meant being chastised and humiliated by one's parents and peers. Contexts of size, height, reach, and high/low energy were given no consideration. All that mattered was being older. If one was older, one should prevail in such altercations. To the degree that this may have worked, given the communal psychology on this, the context of real physical advantage, when obvious, held sway when it needed to, older adversary or not.

The Factor of ConstitEnviron Intersect
In the course of life, constitutional/innate factors and those of one's environment do come together, more often than not, to impact one's life significantly. Similar constitutional factors may and do have different outcomes for life chances, positive or negative, for different individuals, depending on the variables of the social environment. The point or situation where and in which the constitutional and the social/environmental factors meet to so impact an individual's life is what I term the ConstitEnviron intersect. With some scenarios, I will show shortly how this plays out.

The first test of quality life chances is to scale the hurdle of intact physical and mental faculties. For the baby fortunate (blessed by "God") to scale this hurdle, the next hurdle is the environment. Here, the first indication is parental. Did the parents come fully and bountifully equipped mentally and physically? Where this is the case, it means they had the capacity to learn and acquire adequate skills to support and manage their own lives. Also, they had better chances to nourish, parent, and raise their child. Depending on the material resources the parents were or are able to acquire, the child will have more or less and better or worse access to relevant resources that will help determine his/her chances in life. It is pertinent to state here that other factors in the greater social environment—economic, political, and religious harmony or the lack thereof, etc., do greatly impact life chances.

Time and Place (Predominantly Luck) Factors
In life, there are situations in which identically or similarly placed individuals go after the same opportunity but come out with different

results. Certain things that may differ for such opportunity seekers may include the time/season they showed up and the people they had to deal with at the time they did show up seeking such an opportunity.

Nonetheless, there has to be a certain pattern, meaning the same person has to show up at the same or different times and meet the same or different persons for that same opportunity, to truly prove the time and place or luck factor. This does not happen, as people look elsewhere, get what they want, move on, or change course.

A Sampling of Scenarios:
To look at how the factors work or play out in life, I will discuss a number of life scenarios.

Endura: Scenario 1
Endura was born in an East African country. She was the first of six siblings. Her parents were peasant farmers who could only manage to afford a high school education for her. While in high school, Endura developed tremendous athletic skills, winning medals and trophies in competitive sports like the sprint, relay, and mile races. In addition to looking ahead to her own future beyond the ravages of her country's ethnic war, Endura was thinking of ways to help her family and siblings. She was quick to note that her cultural value obliged her to help pull her family up from its economic meagerness. Except for athletic prowess, Endura had little else going for her. Despite the daunting life challenges she faced, Endura just persevered and endured, simply believing she had a chance to break out of and through her economic and environmental constraints. She was a regular feature at her local youth sporting group where she got to meet with an American United Nations Youth aide worker who got to learn of her athletic accomplishments. The aide worker, Ms. Givens, was so impressed by Endura's athletic skills that she decided to link Endura up with opportunities in the United States.

Ms. Givens was eventually able to give Endura something that turned out to afford her the break she had always hoped and wished for—sponsorship for a U.S. visa. The visa application came through, enabling Endura to travel to and reside in the United States. Endura soon became part of a youth summer camp sporting group where she coached the youth in stamina and endurance. This position gave her a chance to participate in a local pre-Olympic amateur sporting event. In this group, Endura met and became friends with Candida, an American-born fellow competitor, who finished ahead of her in competitions in which both of them participated. Though determined to come out first (ahead of Candida), as she had always done in her hometown, Endura found herself falling short of that goal. This record, Endura reasoned, was why the paid position of an assistant athletic coach in the local high school for which both of them had interviewed was offered to Candida, and not her.

To cheer Endura up, Candida tried persuading her that she was still very good at what she did and that she, Candida, may not have necessarily gotten the job over her just based on the record of her prevailing over Endura on those competitions. Not buying that explanation from her friend, whom she saw as always trying hard to make her comfortable, Endura said to her, "But you are always beating me in those competitions."

To this, the six-feet-one-inch Candida responded that as long as she had the height and frame advantage over Endura that afforded her longer strides, plus the good stamina that she had also developed, that she most probably would always prevail over Endura in those racing contests. Then, it seemed to dawn on the five-feet-seven-inch Endura, who suddenly realized that she almost had to double up on her speed to keep pace with Candida as they walked along with each other, that Candida's height advantage made her, Endura, the underdog in those race competitions. She then remarked to herself that she had identical height with, or a little more over, her competitors back in her home country.

Having seen and accepted an aspect of her innate features that contributed to her record in those athletic events in which she was pitched against Candida and which she had not considered before, Endura gradually let go of that feeling of failure and focused on other things. She elicited Candida's insight, as she decided to explore opportunities for jobs like Candida's with other local high schools. With the third high school that she tried, the principal told her that an assistant coach had just retired and they were seeking to replace her. She was asked to produce a reference letter to the head coach. Having received and submitted a very good recommendation letter from Candida whose school's winning record was well noted in the locality, Endura was offered the job. The job paid her well enough to afford her family back in her home country some of the things she had always hoped for.

Endura's case well illustrates different aspects of life chances, including the duo of ConstitEnviron and other factors. First, the limited resources of her parents and the ravaging impact of the ethnic war contracted her social/environmental opportunities and therefore her life chances. Then her innate athletic skills, which were also enhanced by the organized racing competitions of her same environment afforded her a unique outlet and with it a chance at a better opportunity in life. Here, we see how Endura's CostitEnviron factors hurt, limited, and/or helped her life chances. There was the opportunity of meeting Ms. Givens, who was in her environment most probably due to that ethnic war and its attendant ravages, which, though an environmental constraint, doubled for an opportunity that opened the door to the United States for her. There was also the opportunity, stemming from the same innate athletic abilities and the youth sport activity in the United States paving the way to a good job; Endura had the benefit of meeting Candida, and exploring her way to that third high school, while on a job hunt, that just happened to have an opening created by a retiring staff member. Here, in addition to her constitutional factor, Endura was also at the right place(s) at the right time, meeting with the right persons. Whether these situations are attributable to luck or destiny is hard to tell. It is neither clear nor easily demonstrable how luck or destiny work. Somehow, however, they tend to be considered in an effort to explain certain factors that impact life chances that may not fall within the constitutional and the social/environmental.

Joseph Mudd: Scenario 2

This synopsis of Joseph Mudd's—"Joe" to his family and friends— is another that will also illustrate how constitutional and social environmental factors significantly impact lives, positively or negatively. Joe was blessed, by "God," as he turned out physically and mentally intact at birth, and had also developed well thereafter, meeting all his milestones. He was born to parents who, with the benefit of their good material and other endowments, were able to raise him well and afforded him good opportunities at life. Joe, himself, strived well and made good choices in his career and family life. Overall, Joe had good health, except that he had inherited hypertension and diabetes from one of his parents, who died from complications of these. Joe was born in an African nation where medical science had not advanced. This meant that most people were still grappling with life and health issues unscientifically with no understanding that a malfunction in the body subsystem potentially impacts another and/or the whole. Simply put, the norm in his society was spiritism. This meant that issues of good or bad fortune in life, including health, were seen as either a curse or a spell cast upon one by evil neighbors with the powers of witchcraft.

Joe considered his life good until he approached the age of fifty. He had a good education and a good job and income. He was married and had four children with his wife. Joe began to have problems with his wife, which he said was exacerbated by pressure from his in-laws for material things they could not afford at the time. The pressure got to his wife, who was beginning to blame him for not affording those things demanded by her culture when her family—of origin—needed them. According to Joe, his wife became progressively disloyal to their family of marriage/procreation. As she began to go and come as she pleased, Joe suspected that his wife was cheating on him, probably as a means to make more money to deliver for her family. With the growing mistrust, their relationship became openly hostile. Joe's job performance diminished, resulting in his being suspended and then fired. Joe had already begun to experience some health-related issues that began with debilitating and unrelenting headaches.

While he was still at his job, the doctor at his company's medical clinic had diagnosed him with hypertension and prescribed him a regimen of relevant medications that he had complied with for a while. In addition to the new routine of daily pills, Joe was also ordered by his doctor to refrain from meals he had enjoyed eating for years in favor of healthy alternatives that he had difficulty eating. One last health issue Joe discussed with his doctor was intermittent erectile dysfunction (ED). The thought that upon his problems with his wife, he had difficulty achieving and sustaining an erection for sexual intercourse disturbed Joe very much.

As the stress of his problems appeared to have exacerbated his hypertension, his friends convinced him that his wife and her parents had, with the help of a witch doctor, cast some spells on him. Joe abandoned his medication for the alternatives of a Christian spiritual healer and then a traditional medicine man, for the preferred healing of reversing the witchcraft of his wife and her parents.

While on this other course of healing, Joe suffered a stroke that left him substantially paralyzed and bedridden. Despite his critical condition, his immediate family members blamed Joe for not following through with the recommended and "very effective" medicine man from a distant village, whose influence was said to be known beyond the neighboring ones and opting for another who was ineffective. In addition, he was being urged to return the favor of the spell of witchcraft to his in-laws, at least. Not having the benefit of modern medicine, Joe's condition soon worsened. Three weeks later, he expired and passed on, ending the course of his life at about fifty-one years of age. Chances were that had Joe not opted for the communal practice of spiritism and medicine men for treatment and healing, instead of following the recommendations of his medical doctor, his health issues would have had a better chance of improving, allowing him to heal and/or live a longer and healthier life.

Mr. Elder: Scenario 3

Now, contrast Joe's life with that of Mr. Elder, who lived to be ninety years old. For more than fifteen of his ninety years, Mr. Elder was homebound because of issues of geriatric health. He also became blind at age eighty-two, from irreversible damage to his optic nerves. Specifically, Mr. Elder's geriatric health issues were related to severe and crippling arthritis of the knee, elbow, wrist, ankle, and fingers. He also had a heart attack at seventy that weakened him considerably. His living to be ninety after he had the heart attack was attributed to the good quality of modern medical care to which he had access. Mr. Elder had retired from his job as a production manager at age sixty-five. Shortly before he had the cardiac episode at age seventy, he had exhibited some behavior that tended to border on being symptomatic of Alzheimer's, or dementia. He would, although very reluctantly, wake up some mornings and get dressed, and tells his caregivers he was going to work; it was clear he was moody and unexcitable. He was checked into a geriatric care facility, though he strongly resisted leaving his home and insisted on handling his finances. At the request of his oldest son, who was primarily responsible for overseeing his care, a psychiatrist recommended the services of a social worker. The social worker, who employed the tool of the Diagnostic and Statistical Manual (DSM),[1] identified depression as one of Mr. Elder's issues. In dealing in-depth with his issue of depression, the social worker uncovered that Mr. Elder had issues with the loss of status and power and the authority that came with his position at his job and the power that his good salary gave him in his life. It took a good while for Mr. Elder to improve on his depression, as he was very down in spirit and his known demeanor changed for the worse over time.

The Fortuna and the Fate Families: Scenario 4

This Fortuna and Fate Families scenario illustrates how people confronted with the same or similar situations can experience different outcomes. Federico (Freddie) Fortuna and Keith Fate work for the same organization

---

1   The Diagnostic and Statistical Manual (DSM) is a diagnostic tool and guide of the American Psychiatric Association, which, although does not emphasize etiology or cause of conditions, has by identifying criteria for a condition to meet in order to qualify for a particular diagnosis, made it easier to recognize, organize, and focus treatment on myriads of human mental, physical, social, and other health-related conditions.

and have been friends from their high school years. Their friendship so grew that their families—spouses and children—became friends also. Both families routinely planned children and family events together.

In one event that profoundly impacted the lives of the two families, they planned and embarked on an interstate road trip to take two daughters, one from each family, to a college scholarship interview and enjoy a ten-day vacation together afterward. They became involved in an automobile accident. Freddie was driving both families in his camper van along an interstate when suddenly, a truck coming the opposite direction swerved and veered into Freddie's van, narrowly missing a head-on collision. The truck slammed into the rear side of Freddie's van, at the point where Keith Fate and his family sat, instantly killing Keith, his wife, and their eighteen-year-old college-bound daughter, Natalie. Miraculously, two members of the Fate family survived the accident, as ten-year old Keith Jr. and his younger sister, five-year-old Olivia lived. The Fortunas, apparently, were fortunate as they escaped the fate that befell the Fate family, sustaining only minor to slightly major injuries. It was learned that the driver of the truck had been intoxicated.

In the spirit of their long friendship, the Fortunas did much to help the surviving Fate siblings heal. Six months after the incident, the Fortunas had a Thanksgiving service at their church, characteristically inviting the surviving Fate siblings to join them. Back at the Fortunas' home following the church service, Olivia asked her brother Keith Jr. within earshot of Freddie: "Is God dead and not alive and loving for our family like he was for their family?" Olivia deduced this from a remark she had heard from the preacher, as he gave the sermon, that the almighty and loving God was alive for the Fortuna family, as they had not suffered the same fate that the Fate family did.

To echo little Olivia, why was God not alive and loving for the Fate family, causing the calamitous fate it suffered and leaving such a sad imprint in the unfolding lives of young Olivia and her also young brother, Keith Jr., who survived but lost both parents and their older sister? Even at the very young age of five, Olivia asked a question typical of humans over the ages as they attempt to make sense of life and its convoluted experiences. Through what is left of her life, she, as a Christian, will get to hear over and over about the one almighty, all-knowing, all-able, merciful, kind, and loving God. And though she might buy into this spin, it is possible that she will have this question and others at the back of her mind, stemming from this early experience and depending on how her mind unfolds with later life experiences through time, vis-à-vis the cumulative and sophisticated spins her mind encounters along the way.

Bright and Bragg Dudley: Scenario 5

The last of the scenarios is the story of Bright and Bragg Dudley, identical twins, whose lives turned out in diametrically opposing ways, despite both being raised by their parents in the same environment. There were no traces of difference between the twins, according to their story, until about the age of three years when Bragg appeared to need more attention to stay soothed and focused. Even at that, as their story goes, their parents did not think much of it except that they occasionally became frustrated that Bragg got more and more of their attention to the point that they felt too tied up with him; yet, he never showed commensurate response.

As Bright and Bragg reached school age, Bragg got into more altercations with peers and authorities even as his grades lagged. Conversely, Bright would bring home good report cards; he was doing well both in grades and conduct. Mr. and Mrs. Dudley spent a lot of time with Bragg, as they were often invited to the school to conferences on his issues. Instead of getting better, Bragg's issues were exacerbated as he reached teenage years. He was drawn into the gang youth and would "wild out" in the neighborhood. Soon, he began to accumulate arrests in his juvenile justice records. Worried about his life, his parents tried counseling and other interventions that only had occasional short-lived desired outcomes.

His twin brother, Bright, one time confronted him, and he ended up stabbing him with scissors. Increasingly pessimistic that Bragg's behavior would improve and fearful he would end up getting killed, judging by the way he carried on, Mr. Dudley petitioned to have Bragg legally placed in a home for delinquent juveniles. This home had counseling and therapeutic programs and services, in addition to an array of regimented, behavior-modifying programs that included a boot camp. At the juvenile center, Bragg gravitated toward the hard-core youth who did things like rob people in the neighborhood and was eventually caught. Unfortunately for him, he stayed at the center beyond the age of eighteen.

In one group session at the juvenile center, Bragg, who had difficulty trusting or opening up to people, followed the lead of other group members and disclosed that he was aware that he had learning difficulties, causing him to do poorly in academic or other vocation-oriented courses. He said he felt ashamed and humiliated that he did not have what it took to do well like his twin brother, Bright. Prompted by the group leader's clarifying questions, Bragg shared that he had to resort to acting tough, keeping his parents and others from reaching his insecure self, to cover his sense of insecurity and deficiency. Continuing, he said he felt not judged by a peer group who had the same issues as he did and related better with them;

hence, he gravitated toward them for a sense of belonging and support that being a part of that "family" gave him.

Bragg had just turned twenty-three and was having difficulty returning home or being discharged to live independently on his own, having neither acquired the necessary life skills nor the resources for that phase of his life. Upon being arrested for his latest criminal act, he was prosecuted as an adult, found guilty, and jailed for five years. After being released from prison upon completion of his term, Bragg metamorphosed into a career criminal. In a botched armed robbery, he shot his victim who died shortly after in the hospital. As punishment, Bragg was sentenced to prison for many years.

In a televised live interview on a national network, at the prison where he was serving his sentence, a forty-year-old Bragg disclosed that his twin brother Bright had worked and risen to the rank of manager before founding his own company and was making a six-figure annual income for himself. He was living a good life with his family. It was very evident in the interview that Bragg wished things were different for him or that he had had the ability to choose otherwise.

That the lives of the identical Dudley twins ran diametrically opposing courses is rather intriguing. A question that naturally stems from this fact is: how does one explain or account for these divergent outcomes in life for children raised by the same parents in practically the same circumstances?

Here's one more instance of the lopsided fortunes that humans deal with, again from the wrestling world script; this one playing out in how we the citizens of the big, rich, and powerful United States so have it made that we have slated foreigners, particularly from poorer nations of the world, to do those odd jobs we would not do.

A comparatively small wrestler of Latin American origin (about five feet seven) called Rey Mysterio, became the WWE world heavyweight champion as had been scripted. In this drama, Rey Mysterio was in the wrestling ring brandishing his championship belt and proclaiming his conquest of the WWE wrestling world. Soon, he was approached and interrupted by Justin Bradshaw Layfield (JBL for short), a lanky ex-heavyweight champion, who is over six feet tall. With a microphone in his hand as he approached Mysterio, JBL confronted Mysterio verbally, as paraphrased here.

JBL: "Hold on, Rey, and just a minute. You mean you're really standing out here calling yourself the world heavyweight champion?"

Mysterio: "Oh yes, what do you think I'm doing? You have a problem with that?"

JBL: "Don't get me wrong, Rey; I don't have a problem with you being here in America. You just have to know your place. You are welcome to stay in my America as long as you understand your place and stay in it. Without you in my America, who will mow my lawn? In my America, without you, who will babysit my children? In my America, who will throw away my trash without you?"

My Problems Are Other People's Prospects

This section title is one of many aphorisms articulated by my friend Sunday Ezeh, now of blessed and fond memories. Rephrased in another way: "That spot on which I now stand, moaning, groaning, and wailing that I'm hurting, some other people desperate for the opportunity are scampering, and cannot wait to stand on it." I'm reminded of this when, while driving a number of days a week with my wife, through Lower South Street, Peekskill, New York, and crossing over to the town of Buchanan, both in Westchester County, I see many male immigrants most likely of Latin America origin, lurking and hanging around a particular spot. I came to find out that they are day laborers waiting and hoping to be tapped by anyone in need of a laborer to work for them either for a project or for the day. From all indications, it appears that the laborers have no job commitments with an "employer," but just take their chances daily.

An analogy to this in some way is the village markets of my early childhood, which are still held the same way today. The markets are open in public places, like flea markets, as they are termed here in the United States. The difference here is that the laborers are the "goods." They display themselves the way goods and produce are displayed in the village markets, hoping that someone is interested, makes a bid and a good offer, and then buys. It is well known that the United States-born workers would not do the jobs that those immigrants seek, an issue compounded by the very low wages those jobs pay, which those immigrant laborers readily accept. As the United States is generally termed "the land of opportunity," the problem of menial, low-paying jobs for the United States-born worker is clearly the prospect of these immigrant workers; hence, they came in for the "American dream," standing on that spot the United States-born despises.

The Grass Is Not Always Greener on the Other Side

To illustrate the point of this above caption, I will extract from an episode of *Sanford & Son*, a U.S. TV sitcom. Having been part of his father's junk business for so long, Lamont, the son in Sanford & Son, felt he was not being treated well enough. To go for "greener pastures," he took a job with a competitor in the business as a manager. While on the job on this day, Lamont pretended to be visiting his father, Fred Sanford, to see him, and hope he was doing all right without him both in the business and at home, as they both lived alone. In actuality, he was hoping his father would ask him to return. Noticing that Lamont looked haggard, dirty, and weary, Mr. Sanford asked, "Son, how are you, and how is your new job?"

Upon observing that his father was turning to gaze at him, Lamont, who was grimacing in pain, pretended to be speaking authoritatively on the phone to his employer and said, "Oh yes, R. B., as you could see, the guys have done everything I assigned to them this morning already, because they know the consequences if they did not." Then turning to his father he said, "Everything is going great, Pap. You could tell that was R. B. on the phone with me, couldn't you? I have ten people working under me; all I do is give them instructions."

To this, his father, having seen through his hoax, responded; "If you have ten people working under you and you look like this, those ten people under you must be buried. Here; come get some food, son, and don't forget to stop by whenever you feel like and get some food."

Lamont, who was actually the only laborer in R. B.'s employment, ended up returning home with his father and to the Sanford & Son business that same day or the very next day, having been to the other side and discovered that the grass is not always greener on the other side.

Back in 1982, some Nigerians, who arrived in Austin, Texas, to attend the same college that I was attending, decided to return to Nigeria, abandoning their educational pursuit. Lawson, I learned, was one. I was told by a friend, a fellow student, that Lawson had something going for him in Nigeria before he followed his academic goals to the United States like many of us did. Upon spending one or two semesters in Austin, Lawson was said to not actually like what he was seeing, as what he had expected did not match what he was realizing. Then, he began to question his decision to leave what he had to pursue this education. Resolving that he may have to return, he made contacts in Nigeria and found out he could return to what he had, having found out that *the grass is not always greener on the other side*, even in the United States.

Further underscoring the lopsidedness of opportunities in life are these figures from the Economic and Statistics Administration, U.S.

Department of Commerce, tracked by the U.S. Census Bureau, showing in a cross-study of native and foreign-born in the United States, twenty-five years and older, at different job levels, how much income they earn on the average, and the level of education which ordinarily should be a factor notwithstanding:

Region of Birth, Educational Level, Occupational Distribution, and Household Income

			Region of Birth			Latin America	Northern America
	Native	Foreign	Europe	Asia	Africa	Latin America	Northern America
I.(Total%) ▶	84	65	79	84	88	47	84
1.	**More than High School**						
% ▶	49	42	48	63	71	25	56
2.	**High School Only**						
% ▶	35	24	31	21	17	22	29
II. Occupational Distribution							
1.	Managers & Professionals						
% ▶	30	24	38	36	26	11	47
2.	**Technicians, Sales & Administrative Support**						
% ▶	21	22	26	30	32	17	29
3.	**Service & Skilled Workers, Farm & Manual Laborers**						
% ▶	39	54	36	34	42	72	24
III. Median Household Income							
Income ▶	$36,100	$30,000	$31, 300	$42, 900	$31,300	$24, 100	$35,000

Here's the precise story that the study presented in the above chart tells:

▶Despite having the highest level of education, African foreign-born do not hold a commensurate level of jobs; therefore, they do not earn commensurate income.

▶Despite having higher education than the average foreign-born from the other three regions, they only did better than the Latin-American born who has the lowest education.

►Generally, higher education is said to correlate with higher job and professional positions and therefore higher incomes. In this case, both related inversely.

►Confirming again that life chances are not the same for all people, the study bears out in its own way, a statement by the Civil Rights leader and activist Rev. Jessie Jackson that, as a black in America, to be equal, one has to be more than equal.

►This has to validate the joke: "Two Wongs do not make a White," obviously adapted from the saying "Two wrongs do not make a right." Wong is a common Asian (maybe Korean) name. Literally, two Wongs (Asians) do not equal one White (Caucasians).

And, as for the acted scripts of the wrestling world above, it is said that art imitates life; (act in this case) imitates life, and that is the thing I look for in wrestling.

The Thrill of Life
Life is very thrilling for those who have, through their own making and favorable circumstances, found a way to have the resources to have a comfortable living. On the whole, nonetheless, whether or not they are materially bountifully endowed to live comfortably, humans for the most part do not want to die. They obviously are aware and do accept that death awaits all. Still, people do all they can practically and by wishes to avoid dying. The point being that life does become fascinating while, conversely, death is feared. That death is feared means that humans do all in their power to survive and hold on to life. Of course, the more thrilling the life, the more people do to self-preserve, as self-preservation is said to be the first law of nature. Humans abhor suffering and relish and cherish comfort. I personally identify with this, for life shrouded in comfort is soothing, while that in suffering is miserable. For this reason, I posit that humans have the obligation and the duty to find the necessary means to make their lives as comfortable as they can be. A life devoid of comfort is like living in damnation and condemnation. It also has the potential to be short-lived, which, the way I now see it, is better than living long and miserably.

I recall having watched on television a young urban youth who was arrested for gang-related and criminal activities, being interviewed, saying that he did not value living a long life of poverty and misery. Showing no remorse, the young man added that he would have no regret if he died trying the way he knew to have what he needed to live comfortably, instead of a drawn-out life of abject poverty and misery. My orientation and values caused me to then dismiss the young man's position. However, I do now see a sense in that statement and philosophy. Whatever route one ends up taking in attempting to live life the way one sees it, the fact is that humans in general wish for an everlasting life literally. After all, the earth is the only planet they know, despite a rosy religious picture that some have painted of a glorious and everlasting life in the hereafter of heaven, mentally swaying believers with no demonstrable or replicable iota of verifiable proof beyond what groups or individuals perceive in their minds.

The Unpleasant End to an Average Long Life

Looking back at this point to the five scenarios above—Endura, Joseph Mudd, Mr. Elder, the Fortunas and Fates, and the Dudley identical twins—it is clear that they ran different courses, with instances of different durations. As most people pray, wish, and hope for a prolonged life, having lived to be ninety, it would seem that Mr. Elder attained this milestone. Meeting the age number is one thing, but experiencing and dealing with the issues that come with it is another. Beyond the complications identified in Mr. Elder's life, here is a glimpse into a typical route to a hoped-for prolonged life. To be a candidate for a long life, one, of course, has scaled the issues of early and childhood mental and physical disabilities and, generally, had the privilege and benefit of good, caring, and providing parenting. Having been so blessed, like Mr. Elder, these candidates would escape eventful accidental mishap or death and move into adulthood.

Depending upon their education and vocational skills, they would get into good and promising careers, just like Mr. Elder. They get to marry and have families. Every movement they make each day, they face potential dangers inherent in time and place (basic factors of luck). They've got to be sure to make careful and wise choices so as not to have their lives ended abruptly. And for each of those choices they make in favor of enhancing and prolonging their lives, they have played God. This very statement is supported by the fact that humans would pray for a healthy, progressive life that is supported by gainful and rewarding employment/careers. Having made careful choices, they're able to hold on to and advance in their lives and careers. Still in their midlives, they must continue with the demand and the daily routines of their careers to both maintain their good living and sustain this long life they each desired.

Along the way, before or about age fifty, they realize they do not have as much energy as they did a few years earlier. This seeming low energy is not only physical; it is also mental. Minor ailments that healed quickly now take longer to do so. Even with their jobs, which have become routine, they find themselves taking increasingly more time away from work to rest or recuperate from illnesses.

Things they did with relative ease prove more demanding and tasking. Age is beginning to tell, they figure. Some genetically coded illnesses begin to crop up. They must now make substantial adjustments to their lifestyles and routines. This is likely to include changes in eating habits, as the foods they have enjoyed eating over the years suddenly become bad for their health, and they must now force tasteless and bland food into their mouths or risk dying soon from eating those they did and still enjoy eating. In many cases, they must take a variety of pills daily and for the rest of their lives to manage and maintain health. Put differently, instead of choosing the food they eat, their food now chooses them. Suddenly, man gets blamed for taste buds that come with his nature. There's no telling when medical/dietary practice will be taken one notch up to extracting or numbing the taste buds.

In the job domain, they find fewer opportunities for promotion. The job no longer offers challenging, exciting opportunities either. More and more, the job appears boring. If the political environment on the job finds them on the wrong side, going to work becomes a daily drag, as motivation and morale drop steeply. Looking ahead and seeing they have many years before retirement, as early retirement will leave them crippled economically, they must find a way to persist with the job through physical and mental exhaustion. Only two options are open to them—leave the job prematurely and risk losing your home and suffer other consequences or stay put and become "medically disabled." If somehow they find ways to survive this phase, they advance in age and begin to develop diseases and lose some functioning, which comes with aging. These include disabling arthritis and body aches/cramps and diminished hearing and seeing ability. Before too long, the once agile specimen of good looks is wrinkled up and appears repellent and scary. Some are so wrinkled and crumpled up that their faces, hands, and veins—even their entire bodies—look cadaverous. Some, attempting to walk, almost fold over in half as if they were walking on four legs. Practically stopped, the journey that once took forward steps now takes steps in the opposite direction—backward.

This backward journey for one eventually gets back beyond even where one started mentally, as a baby, except that this time, one's children, if one has any, would now "parent him." The role is now reversed. As the worry about and fear of death and dying never stops until one actually draws one's last breath, while one still can, one looks ahead to whether or not whatever one will have as an income upon retirement will be enough to cover expenses to continue (meeting the cost of) living. At that phase of life, medical costs feature even more prominently. Also, someone like myself would still have a high monthly mortgage payment. I'm already pondering options—sell the home then, possibly at a loss, and explore condominium options, assisted living, out of the country, etc. As humans tend to feel colder in older age, I recall folks from my community pushing that age who had to routinely leave the United States for vacations elsewhere overseas, the tropical parts of the world, where the climate is "friendlier." Really, the "run for life" never ends until it's all over.

Not too many years ago, I was working, praying, and hoping to advance in my job and have a successful career. These days, I am counting down to ten years or less to retirement. I have also noticed that in my job, many people around my age and some who are younger but had started on the job earlier and have put in enough years but may not have the age (have the time but not the age) are also counting down. This is an indication that the backward steps are on the horizon and will be here in the not very distant future for me.

Also, because retirement is a kind of initiation into the reverse course of life, counting down to it alerts one to the fact that one's time in life is limited, a fact always known but wished away nonetheless. Someone reading this may ask why I do not see this as a time to look forward to as it will free me from the daily, tedious routine of many years to a deserving downtime that would probably allow me to catch up with certain things for which I did not have the time. My first response would be that there is no catching up this late, as many or some of those things I would have invested my time in otherwise were better done within a certain age range of my life that has passed by. The second and overriding response would be that seeing it as such only recognizes partially the true reality of this life event. To see it in strictly this way would mean being in denial, as the fully realistic fact is that retirement, or approaching it, signifies a life milestone that points out that life is steadily shifting to its final phases for the individual.

An earlier reminder of this for me was when, upon turning fifty, the American Association of Retired People (AARP) sent me a membership invitation package to join. Still in denial, I have yet to respond or join. In addition to physical signs of aging, another reminder that I have that my life may have plateaued is my health. Over ten years ago, I was diagnosed with hypertension; it runs in my genes and actually caused a stroke that killed my father over forty years ago, and my mother has it too.

Last year, 2005, after a bout of exhaustion and low mental and physically energy, preceded by insomnia, I went through a period of about three weeks where I could neither get enough sleep—always needing more—nor have a good appetite for food. Much as I disliked the depletion in physical energy, I was very frustrated by the difficulty I was having doing mental things like reading, writing, and thinking through issues the way I have known myself to. Upon seeing my doctor, I was diagnosed with a severe viral infection and high blood sugar. High blood sugar being a precursor or euphemism for diabetes, I have since been placed on a regime of four pills a day, plus another four for hypertension, having been on two of them for over ten years when I initially was diagnosed with that condition. Diabetes also runs in my family; my older brother Edward also has it. There are days when I feel like skipping those meds but still have to take them. As for food, of course I have been placed on dietary restriction, having to ingest foods that I have no cravings for. Many days, I have to think hard and feel deeply within myself for what food may appeal to me.

Having bought and moved into a new house with my wife in the last year, I, at one point, just reminisced on the house, which my wife and I consider good; we both like it very much. I recall telling my wife that the way life is, there will come a time when we would have to leave or move out of that house we so like, voluntarily or otherwise, because nothing is permanent in life, especially things you cherish with a feeling that you have found yourself a spot that you like and would want to hold on to.

Even though it has not been that bad, I just feel that this current change in my health is not normal for me, but normal in life anyway. Although there has been improvement in the way I feel from that initial bout, I certainly know that there was a marked turning point for me. In almost a year, I have not had certain home-cooked meals and have rarely had others. I still struggle to find food that appeals to me. I am not starving, but whatever food I like, I will eat to the point that it loses favor with me, meaning that I go back to figuring what food to eat next. I still have been hoping and wishing to return to the days when I felt, did, and ate foods that were normal for me. My mother is now in her eighties, and I had said to myself that I would also want to live to be eighty, provided my quality of life remains good. At that age, I still want to be functional and not moribund and a burden to myself and/or others. For at the point where that becomes the case, I would want to go. I do not see a need to hang on to the point where all I can do with any sense that I might still have is ponder and wonder when the dying day is and what it will be like. Changes like the ones I have started experiencing since the spring of 2005, it seems, come with time or circumstance and may manifest through any excuse.

When I had those symptoms in the spring of 2005, I was attributing them to stress from mourning the loss of my very good friend Sunday Ezeh, who died of liver cancer in Albuquerque, New Mexico, and from extending myself tackling other issues I had in my life at that time. Looking back now, I'm beginning to see that as the start of another phase in my life.

A bout of mild stroke that hit my brother, Edward, on September 21, 2006, rattled me considerably. Hearing this about two weeks after it happened was an added shock. Between my two other siblings, my sister Edith, the only surviving and the second of my two sisters (she herself never meeting the first, Georgina, who died the same year she was born) and the youngest, my brother, Chidia. They did not inform me of this in a timely manner. As they explained later, this was inadvertent, as one thought the other had. This made me wonder upon learning about it whether they intentionally kept this bad news from me. The essence of this issue, which explains the depth of my worry, was imagining that it had the potential to break the bonding chain that held us as a family together and helped us pull through the bleak future we faced upon the untimely death of our father when even he, Edward, was a teenager.

This chain and bond, represented by all of us being around and available for each other, has become second nature, and any missing link would prove devastating, irrespective of the fact that the four of us siblings have our own families and are mostly in our midlives. Another symbolic and unsettling point for me is, had this incident with my brother turned out worse, lightning would have struck twice on the same spot. This is because our father had died of the same cause, a massive stroke and aneurysm, at about the same age, fifty-nine to sixty. My mother-in-law, Bona Ezendu, also died of the same complications at a relatively young age in November 2005. That we, the Ogwumas, step-siblings with generational levels, are a very large extended family is a consolation. This does not quite make up for the unique support that siblings of the same mother constitute. And here again, our oldest brother and father figure, Edward, came close to suffering exactly the same fate as our father. As of this writing, my brother is showing no sign of doing worse; instead, he appears to be holding steady and/or improving, thank goodness.

As I go to work every day and observe people at different stages of life heading out also to their daily routines, I see children who, like other members of their families, head out to their daily age-appropriate routines/and "jobs" of various educational programs—pre-kindergarten, kindergarten, primary school, etc. Looking at the preschool and early school kids, I would say to myself: as they accept their age-appropriate duties this early in life as society expects of them, little do these innocent kids know that at a point where they may feel they have done what they needed to do to master living, life will be about to purge them, having used them up. One thought that has most probably cropped up in the minds of many people as they grapple with life would be: *When I thought I had all the answers, they changed all the questions.* The fact is that one sometimes gets to a spot in life where one wishes things not to change—good career, good family, nice and lovely home, good health, good friends and community—for worse, and even for "better;" if greed were not a factor. When I look at and around the home that I now have, that's one of the things that makes me feel like I'm almost at that spot. Then, I tell myself that one day, voluntarily or otherwise, I will not be in that home.

Returning to retirement, it was at his age of retirement, which is not exactly the same age for everyone, that Justice Thurgood Marshall, the first African-American associate justice of the United States Supreme Court responded the way he did to a young journalist's question, as he announced his retirement from the Supreme Court for health reasons. In the event of his announcement, the young journalist had asked him, "What's wrong with you?"

Thurgood Marshall responded, "What's wrong with me? I'm old, and I'm falling apart."

Also, regarding aging and its effects, consider this exchange between an old man and a seemingly inconsiderate and/or naive young man. Finding himself behind the old man buying a ticket from the machine to board a train, the young man, who was in a hurry not to miss the train and needed to buy a ticket also, made a disparaging remark about the old man for being slow within his hearing. Taking yet more time to address that remark, the old man turned to the young man and said, "It is old age. It will happen to you if you're lucky. I have been where you are, and I know."

Whether early or later in old age, nothing signaling the end to life seems good, which the two preceding stories also capture. In those words of Justice Marshall, he seems to associate falling apart with aging and old age. And falling apart indicates that the end is near. The former justice did not live much longer after that encounter, as he has since died. Considered a blessing and good luck, old age, as deduced from those words of Thurgood Marshall, translates to affliction and an abnormality, at some stage. The statement of the unidentified old man to the young man, that it is old age—which could "happen to" (afflict) him (the young man) if he is lucky—that slowed him (the old man) down, also communicates affliction and an undesirable state. In whatever way one dices it, life is oddly littered with unpleasant experiences and sadly ends in death.

Through such above tracks, the backward steps eventually end in and around the house. Backward still, one would be confined within a room in the house, and then on the bed, and finally in a casket and down in the grave, or in a crematorium. Typically, this is the best that comes out of the life that is so loved and cherished and for which thanks and appreciation should be perpetually owed.

Believing like I do now that the case that religions have attempted to make for a guiding pilot of life, as in a God, has not held, I understand and accept that one's luck, for the most part, defines one's lot in life. Having come to this point, I have begun to resolve the loss and the feeling that I have had for years about not having my father feature in my life from my late teens to my adult life, when I would have understood and related better with him. Above all, I do not think that, given the issues I recall him to have been dealing with before his death—health and economic—it would have been better for him to have lived on, as hard as this is to appreciate.

My father had a lot riding on his back. As an eminent person of his generation in my village, by the way of having held what actually were the most high-profile positions among the few in his generation who had the identical educational level that he had, much was obviously expected of him by his community, and this was coupled with the expectation he had for his personal life. Physical evidence abounds that he did his best. There is no question, therefore, that he would've been saddled with an additional burden of feeling that he had failed—physically and economically—had his life dragged on as a paralyzed person. In all, Life seems like a graveyard-bound tunnel train, with involuntary passengers loaded and riding, some lucky to have with them some self-soothing amenities at the time of being loaded, with no choice or door for a passenger to opt out, except to be unloaded and deposited in his grave.

Chapter 3

The Purpose of Life

That life is tentative and tasking, yet purges and gets rid of humans, warrants asking what the purpose of life is. Before accepting the many answers to this question that have been posited from different and diverse sources, looking into the definition of *purpose* is warranted. *Purpose*, according to Webster's New Ideal Dictionary, "is something set as an end to be attained; an object or result aimed at or achieved." Now that some working definition has been established, let me make a further attempt at exploring what that means. One meaning inherent or apparent here is that an entity sets out to get something accomplished.

Also, an implication here is that accomplishment brings some fulfillment or satisfaction to that objective-setting entity. Inferred here is that not attaining that objective or goal brings dissatisfaction or some sense of failure to the purpose-setting entity. An overarching consideration is that only the sense or feeling of the entity that sets out to accomplish and embarks on steps to realize this desire is material or matters. That concept, desire, or objective to be realized, no matter how significant or iconic it turns out to be, like humans as a supposed object of God did, is not taken into account, neither is it given due consideration when purpose accomplishment is being evaluated. Everything that I have discussed thus far, and on the level that I have, fits into the purpose of life for the source of life and not even for an object that has self-awareness, spirit, feeling, and soul, as part of the purpose for their source.

"God," nature, or whatever other terms are fancied, of course, is this source here. Because there is no physical or concrete relationship or interaction with man and his source, the right of man to probe with his source whether or not man in his manifested form should have been factored into meeting an empathic consideration of purpose is forfeited. This probably forms the basis for many religious groups holding the position that man must not question God; although the practical and realistic reason is that man's relationship with God, in the strict sense, is a one-way street. This fact is captured in this first verse of the Serenity Prayer, which is potent enough, with or without a religious slant:

God grant me the serenity to accept the things I cannot change;
Courage to change the things I can;
And the wisdom to know the difference.

This, the first verse of what is a longer prayer, I consider thorough enough and fitting for this discourse. There is no message of irony here, as a reader might be tempted to see, considering the background of the rhetorical questioning of this discourse. This put in perspective, and considering that I identified and separated the exploration of the purpose of life into two domains, the first, addressed above, for man's source; I will now return to exploring the second, the purpose of life for man that turned out to be iconic, given his attributes of self-awareness, spirit, soul, feelings, reasoning, judgment, etc. After all, this discourse is about man and his life by man. Many people may claim they know what the purpose of life is. For me, it is still not clear what the actual purpose of life—life's outcome in the final analysis of things—really is. From the above working definition of purpose, I want to be clear here that there is a difference between a purpose in life and the purpose of life.

A Purpose in Life

A purpose in life speaks to a fitting or fulfilling role an individual identifies for him/herself. In that role, that individual would, generally by fulfilling his/her own needs, be engaged in productive skills that very probably help meet the needs of others. The skills and knowledge are acquired through educational and vocational training, as well as through hands-on experience. If one likes, excels, and becomes fulfilled in a particular endeavor, that individual in many cases feels and expresses satisfaction in having found his/her niche or purpose in life. People are also known to find fulfillment in helping meet the needs of others altruistically. On this level, the helping individual realizes no material benefit, at least directly, in his/her deed. Here again, the individual very likely has had his/her material needs met and engages in the altruistic deeds for spiritual and mental fulfillment.

The Purpose of Life

To understand my idea of the purpose of life, one would have to visualize the life of an individual over time, starting from when an individual enters the sphere of life and then lives a while and dies—wasted, as it were. From the perspective of that individual, what really was all that about—the so-called life? Had the individual the capacity to establish a purpose of life for himself and not just being a purpose in the "life" of his source, would he have set an objective to end wasted? For all that is ever really known, humans do what they know to do to sustain the life they find themselves in. They have taken it upon themselves to delve and make forays into spheres that primarily encompass inquiry into things that may seem obvious but give little or no clue for the curious and inquisitive mind.

Doing this, humans have evolved and embraced fields like science, logic, philosophy, and religion, etc.—purposes in life, fittingly. In the process of this endeavor, they have invented all sorts of careers and professions that are all targeted at serving human purpose or meeting myriads of human needs. These efforts have translated to individuals getting to meet their personal needs for the purpose of sustaining and prolonging life. As the individual ends his/her course in life and gets wasted, however, does anyone, including that individual, really know why he or she was here in life beyond the reason of finding him/herself in life and having to take care of him/herself and do what other humans do, many of whom raise families, among other things?

And for humanity in general, the point that humans replenish themselves as much as, or more than, they are wasted is noted. Considering that all life will potentially end, the question here again is: what really was achieved for whom in the end and for what purpose? Other than to live for a while—where that applies because not all who arrive in life get that chance—and die; no one apparently has been able to prove the purpose of life. Bear in mind that even the many inventions that have contributed enormously to improving human life fall into finding a purpose in life and do not speak to what becomes of humans beyond the living experience.

While what I have just described in the preceding sentence may meet the premise of the purpose of life for some, it does not do it for me. It is one thing to find oneself in life and adapt to the living environment in ways that include looking for and finding ways to self-soothe, sustain, and prolong life. It is something else entirely to come to terms with the idea that life ought to end and not be indefinite, whether or not one is ready or would have preferred an option not allowed in his current nature. It seems, therefore, that the purpose of life is to live and die. This is a purpose that was destined for humans from their source.

To see and accept it as a purpose that suits the fancy of "God," as it appears, is like imagining a gardener (neither garden nor flower is valued or placed at par with human life) who cultivates and tends a vibrant, attractive, and beautiful garden of flowers, just that they may die because that's what he fancies. This certainly would sound selfish and/or crazy. It is a purpose that I think many humans would not have wished for, as it is known that people do a lot to avoid that fateful dying day. An exception to this would be in instances of suicide and terminating life because of very old age and irreversible, painful, and disabling illnesses, where the individual gives up and accepts the liberation of death. In suicide cases, those who choose that path are considered troubled and/or "sick." This, again, is because humans normally would want to hold on to life.

As expected, a believer in the Christian faith, for instance, would look at this and counter that Christ and the Bible have all the answers for whoever is listening and has faith. That answer here is life in the hereafter of heaven. Heaven has been or is described as a place where there is no suffering, hurt/pain, want, toiling, grief, sorrow, or dying. In other words, life, for the Christian, continues beyond the living experience in the here and now of earth. Taken this way, life in heaven sounds similar to life in the physical realm, except the absence of those characteristics that constrain life on earth. To underscore the difference between life on earth and in heaven, the religious-faith proponents would take the heavenly experience to a higher realm of the spirit and soul and would emphasize that while the body dies here on earth, the spirit of the believer soars and is received by "God" and then is secured in an everlasting life in the serene and pure environment of heaven. For those who buy into this, it gives them the ultimate purpose of life.

Assuming for a moment that this is the case, it means that even the Christian agrees with me that it is not clear what the purpose of life is upon its end here on earth, except to live and die, which apparently no one desires or looks forward to doing. This has to be the idea behind life in the hereafter of heaven, giving a purpose of sorts to life. Summing these up in different words, even Christians take issue, like I do, with the end result of life here on earth. They, too, look at what is not and ask why not, implying that an all-knowing, all-able, and particularly loving God should have done better. In a wish to realize an ideal state not feasible in the here and now of life on earth, therefore, they created an imaginary and endless life in the equally imaginary and reality-of-earth-conditions-free domain of heaven. It is reasonable to assume that had the condition and the outcome of life been different; there would have been no basis for a wish of heaven, let alone creating an imaginary one.

**A Preacher Wiggling out of an Invitation
by God to Come Home to Heaven**

"Everybody wants to go to heaven, but nobody wants to die" are the lyrics of
"Equal Rights," the renowned song by Reggae legend Peter Tosh. The fact,
apparently, that no one goes to heaven in this form of life notwithstanding,
as one must die to do so, there are indications that even preachers appear
to shy away from making the dying transition to the heaven that they sell
to and advocate for their congregants and flock. A case in point is the
Oral Roberts' "bombshell" of a story in 1987. In one of his fundraising
campaigns and efforts, Roberts, the renowned American televangelist,
made a desperate and fervent plea for money that he may beat a deadline
God had set for him to raise enough money to complete a phase of the
project of his Oral Roberts University (ORU) and City of Faith Medical
and Research Center, or be called home. In plain language, to be called
home is to die, but euphemized. It was clear from his desperation that he
wanted nothing to do with going home to God. Roberts got the attention
of a millionaire who donated the entire amount he said he needed, or most
of it. His donor and rescuer also advised that he seek psychiatric help,
apparently sensing something wrong about the way he carried on with his
plea for that fund.

Earlier in 1977, Oral Roberts claimed he saw a nine-hundred-foot-tall
Jesus who told him to build his City of Faith Medical and Research Center
and that the hospital would be a success. A nine-hundred-foot Jesus! That's
a whole lot of Jesus to behold for crying out loud! Imagine the lingering
after-image of that sight; it could freak out anybody's mind. Not done
with his divine revelations and directives; according to Wikipedia-on-
line, "Roberts again in 1980 said he had a vision which encouraged him
to continue with the construction of the said City of Faith Medical and
Research Center in Oklahoma." Another Roberts' controversy, from the
same Wikipedia-on-line, is this reported by *Time* news magazine in 1987
that he and his son, Richard Roberts as witness, claimed that he had seen
his father raise a child from the dead.

The moral of the Roberts story is that for a Christian preacher to fear
and avoid being called home by God to heaven leaves much to be desired.
As someone who does not recall ever having seen God or Jesus Christ
myself, for Oral Roberts who claims to have seen a nine-hundred-foot Jesus
giving him directives and endowing him with the power to raise the dead
back to life just like Christ himself had risen, to shy away from an offer of
coming home to heaven by God is a hypocritical bombshell. Having spent
his life serving God and winning him converts, what better reward than
the kingdom of heaven, sharing in an everlasting life, was there for Oral

Roberts? *What more fitting purpose of life would he expect?* He could not have used the excuse that the order or command to complete a phase of the project in his university superseded his going home to heaven because his heir apparent, Richard Roberts, his son whom he had groomed in his ministry trade, would have followed through in completing the project. All he needed to do was persuade him it was a direct order from Jesus. That chapter in Oral Roberts' life must have sent a message of doubt to his teeming followers about the reality of everlasting life in the hereafter of heaven. It was a missed opportunity for someone to have told him, "Farewell to a deserved journey, Robert."

A Thought on the Nine-Hundred-Foot Jesus
Either that Jesus has his height stamped/etched in his forehead or Roberts has a knack for precisely figuring heights for him to know he was nine hundred feet tall. Anything is possible in delusion or hallucination, apparently. To imagine the body mass to hold up and sustain a nine-hundred-foot height is another thing. How Jesus grew from the pictures of him that have circulated for ages to this monumentally humongous size must be the mother of all giant sprouts. Apparently, he was not intimidating enough while here on earth, making it possible for his detractors to be able to physically subdue and kill him. Having learned a thing or two from that experience, he made sure a few would have no chance at repeating that feat when he makes his way back. The suggestion to Roberts in 1987 by his millionaire donor/rescuer to seek psychiatric help, like that by Bill Maher to a caller asking what Maher would do if God were to talk to him, was ten years late. This is because his nine-hundred-foot Jesus vision was ten years earlier in 1977. As for Roberts putting any stock in that suggestion, he could as well have told his rescuer to step back and mind his business, because unless he had shared in the world of the faithful believers, he was in no position to understand. For a rational mind, such a world must be in a delusional mind.

By choosing to decline God's call home to heaven for a little longer life here on earth, the problems with life on earth notwithstanding, Oral Roberts demonstrated that he knew nothing about the existence of heaven, contrary to purporting to know such in his preaching. Obviously, the fear of the unknown was at play for him and prevailed. This places him along with others, the agnostics, who accept, in humility, that they do not know the truth about the existence of a heaven and other things that have defied human knowledge thus far. While they, the agnostics, take such a middle-of-the-road position, they still hold out some ray of hope that there may be a possibility of knowing certain aspects of manifestation in that category.

Although he, Oral Roberts, like many others, has the option of staying in the column of not knowing for sure about heaven and things in that category, just like an agnostic who still rhetorically asks, his professing openly to know rules this out for him. Oral Roberts avoided his call, if he were to be believed, while some other religious adherents have even taken hastened actions to heaven, by following through with the dictates of their doctrines or leaders. Examples are Jonestown and the Heaven's Gate group. Although those groups ended their lives here on earth believing they would end up in heaven, their action is seen as a human tragedy. Their assumption of being in heaven or the assertion that they died tragically may never be verified. It would take verification by God to prove which of the two positions is right. Going by the human experience, this would never happen. In all of these, the danger of dogmatism—not having a somewhat open mind about not knowing some things—complicates matters. Sheer faith has its limits indeed.

That there is or may be life in the hereafter of heaven, whether comparative to the one in the here and now of the earth but devoid of its baggage or in the higher realm of spirit and the soul, may be a continuation of the song-and-dance chase after some idealistic state. Even at that, it also factors in to the fact that the answer to the purpose of life is still not met by a purpose in life for many of us humans. The wish for the life in the hereafter of heaven persists and endures for a number of reasons. Many people have been conditioned to expect and accept answers to many of the mysteries in which life is shrouded. Seizing upon this, religious and other gurus assumed the role of coming up with answers for the many that dare not endure the "torture" of ambivalence or a state of no answers, which life does impose. Apparently, many in their minds are happier remaining in the center with the answers to practical life experiences given to them, answers that have worked for them, than allowing themselves to move to the periphery where following through with their thoughts in questioning leaves them with no answers and might scare the living daylights out of them. In one sense, I can identify with this, for I am a believer of finding a comfort zone in life, as that is hard to find, and holding on to it. However, for those who are prompted by their unique nature to question and probe, they ought to feel free to so pursue, as that may be a purpose in life for them.

A question that arises, or a fact that needs to be noted, is that knowing, as he should or does, that considering just his purpose in making man, God is selfish. For the way man turned out, that this fact is stated or would come up cannot be wished away. Yes, no other resolution will come of this, and the serenity prayer applies here. If rationalizing, rhetorically laying out facts, and asking questions bring a satisfaction of sorts to the thinking mind, and I submit that they do, then a goal is accomplished. As to the quality of selfishness in God here, that only holds if God, nature, or the source of man is of those qualities repeatedly referred to in this discussion—omniscient, omnipotent, encapsulated in a human-like body, male, loving, caring, forgiving, conscious, conscientious, moral, just, and fair. If, as logic would dictate, an entity with those qualities and characteristics would be likely to do things differently, the questioning of the existence of that God would persist and fit into the puzzle that life continues to be.

Chapter 4

Morality

As defined in Webster's New Ideal Dictionary,"Morality is about the principles of right and wrong in behavior; expressing or teaching a conception of right behavior; conforming to a standard of right behavior; virtuous, good"

Morality cuts right into the fabric of human interactions, relations, and exchanges, as the trampling upon, and the subjugation, violation, and degradation of humans by humans characterize human history. Where these vices are not visited upon man by man, nature's scourge upon man has more than made up for them. Immorality in the human experience, therefore, is traceable to man and his nature. Interestingly, the good side of man prompted him, innately, to play God, this time to seek ways to address immorality, in a situation where God left a void as he did upon the birth of man. It could be deduced that man evolved a sense of morality as he felt empathy for his precarious situation in life as a way to encourage human trust and bonding, which are critical for his survival. As man is a mirror image of "God," inheriting "his" good and bad sides, life swirls in paradoxes. This principle is behind "God" initiating many good things, which appears to be neutralized by the bad things "he" allowed into reality. Morality appears to precede formal laws, and there is necessarily no enforcement authority of moral conduct. The principle behind the modern criminal and civil laws must emanate from man's desire for ways to curb human excess, as leaving things just to the whims and consciences of man would not suffice.

Ethics go hand in hand with morality, and it would be difficult to wade into morality without addressing ethics. Ethics, according to Webster's

New Ideal Dictionary also, is (1): "A branch of philosophy dealing with what is good or bad and with moral duty or obligation; (2): the principles of moral conduct governing an individual or group."

Even as religious and other groups formalized codes and rules capturing aspects of morality and ethics, the codes so formalized merely mirror what respective human societies have already identified as being of moral importance before the advent of such organized groups and their formalized codes. It is because morality is of this primary importance that one hears terms like supreme moral authority. And when people take such positions, they generally are alluding to "God" being the supreme authority and the author of morality. It is as clear as night and day, however, that God as conceived and created by human and religious tenets is neither verified nor confirmed. As I infer and add the qualities of conscientiousness to "God," I do so because it takes that quality to be moral and being moral would compel the assumed conscious God to put an end to the vices, sufferings, and tribulations of man, including death. Need I restate that "he" should have configured and manifested man, life, and reality differently? As I make this point, the thought of the packaged but tired and boring spin of "No one can second-guess God as he is infinite in his wisdom and did things his way" flashed through my mind. Enough already to that, I would add. That packaged response has never proved anything; it does not now, nor will it in the future. Morality, therefore, cannot emanate from the conventional God. It can only be so to the extent that humans, the originators of morality and ethics, are part of life's manifestation from a "supreme author of life." One way to assert accordingly is to look again at all the ills, man-made and from natural sources, which have befallen mankind.

Anything or body with a smack of morality about it or him, capable of doing better, would not allow this to be the fate of humanity. Therefore to attribute morality to such is a nonstarter. It is because humans find it difficult to accept that an amazing God that they conceived of and created in their imagination could also be this evil that they have invented the devil as being separate and apart from God, even as they assert that God had no competition when it came to originating all reality.

Although I have given the credit for morality to humans, it is clear that humans do have their share of evil. Humans are so determined to hang and hold on to life that over-ambition and greed, in many cases, seem to have caused them to lose sight of the fact that life is temporary. This means that people have hurt each other in the process of amassing and "hugging"/attempting to monopolize materials beyond what is reasonable. As humans learned to organize for effect, either on an individual, group, community, national, or regional level, they have become so ambitious as to overstep and invade, virtually or physically, others' territory. The powerful ones have found ways to articulate and justify these acts that have potentially driven wedges between people and nations and along with them psychological, ideological, and real wars and destruction.

In a way, humans are evil twins of nature as much as they are nature's good twins, having inherited its two sides—good and evil. Those amazingly good things about nature must emanate from its good side, while those disgusting things that take away from those that are great about it have to emanate from its evil side. Certain human attributes help degrade the morality quality in choices that people make. These include individualism and selfishness; power and control; social, economic, and material values; organized in-groups and out-group ambitions.

The Morality Challenge

While humans are duty bound to seek the resources to support living comfortably, I caution that they are also morally bound not to infringe upon others as they seek to fulfill this duty. The fact is that humans are bound in or by the same fate; having found themselves thrust into life configured the way they are—subject to diseases, pain and hurt, with physiological and physiological needs, aging and disintegrating, and dying—imposes this challenge. It would have been a totally different reality had humans manifested differently—if humans needed to be made to manifest—devoid of those negatives inherent in their state. This not being the case, humans are in this quagmire of life together and the human race should be empathetic of their common fate. The human race, therefore, owes it to itself to be bound by morality and goodwill as it goes about the business of living. There is a good chance that this thought may have cropped up in the human consciousness, prompting the conceiving and evolvement of conscience and morality.

This morality challenge is captured thus:

- Choose to live to soothe the physical and spiritual senses in the here and now and seek the resources to do so.
- Add not to the burdens and distresses of others in pursuit of self-soothing; rather be morally obliged to help ease the distress of others, if in a position to do so.

These principles/laws should be imbibed in human transactions, exchanges, and relationships, given the above facts. Unfortunately and as I will show later, this is not always the case, as individuals, societies, and nations, either by evil/animal instinct or by plain addiction to luxury or control, have stepped on and all over fellow humans as they seek to live this all-too-temporary life.

Morality Compromised by Individualism and Selfishness

As humans overindulge in and become too consumed by selfish and individual pursuits, it seems they lose sight and the feeling of empathy. As a result, the moral obligation becomes either ignored or trampled upon. While the commonality of existence and fate caused humans to feel empathy and evolve consciences and morality, separation and individuality caused them to also negate these substantially. This separation and individualism are seen on levels. Beginning with the individual body, mind, and ego, there is the level of family and kinship and then community. There is also the racial separation and the separation of the world's citizens by geography. Besides the forgoing separations, humans added those of nation-states and regional alliances. As each has its advantages for the survival and thriving of human life, each has also fostered competition of an in-group on one side and an out-group on the other. As the strength on any higher level enhances thriving and the pool of resources with it, this in turn reinforces the desire for more and along with it the depersonalization of and apathy for the out-group. It becomes worse and dangerous when a group feels superior to another and becomes condescending to the other's culture, values, and needs. While the above picture depicts issues of morality on a group level, there are also issues on the individual level.

Speaking of groups, instances abound where a more materially successful group may attempt to show some support to the less successful or needier group, prompted, it would seem, by remnants of morality and compassion. When that group does show some support, it does so on its terms and probably for selfish reasons—selfish altruism as it were— and would expect or demand more, directly or indirectly, in return. That successful group courts power and dominance and expects to be so reciprocated. Here is a brief look into some of the factors that impact or prompt some morality questions.

Value

One other factor that seems to nibble away at morality is value. Yes, the thread of humanity binds all humans together. However, like those things that segment humans and separate them, values are not universally shared, as some people may hold dear, or value highly, what others may not. Value is defined, for this purpose, in Webster's New Ideal Dictionary, 3 and 8 (b), as a relative worth, utility, or importance; to rate or scale in usefulness, importance, or general worth.

The above becomes clear and critical when one looks at contentions between individuals, people, and societies of differing and divergent backgrounds. People may choose to invest interest and/or energy and vice versa, on things, issues, and matters according to the value they attach to them. In the arena of life and living and the scouring and scampering (competing) for resources that seem increasingly insufficient for competing interests, the compartments of individuality and ego and the attendant judgment, condescending attitudes, and snubbing of cells against cells of human groups foster debased morals in the treatment of "others." In the mix are human excesses and the inability to control or powerlessness over certain urges. This is the reason, for instance, the premium, based on value, some societies place on sexual abstinence before marriage appears to be misplaced. For while there may still be a few individuals who may so hold themselves, a great many are not able to, because the sexual drive is biological and may also be physiological. After puberty, the hormones seem to determine this urge.

Even adultery, which could be narrowly defined as sexual intercourse outside marriage, especially by married people, which matrimonial laws of some societies capture and enforce as grounds for divorce, seems to be pervasive. On some other immoral acts, as determined by societies, like petty theft, for instance, the motivation for such immoral acts can reveal a lot. A poor and hungry person, who steals food or food items to satisfy hunger, an immoral act nonetheless, still attracts social condemnation. I still recall from my early years growing up in my rural village, Umuawala, Abayi Ngwa-ukwu, where people caught stealing yam or cassava or other food crops from other people's farms or barns were apprehended and humiliated in fashions that included hoisting and parading them in markets or other community squares. In some cases, the culprit was excommunicated, banished, or exiled from the community. This was the custom spanning far beyond Umuawala to the larger community and the adjoining ones. If there were degrees, in a range of minimal to egregious, placed on the acts of immorality, stealing to satisfy hunger may be ranked low, close to the minimal range. Conversely, immoral and criminal acts of robbery to satisfy greed and support grandiose lifestyles would rank very high and close to the egregious and also attract comparable punishment from society.

Individualism and Selfishness

Individualism, according to Webster's New Ideal Dictionary, is an ethical doctrine that the interests of the individual are primary. Selfish(ness), according to the same dictionary," is being concerned excessively or exclusively with oneself; seeking or concentrating on one's own advantage, pleasure, or well-being without regard for others; arising from concern with one's welfare or advantage in disregard of others." There is no question that humans have innate attributes of individualism and selfishness, again, as self-preservation is said to be the first law of nature. Species that do not self-preserve will not be around for long, as they would become extinct and become committed to the fossils of time. However, the point at which self-interest becomes excessive and obsessive, it becomes an issue that crosses the morality line. Where this is an act of individual behavior, mental health and human behaviorists may question that individual's self-control and lack of willpower. When a group or nations cross this line, questions of power and control and/or addiction to such status might be considered.

Power
Power is the possession of control, authority, or influence over others (Webster's New Ideal Dictionary). In human interactions and relations, the power factor is an everyday fact of life, whether on an individual, group, or organizational basis. Power does become misused, addictive, and abused. When this is the case, it compounds the misery of those who are the target of abusive power. On intranational and international relations levels, there are indications that either divergent values or outright greed have resulted in behaviors and the treatment of others that must prompt questions of morality. There are also indications that power and control are driving some nations to stick it to others. A closer look at the heightened insecurity some nations are feeling today, which certain of those nations only trace back to September 11, 2001, and the bombings of landmark buildings in the United States and with it the loss of thousands of lives, shows some underlying questions of morality.

The obvious issue of morality in this instance, especially as propagated by our nation, the United States, and other nations in her camp (her allies), is the loss of those human lives plus material capital. From this camp, the morality of those termed "radical Islamists" and "Muslim extremists" are questioned; their religious faiths are judged, condemned, and cited as being at the root of their "extremism." On their part, the perpetrators of those acts of September 11, 2001, simply termed 9-11, would argue and have always argued that the moral questions surrounding what they did go beyond their actions on that day and the resulting tragedies. It is on record that they take issue with the power, influence, and the control, for the most part, that the West has over their territories, their world, and, yes, their lives.

Chapter 5

Religion

To simply state that life is one big puzzle is an understatement; for it is also an enigma that could be, and has been, as overwhelming as it is stressfully catastrophic. A lot about life is unknown and potentially unknowable. As humans deal with it, they would ideally wish they were in control or had more control; that way, they would take necessary steps to get life to work the way they desired. Against that background, humans in their nature, which apparently emanates from the enigma that is the universe, have through the ages grappled with getting some grasp of the mysterious and the illusive nature of life. Prompted by curiosity and inquisitiveness, they have evolved many and different approaches to dealing with life in the physical and the more in-depth realms, hence the philosophical, religious, mystical, metaphysical, esoteric, astrological, cosmological, and other thoughts and approaches or schools. Some of these different schools do intersect and share common understanding in some areas, and others are diverse and divergent.

Per Wikipedia online, from the knowledge discerned through cosmology and physics, for instance, philosophy and certain religious beliefs do proffer answers to some questions on the nature of the universe, of humanity, of the divine, of being, and of the purpose of life. While philosophy avers that logic holds the key to gaining enlightenment, mysticism asserts that certain mental and physical disciplines help alter the state of consciousness, therefore improving insight in a way that logic could never match. To support this assertion, mysticism argues that mysticism is about being in communion with, or attaining "conscious awareness of the ultimate reality, the spiritual truth, the divine, or God, through direct, personal experience, intuition or insight, and not rational thought," adding that such experience is a genuine and important source of knowledge. Contrasting itself with religion and philosophy, esotericism's preference is to rely on intellectual understanding rather than faith, and proponents of esotericism consider it more sophisticated than religion. With this, I totally agree. It also speaks of improving on philosophy, on its emphasis on psycho-spiritual transformation—esoteric cosmology. The focus of esotericism is on hidden knowledge that is available only to one who is advanced, privileged, or initiated, as opposed to public, exoteric, knowledge, which, of course, is available to anyone. Esotericism was the prevalent mystery religion of ancient Greece. That ancient Greek philosophers and philosophy formed the bedrock of Western thought gives credence to the significance of esotericism.

As in ancient Greece, there were also mystery schools in the Middle East, and Jesus Christ was said to have been a student of such school(s) in some period of his life. It must be due to the discipline and devotion required of the students of those schools, as a select few embraced ideas that were ahead of their time, which would revolutionize their societies and eventually the world and would become broadly embraced, that they were conducted in secrecy. Holding those teachings and studying openly, given their unorthodox and in-depth nature, might have subjected them to opposition, persecution, and destruction by the uninitiated and the authorities. So in the interest of freedom to pursue that came intuitively for the curious, inquisitive mind, only people of like mind were acceptable to these mystery religions and studies. I am persuaded that similar groups in modern times in my native nation were demagogued and labeled "secret societies" by the Christian groups, who must have feared the rise of another philosophy that would grow and pose a challenge to them. Having spent decades tearing down the ethnic religions of the people using any and all means, including calling them the worship of idols and of other gods, they dare not drop their guard and allow a new challenge anywhere on the horizon.

A discussion of philosophy and religion as a way of dealing and relating with the natural phenomenon would be incomplete without the mention of mythology. According to Wikipedia online, mythology has several meanings, including these three:

1. A traditional story of ostensibly historical events that serves to unfold part of the world view of a people or explain a practice, belief, or natural phenomenon;

2. A person or thing having only an imaginary or unverifiable existence;
3. A metaphor for the spiritual potentiality in the human being.

Continuing, Wikipedia online has it that:

> Religions of pre-industrial peoples, or culture in development, are similarly called "myths" in the anthropology of religions. The term "myth" can be used pejoratively by both religious and non-religious people. By defining another person's religious stories and beliefs as mythology, one implies that they are less real or true than one's own religious stories and beliefs. Joseph Campbell, American Mythologist, remarked that "Mythology is often thought of as *other people's* religions, and religion can be defined as misinterpreted mythology.

Organized religion, whether supported and/or established by states or private groups, has historically competed for influence and taken oppressive steps to whip members into shape. Defining and terming another person's religious stories and beliefs as mythology, as I am sure it has been done, might even be the mildest among the ways used to destroy those other religions. That humanists believe that all religion is based on myth, meaning that it is based on legendary stories that are not in fact true is rather relevant here. However, the acclaimed death and resurrection of Jesus Christ by Christians is cited as an example that in sociology, the term *myth* is defined as a story that is important for the group whether or not it is objectively or provably true. While instead, the symbolism of the death of an old "life" and the start of a new "life" is what is most significant. Sociology really has it better here because it better explains the relationship people have with their beliefs than those stories ever would.

Philosophers and Revolutionizing Ideas
Given that life is a puzzle, humans, through the ages, have sought ways to help fill in its missing pieces. From the human endeavors in that domain have emerged thinkers and philosophers, some of whom became outstanding and great. Socrates, a foremost world-renowned Greek philosopher, whose philosophy demands the quest for truth, is one.

As truth could be both elusive and subjective, Socrates devoted his ways to the quest for truth, using his "dialogue," a process in which he engaged individuals, groups, and even the authorities of his time in rational questions that demand answers to get them to see for themselves that some assertions they made and assumed to be the truth had no basis and were indeed fallacious. Another of these great thinkers was the Buddha, and his philosophy demands insight through illuminated minds to see or behold things essentially beyond the five senses. As there is more to life and "reality" than what is registered in the five senses; this state, to be achieved through sustained discipline and evolved spirituality, supposedly helps one achieve a more fulfilling life. Jesus has emerged as the symbol of the world's largest single religion. The crux of the Christian faith is salvation. Salvation must be from the ruins/damages of this life; although the Christians say it is from our sins, from being conceived in sin— for just being born humans. Education is underscored as the demand of Confucius, the great Chinese philosopher, who placed much stock in education, as an educated mind has commensurate knowledge and skill for independent thinking. Confucius spent a considerable amount of time achieving education himself. Confucius, among other things, was famous for this rule of conduct: "What you don't want done to yourself, don't do to others." This is also captured in his teachings on character and personality and on relationships: "Do not impose on others what you yourself do not desire."

The Confucius rule of conduct has something in common with the tenets of Ọfọ-na-Ogu (like the law of retributive justice) of my Igbo heritage. In Ọfọ-na-Ogu, one espouses not to do and/or have done, any wrong to others, wishing on others what one wishes for oneself, as one libates (pours libation). In the line of great philosophers, like Jesus Christ, who lived and died after Confucius; Ọfọ-na-Ogu, imbibes the golden rule, similar to that documented in the Christian Bible, along the lines of Confucius' moral code.

One thought that still stands out in physics is that of Isaac Newton's description of universal gravitation and the three laws of motion. To an ordinary mind, there's nothing to an apple falling from an apple tree downward, for it is a norm that is expected. To a mind like Newton's, however, the falling of the apple at that particular time he sat by the apple tree triggered some thoughts as to why it did not or could not fall in any other direction. That this thought was pursued culminated in the knowledge of the earth's gravitational pull. One thing in the modern scientific age that demonstrates or proves this law to non-scientists who have not engaged in or participated in an experiment to prove it is watching the astronauts and everything else in the space shuttle float and drift when their images/ pictures are beamed to viewers from outside the confines of the earth in space.

An array of religions arose from the thoughts, mainly philosophical, and the teachings of these great thinkers—Buddhism, Confucianism, Christianity, Hinduism, etc.—whose followers had even documented, gathered, collated, and published their teachings, using them to formalize and establish those religions. Because those leaders had the gift of insight beyond the ordinary, using the term *inspiration* to define the source and depth of their thoughts is proper. The Christians, I am sure, would be offended by any notion that lumps Jesus Christ with the others as a philosopher, as they see him as a non-human, the only son of God, who was made to incarnate as a human born of the virgin Mary, that he may dwell among mortals here on earth in order to salvage them from everlasting damnation because of their sins.

Islam is on record to disagree with that claim and regards Jesus Christ as one of God's prophets, like Mohammed, the founder and the symbol of the religion of Islam. Many revolutionizing leaders of thought have had unfortunate fates visited upon them, as they had to deal with the challenges and disapproval of the authorities of their societies and times who felt threatened by the liberating teachings and enlightenment those thinkers brought to their followers and the citizens. And this is in different parts of the world. Some paid the ultimate price—their lives—as others came close to doing so. Socrates of Greece and Jesus Christ of the Middle East were persecuted and killed; Socrates made to drink hemlock and dying from it, and Jesus Christ crucified/nailed to the cross. Confucius of China ran out of favor with the king he advised and had to spend years going from one Chinese state to another seeking out another king who would engage him to work for him. In the end, he died poor, although his spirit was hardly broken. In modern times, Martin Luther King Jr. of the United States of America was assassinated for challenging, through nonviolent activism, the morality of the laws of his country that enslaved humans and made humans sub-humans and properties. Nelson Mandela of South Africa came close to being killed, suffering the anguish of a thirty-seven-year prison sentence with hard labor which failed to break his spirit also for challenging the morality of the apartheid laws of his country.

Human Nature

It is "normal" for humans to avoid hardships, difficult situations, and the strenuous, torturous, and grinding things in life. Ultimately, humans would wish death and dying were not part of the human experience. Life as depicted here would be in a state of perfection or have attributes thereof. So, it will be correct to say that what humans, by their nature, desire is not a less flawed but a perfect life. I feel confident to say that most people would agree with this.

Going from the ideal above, here are what some attributes of life and the human experience really are. Humans must be up and doing in all aspects of life, lest they be mired more in some or all of the undesirables of life, including untimely death. Put differently, life is hostile, but for the human and individual efforts to make it somewhat bearable and better for humanity and for the individual respectively. Essentially, life is really flawed. Contrary to the human wish for a life devoid of stressors, ailments, and death, my sense is that more people would take issue with this. The reasons might vary, but would be based more on religious grounds. Religion has been around about as long as humans have been seeking meaning in and answers to life. That a whole lot about life is shrouded in mystery and the practical human experience is replete with discomfort and unwelcome outcomes and ends make it natural that humans seek religious and spiritual strength. Therefore, religion has played a notable role in helping believers cope to some degree with life's pains and stressors. Seizing on this coping role, however, organized religion has arrogated tremendous knowledge to itself and has become enormously powerful in the life of humans. It is one thing to help people deal with hurt; it is another to profess conclusive and finite knowledge of God, his plan, and his ways.

It is accepted by most people that life has a source. As life and the manifestations thereof are flawed, as far as the way they impact humans go, if humans do not proactively seek ways to mitigate them, wouldn't it be correct to infer that the source of life is also flawed?

Ordinarily, most people would agree. The adherents of major religions would be angered by any notion that their God is not perfect. The problem here may stem from the quantification and qualifications of God by these religions, first as encapsulated in a male body. They go on to ascribe to him the attributes of immortality, omniscience, omnipotence, omnipresence, consciousness, conscientiousness, generosity in providing, compassion, love, justice and fairness, and forgiveness. It only takes juxtaposing these attributes of God to the flaws in his creation to highlight and point out the very obvious contradiction and the illogic to trigger the anger of the adherents of those religions. Nonetheless, the facts speak for themselves for anyone who is not locked into the myopia and trapped in the demagoguery of religions to see. It bears repeating that out of perfection, imperfection does not emanate and the so evident flaw. Therefore, if these religions insist that the God that they have so quantified and qualified is the sole creator, and nothing has been said about him having any competitor, then he is imperfect and flawed. The recourse open to them here is that they stop avowing to the knowledge of this God as an incontrovertible truth. This is what many people who have not ceded their ability and right to reason to others and have therefore accepted that nothing has demonstrated a conclusive knowledge of "the source of life" and all manifestations have done. Unfortunately, to ask a religious adherent to do this is to ask him/her to commit religious suicide.

Let me articulate the paradox about which I speak here using this metaphor of my Igbo (Ngwa) people: *"Ọbu onye nu l'ọdi (na ọdi) iri ya achiba l'akpa?"* ("Does one just pocket upon hearing that it is ten?") This is about checking to be sure or checking to confirm or for proof. Upon checking and finding out that it is seven and not ten, for instance, one is supposed to say so. To not say so is to accept to be shortchanged, or speaks to one's cowardice or impairment. Organized religion and the "faithful" dictate and demand that people not count and if somehow they do and discover a shortage, that they dare not so affirm or ask questions about it.

Religion has evolved over time in different human societies and cultures and features prominently in the lives and times of these people. Many religious adherents of later years may be oblivious of the evolution of different religions through time. It is proper, therefore, to get some definition of religion and probably take a brief look at some history of religion and its cultural base. This way, it could be assessed against the claim of religion being a creation of a universal God, which is what the Christian faith with which I am more familiar avows and preaches.

Religion, according to Webster's New Ideal Dictionary, "is the service and worship of God or the supernatural; belief in or devotion to religious faith or observance; set or system of religious attitudes, beliefs, and practices; a cause, principle, or system of beliefs held to with ardor and faith." And Wikipedia online defines and describes religion in the following ways:

> Religion is a system of social coherence based on groups of beliefs or attitudes concerning an object, person, unseen being, or system of thought considered to be supernatural, sacred, divine or highest truth, and the moral codes practices, values, institutions, and rituals associated with such belief or system of thought. It is sometimes used interchangeably with faith or belief system, but is more socially defined than that of personal convictions.

There is more from the same source:

> A **religion** is a set of beliefs and practices generally held
> by a human community, involving adherence to codified
> beliefs and rituals and study of ancestral or cultural
> traditions, writings, history, and mythology, as well as
> personal faith and mystic experience. The term "religion"
> refers to both the personal practices related to communal
> faith and to group rituals and communication stemming
> from shared conviction.

All patriarchal religions present a common quality, the hallmark of patriarchal religious thought: the division of the world in two comprehensive domains, one sacred, the other profane. Religion is often described as a communal system for the coherence of belief focusing on a system of thought, unseen being, person, or object, that is considered to be supernatural, sacred, divine, or of the highest truth. Moral codes, practices, values, institutions, tradition, rituals, and scriptures are often traditionally associated with the core belief, and these may have some overlap with concepts in secular philosophy. Religion is also often described as a way of life.

The development of religion has taken many forms in various cultures. "Organized religion" generally refers to an organization of people supporting the exercise of some religion with a prescribed set of beliefs, often taking the form of a legal entity (see religion-supporting organization). Other religions believe in personal revelation and responsibility. "Religion" is sometimes used interchangeably with "faith" or "belief system, but is more socially defined than that of personal convictions."

In the foregoing contexts of religion, it is clear that people and societies originate religion, and it is what the culture and society makes it. It is, therefore, not scripted by any one God, much less one universal God. For me, bringing this much context to describing religion is critical. It is critical considering the background that I grew up in. It is an environment where Christianity held and still holds sway, with most of the people still believing they have been saved by Christianity, and many recently bringing more damage to the cultural and the traditional ways that did more for morality and decency than Christianity, any other religion foreign to the society, or a combination thereof, could ever achieve.

Imagine then the truth to a claim and assertion of the Christian God being "the God," through whose only son any soul or life would be saved, especially in the context of "Religious Groups as a Population of the World in 2005," according to Encyclopedia Britannica, found in Wikipedia online, showing that Christianity, although the single largest religion, is but one-third of the world's religions. Does this not show that God as a being remains incapable of having the rest and the majority of his children, two-thirds of the world's population—those who are not Christians—follow his only son and their redeemer and does not care either that they would perish and not be saved? If this is fine with this God, why would the majority, the non-Christians, bother? Why would that God prefer that they perish over living up to his abilities to have all comply and conform to the one and the right religion to guarantee his salvation for all? Put differently, anyone for whom browsing the table and the chart does not prompt a thought or a question of why and how so many non-Christian religions exist side by side with Christianity, the God's ordained religion, and what that means to the souls of those non-Christians who, apparently, could never inherit the kingdom of God, has no thinking faculty, or at least no attributes of curiosity normal to rational minds.

Demagogy/Demagoguery

One tool that religion has used to effectively check the believer's freedom to think is the stifling and numbing fear of religious demagogy: "One preaching doctrines one knows to be untrue to men he knows to be idiots," according to H. L. Mencken, a twentieth-century American social critic and humorist.

Here's one formal definition of demagogy by Wikipedia on-line:

> A strategy for gaining political power by appealing to the prejudices, emotions, fears and expectations of the public— typically via impassioned rhetoric and propaganda ...

Because in religion, attendant in demagoguery is the fear of offending God and incurring his infamous wrath; here, then, is how I define demagogy: Bullying into submission by dangling and wielding a damaging consequence hammer and axe over the skull of anyone who dares to question the authoritative assumptions and impositions about God that do not stand up to experience and facts.

I am not sure what offending God and its consequences still mean, given that all humans are already condemned to die by him, come what may; "For all have sinned, and come short of the glory of God," Romans 3:23; "Therefore, just as through one man sin entered the world, and death through sin, and thus death spread to all men, because all sinned..." (Romans 5:12).

There is a saying that one who is down fears no fall. So, why all this fear of falling when all have already fallen? As if ignoring God's decrees, believers still carry on with the wish, or hope, of being rescued and invited to live an everlasting life with God in the delusive kingdom of heaven, paved with gold and silver. This means that God's words, or some of them, shall not come to pass, contrary to religious doctrines. This, the delusive heaven, is at best the "catch" and the glue of the clever packaging of Christianity that was conceived of to perpetuate the demagogy.

One demagogical line of the religious demagogue is, and I paraphrase: *The devil is adept at even quoting the Bible/the scriptures.* This becomes relevant here given that I cited "the scriptures" above by stating "for all have sinned and become short of the glory of God." And recently, an elder of my community, defending his religion in a discussion I was having with him, used that line in response to a statement that I had made. For the most part, though, demagoguery delivers for the demagogues; hence, the faithful will remain stifled and contained for the benefit of religion. Even at that, others do catch on to the game, albeit not in significant enough numbers to worry the institution of religion or endanger its goals.

Catching on, pop culture, as shown in this expression in the Ebonics English of a stand-up comedian that I watched on TV, sees the danger in religious demagogy enough to poke this joke at it: *Two types of people go to church; those who took and those who got took.*

I find myself lately having more respect for those "tookers" than for the teaming masses of the "took," as morally wrong as I think it is for any person to "take" another in the name of "God." I probably could understand the "taking" of anyone in the early days of the advent of organized religion, whatever those days may have been like.

Over time, however, after there was enough time to take stock of religion vis-à-vis enlightenment, that people remain scared to engage their minds but lend themselves to be taken in the name of religion and/or God causes me to not want to care when they are so taken. The reason that I find myself leaning with respect toward the "tookers" is that they have the ability to assess aspects of human psychology in terms of fears and spiritual needs, particularly when the times are harsh and fraught with economic/ material lack, poor health, etc. Taking undue advantage of these human situations, unfortunately, the "tookers" methodically conceive of products/ services, package them well, and target them carefully to provide mostly psychological placebos or succor to their target mass audience whom they end up fleecing.

As I make this point here, my mind flashes to two Nigerian musicians who were popular, as they produced hit music, with Nigerians of my generation in the 1970s and early 1980s. As the now globally renowned corrupt Nigerian politicians plundered the nation into dismal and abject poverty and hopelessness and crime took hold of the nation, organized religion resurged in quantum leaps. As religion became the emerging market, the two popular musicians to whom I alluded above, along with many other artistic entrepreneurs, reinvented themselves and reincarnated as ordained religious priests and evangelists, making religious music and ministering to huge congregations. Doing this, they remain popular and are probably rich and famous, even as the mass of their fans and followers remain poor and in physical pain.

There might be some chance that there is a God. Should this ever turn out to be true; that God could not be as has been depicted. If he is as has been depicted, he neither merits nor deserves the respect of any person with a mind that he or she feels empowered to engage the way a mind is meant to be engaged, not to mention the praise. For that God is mindless and devoid of conscience. If he had these, then he is one narcissistic egomaniac who personifies the devil and would have been seen and recognized as the devil by most people, except that he has been labeled God, with all the attendant fear of speaking up and out about him.

As I was driving to work on the bright and sunny but cold morning of Thursday, January 21, 2008, I noticed a sticker on the rear bumper of a car directly ahead of me that apparently captures the "reality" that the driver confronted every day of his life: "Work sucks!" Work sucks because life sucks, requiring the sucking work to live it. Life sucks because God sucks; if he didn't, he wouldn't let life suck. *The fear of God* and *fear God* are two favorable lines of religion and religious adherents. I, personally, could not reconcile why I should be fearful of my loving and caring father who should, by nurturing me, have a personable relationship with me. My sense is also that my loving father would not be intimidating me and would not expect me to tremble before and/or around him. My parents and my heroes, Aaron Alozieuwa (A. A. to his peers and contemporaries) and Abigail Nnena Nwanyinma Ogwuma, earned my respect for loving, caring, protecting, and providing for me. I know that they never extorted fear from me and my siblings. "Praise God and "God is great" are two prominent slogans or prayer calls of the Christian and the Islamic faiths respectively. To these, lately, my thoughts in response are: for what, and how so?

Among other purposes, the table and chart in the next pages, showing the religions of the world grouped into subcategories with their shares of the world's population as of the year 2005, help raise the question of how and why all this jumbling of religious faith could defy the will of the one great God. Or, does this not demonstrate and support the fact that, humans, stemming from their cultures and values, founded their religions and their gods so that they fit into their familiar human experiences?

One aspect of what is familiar with humans, beginning with "life in the state of nature," is that the male by nature generally is physically bigger and stronger than the female. As if this fact needs proving here, my wife and I were recently watching a TV program, with an animal biologist, or wildlife expert, studying the life and socialization of a particular species of large animal. As a pack, apparently a family, of that animal approached a road intersection and paused, a minute or less after, one of them, in front of the pack, jumped across to the other side and turned, facing the rest of the pack still on the other side. Immediately after what seemed like a gesture from the one animal, the rest, including the young ones, followed suit and jumped. Narrating what had just transpired, the expert explained that the male had taken the lead to venture over to the other side of the terrain and signaled the rest of the pack/family to join him. To this, my wife stated that the male is the head of the household everywhere, even in the animal world.

And so with humans dating back to those earlier times, for survival and adaptation reasons, the male went out and about hunting, killing, and gathering food and provided security and safety for the family that included the female and the offspring. The man also, in a society of humans that progressively became organized over time, was in charge and in control. Therefore, when man created God, it had to be in man's (human) image— the familiar—and a male, of course. This position obviously flies in the face of the convention that "God created man in his image." If "God is a spirit," and "those who worship him do so in spirit," according to this biblical line, his image in which he created man must also be his spiritual image, as he does not physically exist and would have no physical image. That we humans have a physical existence and image, unlike our maker, almighty God in whose image we are made, negates his having created us in his image.

Does the concept of a physical image of a non-physical phenomenon then hold?

To the majority of us humans who still insist otherwise, is it not bad enough that the almighty God, by choosing and still refusing to relate and appear to us physically, from the days when only Adam and Eve, his supposedly first created duo, roamed all over planet earth in the Garden of Eden, leaves us no choice but to ask and guess? Yet, even with the failed rescue mission of Jesus Christ, he still would not show up, seeing that his absence here may have exacerbated the woes on earth.

A Changeless God of the Ever-Changing World

To assert here that God should have been, or should become, dynamic and responsive to change would automatically trigger this other well rehearsed, rehashed, and ubiquitous religious spin: God is changeless. A permanent slogan in the weekly church program of St. Luke's Episcopal (Parish) Church in the Bronx, New York, which my wife and I used to attend reads, and I paraphrase, "... years of preaching the changeless God in the ever-changing world." When I first read this, I was impressed by it as a masterly coined preaching line. To me, it was the genius in the training and the skills of a seasoned preacher, who, versed in semantics, came up with this impressive line. It still reminds me of how creative, oratorical, and otherwise, preachers must be to keep doing what they do best: hoodwinking and grabbing the attention of followers and in the process and return, giving them the hope and coping tools they desperately need. And to that point of this oxymoron of a "changeless God," what else could be a better recipe for catastrophe in an ever-changing world than the changelessness of God, the only master of the very world and the life in it? Who's better to know than the omniscient and the omnipotent one that something needs to give in the resulting misery, as humans contend with an experience where the only constant is change, as they slip, trip, fall, and struggle back up to continue, because a changeless God is in charge of an ever-changing world?

Staggering and frustrating, an expression that is likely to follow this experience is: "When I thought I had all the answers, they changed all the questions." It is then a clear paradox that their God and maker goes through no necessary changes to meet their needs. Imagine in the human experience, which is the only thing that humans have to go by, an individual employed in a job in which he has the authority over and the responsibility to keep track of some function that is susceptible to change, taking the position that for one reason or another, all that should be expected of him is the ground rules he laid out on his first day on the job and nothing else matters beyond that. He would soon be out of a job and with that incur all the attendant consequences that he has the rest of his life to regret. Of course, he is not "God."

To communicate the information captured in the graphs and charts of the world's religions in the next pages below graphically, the pie chart illustrates the size, in percentage, of each religion in relation to the others. As the table does show, different religions and religious groups in the subgroupings support their geographic origins, based on the region of the world from where the leader after whom each was founded hailed. This does underscore the cultural root of religions. So, the Abrahamic group of Christianity, Islam, Judaism, and the Baha'i faith are rooted in the Middle East and its values and culture. Those identified or classified as the Indian region group of Hinduism, Buddhism, Sikhism, and the Far-Eastern group include Confucianism, after the great Confucius, the Chinese sage and teacher, while the ethnics, which must include Ọfọ-na-Ogú of my foreparents, are those that I consider less organized and are practiced more in and by the ethnic groups of Africa, the Americas, and even India and Asia. Notably, the industrialized nations of the Western world embraced Christianity and its philosophy earlier, although Islam has made some inroads unimagined there in the past.

That many or some among the religious adherents, including Christians and their faith of salvation only through Christ in the case I discussed earlier here, might be aware of the facts captured in the following table and chart and still hold on tightly to their "reality" speaks to the nature of reality. According to Dr. Phil McGraw of TV's *Dr. Phil*, there is no reality, only perceptions. To this, I say, "Reality is perception, as perception is reality." It is this nature of reality that allows people to use concepts, including those that stem from conspiracies, to take advantage of people, their fears and vulnerabilities. Conceptions do get to be as concrete as physical superstructures in the mind; more so in the minds of the gullible target group. For any such perceived superstructures (perceived because it's all in the mind) that could register as concrete as an iron and metal scaffold or building, could also be deconstructed and brought to a state of physical nothingness, the way it was before that mental superstructure was put in place. Many of the theories and principles that operate in the world, from politics, economics, and social engineering, that have defined the way people live and have controlled their lives over long periods of time would qualify as forms of one conspiracy or another that has been pushed, sold, and propagated as "real."

Perhaps more than in any other domain, religion thrives on mind control and will continue to skillfully create ways to achieve that. Religions and those who desire power and control will continue to recycle the control mechanisms that still work and deliver, while seeking ways to adapt to the trend of the times so as to appeal to the succeeding generations of humanity for sustenance and continuity.

Demographic Distribution of the Major Religious Groups, as a Percentage of the World Population in 2005

Name of Group	Name of Religion	Number of Followers	Date of Origin	Main Regions Covered
Abrahamic religions 3.4 billion	Christianity	2.1 billion	1st c.	Worldwide except Northwest Africa, the Arabian Peninsula, and parts of Central, East, and Southeast Asia.
	Islam	1.5 billion	7th c.	Middle East, Northern Africa, Central Asia, South Asia, Western Africa, Eastern Africa, Indian subcontinent, Russia, China, Balkans, Malay Archipelago
	Judaism	14 million	Iron Age	Israel, USA, Europe
	Bahá'í Faith	7 million	19th c.	Dispersed worldwide with no major population centers
Indian religions 1.4 billion	Hinduism	900 million	no known founder	Indian subcontinent, Fiji, Guyana and Mauritius
	Buddhism	376 million	Iron Age	Indian subcontinent, East Asia, Indochina, regions of Russia.
	Sikhism	23 million	16th c.	India, Pakistan, Africa, Canada, USA, United Kingdom
	Jainism	4.2 million	Iron Age	India and East Africa
Far Eastern religions 500 million	Taoism	unknown	Spring and Autumn Period	China and the Chinese Diaspora
	Confucianism	unknown	Spring and Autumn Period	China, Korea, Vietnam and the Chinese and Vietnamese diasporas
	Shinto	4 million	no known founder	Japan
	Caodaism	1–2 million	1925	Vietnam
	Chondogyo	1.13 million	1812	Korea
	Yiguandao	1-2 million	c. 1900	Taiwan
	Chinese folk religion	394 million	no known founder	China
Ethnic/ tribal 400 million	Primal indigenous	300 million	no known founder	India, Asia
	African traditional and diasporic	100 million	no known founder	Africa, Americas

Groups estimated to exceed 500,000 adherents that are not listed under any of the categories above are the following:

- Juche (North Korea): 19 million
- Spiritism (not an organized religion): 15 million
- Neopaganism: 1 million
- Unitarian-Universalism: 800,000
- Rastafarianism: 600,000

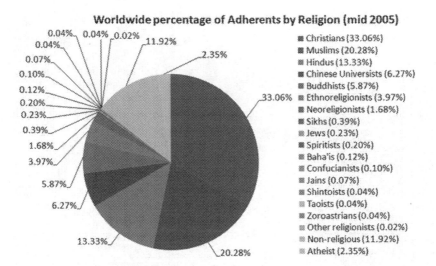

Worldwide percentage of Adherents by Religion (mid 2005)

- Christians (33.06%)
- Muslims (20.28%)
- Hindus (13.33%)
- Chinese Universists (6.27%)
- Buddhists (5.87%)
- Ethnoreligionists (3.97%)
- Neoreligionists (1.68%)
- Sikhs (0.39%)
- Jews (0.23%)
- Spiritists (0.20%)
- Baha'is (0.12%)
- Confucianists (0.10%)
- Jains (0.07%)
- Shintoists (0.04%)
- Taoists (0.04%)
- Zoroastrians (0.04%)
- Other religionists (0.02%)
- Non-religious (11.92%)
- Atheist (2.35%)

Again, which one of the gods of the above religions is the one and the almighty? Could this be the Christian God because that religion has about one-third of the world's population, per this chart and graph? Does he then need to wheel and deal with these other gods, or slug it out with them, to take total and complete control? Or is he just one of the gods that is also created by humans in their image, derived from their cultures?

There has not been and may never be a reconciling of the gods. People would carry on the way they always have anyway. "So why bother with these questions?" some would ask. To this, I will respond that these questions or the variations thereof, have been asked throughout the ages and will continue to be asked by the succeeding generations of humans for as long as the convolutions of reality are part of the human experience. Asking that question does also bring a resolution of sorts in the mind of the inquirer—I, in this case. Essentially, this re-examining is about re-examining illogical assumptions about life. Should it become incrementally widely embraced, it would help reduce the amount of puzzlement that gets in the way of a thinking mind, allowing for aspects of life to be filed away in the columns of the unknown, unknowable, etc., freeing it to move into other agitating things on which precious time and energy should be more productively invested. Also, religious faith and beliefs, which are subjective and should really be an internal and personal matter of the individual, have been pushed to feature prominently and dominantly in the larger human communal living to the point that they have become dangerous, getting in the way of interhuman dealings. If nothing else warrants it, such negative consequences that help compound the distortion in life are enough to subject religious faiths, attitudes, and practices to continuous re-examination.

Founding religions is important in the concept of the human role of playing God for succor in the spiritual realm. But going from this to conceive of and create a definitively living God is an assertion that flies in the face of logic, rationale, or demonstrable evidence. Speaking of evidence, I am aware of the innumerable spins and lines about God and faith not being subject to reasoning, as God is said to know what he did and does in choosing to do whatever he wants in his infinite wisdom and has chosen not to either make humans his equal or clue them in to what makes him God. With whatever gift of thinking I may have, I have chosen to rely more on logic and reasoning in life, which though not 100 percent foolproof, have been shown to work better for humans than blind faith. For on a scale of one hundred of what approach has served life needs better, I rank the logic and reasoning (scientific) approach at about ninety-five and that of God/faith, at five. Given a choice between Nostradamus and algorithm, I'll choose algorithm hands down algorithm. I have been ready and willing to give up that five in favor of keeping my ninety-five, because, logically, it makes no sense to choose the flip side. Moreover, in life, one wins some and loses some. For me, losing the five still leaves me with much and good enough winnings.

By coincidence, this aligns with the philosophical approach of pragmatism, propounded by the American philosopher William James, to reconcile scientific with religious knowledge in an era of intense religious and scientific conflict. Pragmatism, here, basically holds that the truth of a set of beliefs can be indicated by its usefulness in helping people cope with a particular context of life. Therefore, that scientific principles and methodology are useful in predicting observations in the physical world can prove the authenticity of the scientific theories. Also, that religious belief can be useful in helping people cope with difficult emotions or moral decisions can indicate a certain truth for those beliefs, for the believer.

As people swear and die by the belief that their faith/religion is ordained by the one, almighty God, they lose sight of the fact that whatever the mind believes, about which others who do not so believe might be indignant, works for them and prompts them to do things that those others might consider crazy, stupid, etc., hence sayings like *one person's treasure is another's trash*. For instance, while organized religion could hardly compel me to imbibe any values, characteristics, or behavior patterns; others wear turbans, robes, veils, Yakamas, or wool coats even in scorching, humid 100-degree temperatures; grow lengthy, bushy beards; and do other things unique to their faith. It is amazing what people unwittingly or enthusiastically embrace and imbibe in the name of religion.

It would help if progress is made along the path of a broad recognition of the fact that religious faith is based on a people and their culture and serves the believer better on those grounds. Saying this here warrants some discussion of Ọfọ na Ogú, the authentic spiritual medium of my heritage—the Igbo of Southeast Nigeria. This discussion will include some of the ways the Christian religion has impacted Nigeria and her communities since it was exported there. Following that, I will yet take Christianity to some more, but focused, task; using some of its widely acclaimed beliefs, as captured in biblical stories.

Ọfọ-na-Ogú

Ọfọ-na-Ogú is the principle, tenet, and symbol at the base/root of the Igbo spirituality. It may not fit into the mold of religion that is widely known and identified when religion is formally discussed. As far as a formal definition goes, it would fit more into this one by Webster's New Ideal Dictionary: "A cause, principle, or system of beliefs held to with ardor and faith." For the fact that this faith and practice is news to many, much as it is "strange" to teeming succeeding Igbo generations, an introduction and a brief discussion are in order here.

In the physical and spiritual realms, the Igbo values communal and kinship bonding, not just with the living, but also with the spirits of departed ancestors down the generational line. They truly believe that communal and kinship healthy relating is fundamental in life. Important also is the dignified and revered place of the elderly, who are seen as the embodiment of knowledge and wisdom, the custodians of culture, and the link with the departed generation, without whom history and the ways of life would be lost. To understand the significance of human behavior in the social environment is to understand the critical place of this value in the Igbo life and world.

On the subcommunity level, men known for integrity who are highly respected are the custodians of Ọfọ, the symbol of purity and of virtue. These men have earned the trust of the community as people who wish and do no evil. Ọfọ-na-Ogú subjects an adherent to a self-atoning and self-cleansing life. In the ritual of libation, which features prominently in the Igbo spiritual life, the individual, mostly but not always with wine, first reveres, pays homage to, and seeks spiritual contact with the departed ancestors. Continuing, the individual atones by proclaiming his goodwill on others and professing not to have brought about ill will or harm unto any, before asking and expressing a wish for good fortunes. This ritual exercise in essence is about expressing and imbibing the principle that what one wishes upon others becomes one's fate also—the law of karma of one reaping what one sows.

The underlying spirit in Ọfọ-na-Ogú is constructive coexistence. In the aforementioned libation ritual, carefully chosen utterances and expressions like, *"Egbe bere ugo bere; nke si ibe ya ebela, nku kwaa ya n'ike,"* are stated. Translated into English, it means, "Let the eagle perch, let the hawk perch, whichever says the other shall not perch, may its wing break forcefully."

This, in my experience, ranks among the highest virtue of any religion. A significant drawback of Ọfọ-na-Ogú is similar to that of other religions in one main way; it is devoid of a "scientific" approach to things. This may mean that by imagination and assumption, and no concrete knowledge or verifiable evidence, people could and do perceive and conclude others to have wronged them or be behind their physical and other ailments, before proceeding in instances to atone and libate. On such assumed moral grounds, they justify invoking the good spirit of the departed ancestors and the source of life and appeal to them for favors. As is already evident in human psychology, assumptions and perceptions along these lines do validate one's predispositions. This does bode real enmity in one's mind and damages interpersonal relationships. However, for those not compromised by any tangled relationships with neighbors or others, the experience and feeling are exhilarating and worth it. In the larger context of the role of religion in the area of fermenting and wreaking mass damage on the naïve or innocent, the contribution of Ọfọ-na-Ogú pales in comparison to that of many other religions.

One reason for this is that unlike those others, Ọfọ-na-Ogú is neither organized nor packaged and pushed even within the locality, let alone beyond it. Its impact is rather limited to the immediate environment and within the individual and groups. Although its principle generally applies across the Igbo nation, aspects of it may vary in Igbo subcommunities. A victim of misinterpretation by condescending foreign religions, Ọfọ-na-Ogú withered even more by the neglect and abandonment of Igbo generations who were swayed mostly by the opportunities, real or imagined, offered by foreign influences, who very probably, had ulterior motives to control them.

An indelible and still being inflicted *black eye* to Ọfọ-na-Ogú is the so-called *"igbu muọ," "ikpọ muọ ọkú"* ("the burning of the gods"), orchestrated and carried out by the agents of the invading, foreign, Christian religion across the Igbo nation around 1918. Those agents convinced converted and converting indigenes that shrines and artistic symbols of the Igbo faith and practices constituted lesser gods than the one and the almighty, and was idol worship that needed to be destroyed if their rejection of them and conversion to the Christian faith would be complete. Juxtapose this to the fact that the Christians wear images of their saints and display them on the walls, shrines, and alters of their places of worship. As a good number of educated and deciphering Igbos (ndi-Igbo) clamor for the embracing of their Ọfọ-na-Ogú heritage, refining and repackaging it where necessary, encountering Igbo Christians who want nothing to do with libating—the ritual of pouring libation—is a routine occurrence. Lately, as times and life in Nigeria have become desperate in recent years due to the challenges of nurturing and solidifying the framework for a modern human society and nation-state, Nigeria has become a fertile ground for religion and the escape from everyday reality it brings—an opiate, as attributed to Karl Max. And for the Igbo nation of the modern generation, the favored religion has been and remains Christianity.

With the current religious resurgence amidst the hopelessness, the Igbo nation is again witnessing the return of the charade of routing out perceived traits or remnants of "devil/idol worshipping" and witchcraft. Among other things, converted leaders and members of these perceived devilish groups take church leaders from community to community to identify other members and their victims. Another route is said to be the cutting down of large trees, many of which constitute a community gathering point and landmark, because they are now said to be the shrines and performing points for voodoo and witchcraft artists who are perpetuating bad luck, poverty, joblessness, and the lack of suitors for women of marriage age. All these are happening, believe it or not, this year, in 2006. The evidence said to be cited to prove this is that people in those communities where those trees stand are not prospering in life.

The success that the religions foreign to the Igbo have enjoyed can be explained by the fact that they are highly organized and packaged and have motives and goals beyond the focus of Ọfọ-na-Ogú. While Ọfọ-na-Ogú is mainly about the morals and the conscience of the individual and kinship communities as they impact mutual existence, those others aim at regional and global control and have transcended racial, national, and regional boundaries to make inroads in places beyond where they originated. Ọfọ-na-Ogú has also not professed to have, share, or spread the knowledge of the one almighty God, much less arrogate superiority of that God over those of other religions. It has not sought to hold an ironclad superior knowledge of the origin of man and life and embark on a crusade to preach, persuade, and convert minds and souls. To the Igbo, Chi is attributed with being the source of humans and of life. In a way, it is the answer to the question of how life and being came about. Seemingly, this is an acknowledgment and acceptance of the fact that an absolute knowledge of the source of life and being has eluded and continues to elude mankind. Beyond the global Chi, there is *Chi-na-Eke*, which is personal and individualistic. One way to look at *Chi-na-Eke* is to explain its root words and meaning: God (Chi) and (na) Fortune (Eke). The notion here is that the individual's place in life is shrouded or scripted by one's personal God and one's individual fortune, hence, the Igbo names *Chi Ọma* and *Eke Ọma*—Good God and Good Fortune, respectively. Generations of Igbos over time have, mostly unwittingly, corrupted Chi na Eke, (*Chin'eke* in shortened form) for *Chi okike*, literally the universal *creation God*, as in Chi (God) na (that) eke (creates).

Christianity

A highly and successfully organized religion like Christianity would most probably not be where it is without the factor of illusionary hope for escape from the very flawed life to which humans are subjected. This illusion is potent opium. This is why the believer is contented that Christ and the Bible have all the answers in the form of life in the hereafter, in heaven, for whoever would listen and believe. Heaven has been or is described as a place where there is no suffering, hurt/pain, want, toiling, grief, sorrow, or dying. In other words, life, for the Christian, continues beyond the living experience in the here and now of the earth. This would mean that life in heaven is similar to life in the physical realm, except for the absence of those characteristics that constrain life on earth. To underscore the difference between life on earth and in heaven, the religious faith proponents would take the heavenly experience to a higher realm of the spirit and the soul and would emphasize that while the body dies here on earth, the spirit of the believer soars and is received by God; it is then secure in an everlasting life in the serene and pure environment of heaven. For those who buy into this, this gives them the ultimate purpose of life.

Assuming for a moment that this is the case, it means that even the Christian agrees with me that it is not clear what the purpose of life is upon the end of life here on earth, except to live and die, and no one looks forward to or desires death. This has to be the idea behind life in the hereafter of heaven, giving a purpose of sorts to life. Summing these up, even Christians take issue, like I do, with the end result of life here on earth. They, too, look at what is not and ask why not, implying that an all-knowing, all-able, and particularly loving God should have done better. In a wish to realize an ideal state not feasible in the here and now of life on earth, therefore, they created an imaginary and endless life in the imaginary and reality-of-earth-conditions-free domain of heaven. It is reasonable to infer from this that had the condition and the outcome of life been different, there would have been no basis for a wish of heaven, let alone creating an imaginary one.

Considering all this, does it not seem that humans are but pawns in the game of God? As the story is told, he just got up one day and decided he would create life and humans as part of it. He made Adam perfect initially. For food, he threw in fruits but had to leave one in the midst with a caveat, warning that Adam must not eat it. Then he added Eve, a would-be weak link, to Adam's life. Lastly, to ensure that the doom is complete, he let the serpent, a.k.a. Satan or the devil, loose in the abode of Adam and Eve. Cleverly, the serpent understood that the easiest way to complete God's script of doom for Adam and all humanity for life is through Eve. With the fear of the dangers and hazards of life and of death ultimately hanging over their heads, God ensures that humans would forever beseech and beg him to spare them of the dangers of life and of death and would be thanking him for every day they did not have to be irreparably damaged or die.

There is clearly an irony to this circus of begging, pleading, and thanking God. The biblical scriptures are clear that "all have sinned and become short of the glory of God"; that "the wages of sin is death"; and the like. As if disbelieving that the "word of God never fails" and "must come to pass," humans are embroiled in this wish and hope of being saved.

Again, as has been preached and propagated, God decreed that death and destruction are unto man. Therefore all evils, suffering, and death from any source or cause that befall man must be doing the work of God. It also follows then that deaths and destruction from natural disasters like earthquakes, tornados, volcanoes, tsunamis, and the like (to be blamed on the curse of Adam, huh) must be doing what God intended by helping him in their own ways.

In recent times, natural disasters (Acts of God) of earthquakes, Tornados, Tsunamis, Volcanoes and the like have increased, wreaking devastations and destruction of lives. With these, apocalyptic prophets of the Christian faith are spreading messages of end time and the return of Christ. That the return of Christ is linked with brutal, ruthless decimation of humans must lend credence to the Christian faith articulation that humans just amount to worthless and undeserving sinners. In that regard, humans are but a mass of rubbish to God, hence he wastes them the way he does. That us humans have soul and feeling makes no difference.

Going by the mentality of believers, tragic incidents like the deadly shootings by Matthew J. Murray in Colorado churches could be put in a different perspective. The victims (they must still be aware since the belief is such that there is life after death), their families, and fellow congregants of the church, by taking the preachers' spinning ways one notch up, might be grateful and thankful to God that his deed and will are done and that the victims' place in heaven is even more secure by their exiting the earth to heaven through God's house—the place of worship—where the shooting occurred, instead of mourning their loss. In the mind of the believer, could this and all other horrific deadly incidents simply be the undesirable work of the devil? If they are, could it not mean that Satan continues to prevail over God and unlike God, readily answers prayers to him for those who seek evil upon others, while God may vacillate and pick and choose from the prayers to him on which to give favors? If this is the case, is it not understandable why it appears that more people have chosen to seek Satan and his will and favor for whatever objective they fancy?

Here's is a recent experience on praising God that left me wondering about the true state of mind of the religious faithful. On the evening of Saturday, January 5, 2008, I stopped over by the home of my community members to again see the wife, the current vice president of my organized New York community, who had had a knee replacement surgery about two months earlier. While there, I met five members of their Seventh-Day Adventist church—three females and two males, one of whom was a boy of about five years old. Shortly after I got there, the group, led by one of the females, later identified to me by the host as a church elder and a "prayer warrior," started a full prayer session, complete with Holy Communion (given only to the sick host and I), singing of songs from the church hymn book, and the reading of Bible passages.

At the conclusion of one song, titled "My Lord and I," I think, the prayer warrior/leader asked individuals to share thoughts from the song that stood out for them. One after the other, they did. Then the leader spoke of the love of God and that of his son, Jesus Christ. Continuing, she shared that, as sinners, all humans are unworthy and undeserving of the mercy of God, and yet that, he, Jesus Christ, came down to earth, leaving his coveted

91

kingdom in heaven that is strewn with silver and gold, reducing himself to the human level, only to be humiliated, injured, and nailed to the cross where he had to die. She added that she knows that had she or anyone in the group been the only one here on earth, he would have come to also give his life for her or the other.

Sitting through and partaking at that time in that experience of repeated praises to an imagined God and his assumed son and their abode of the kingdom of heaven strewn in silver and gold, particularly, brought up a thought in my mind that there must be something delusional in the mind of the religious faithful, in religious faith itself, or both. Imagine that all there is for humans to be labeled unworthy sinners, who must immerse themselves in guilt and supplicate mindlessly, is to be born human—to be created by the same God as religions have it. Could this not be likened to children, whose parents chose to have and would expectedly have the responsibility to care and provide for them in any way, including health, safety, and food, having to blame themselves for constituting inconvenient burdens on their parents to whom they must also sorely and pitifully beg for forgiveness and acceptance so that those parents may help provide for them and nurture them to life?

For the five-year-old whom I sensed was the son of a man and woman in the group, it was evident that his initiation into owning up to sins he committed just for being born, therefore his contribution to making "God's" otherwise perfect world the evil that it is, and bearing the overwhelming burden and the indulgence in a lifelong profuse pleading with "God" had been effected. That experience was just one in a series that lie ahead in his path in life. There must be a better way, though, that this boy can learn of the fate that awaits all in life that does not subject him to needlessly carrying the weight of a misplaced guilt throughout his life.

The Adam and Lucifer Factors
The perfect and flawless God also created a perfect world. Adam, through Lucifer, is the flaw that afflicts and permeates life. It is because of Adam and Lucifer that life and humans in it suffer and die the way they do.

Adam would probably have been good with his life and the proclamation of God, except that his wife, Eve, succumbed to the temptation of the serpent that successfully persuaded her to eat that particular fruit that God had forbidden them to eat. Adam was to incur the wrath of God for succumbing to his wife's temptation by eating that same fruit. For this, God cursed him and all the generations of his children to be ever born. This includes all humans today, who never knew Adam and/or what he was about, let alone partook in eating the said forbidden fruit.

And as for Lucifer, a onetime archangel in God's abode of heaven, the devil entered into him and he became rebellious and a challenge to God. To solve that problem in heaven, God flushed him out of heaven and sent him down here to earth, where he has continued with his evil ways, causing people to err and their punishment, on top of those woes through Adam, to worsen.

Then enters Christ in the mix; not being a Bible or religion scholar, I'm not clear as to the sequence or chronology in which Adam, Lucifer, and Christ entered the sphere of earth. Considering, however, that Christ is said to have been sent for the purpose of redeeming mankind, I assume he came after the two have triggered and perpetuated untold woes on humanity.

From the above arises the question of whether the Bible and its many stories should be taken literally. In other words, are those stories all truthful, and should they be taken concretely or be seen as metaphors? As my mother, a devout Christian of the Anglican (Episcopal) denomination, would say, the Bible was written to teach humans lessons. My sense is that this statement stems from her catechism classes, as Anglicans are required to take and pass those classes to be "confirmed" to receive Holy Communion. Because Christians, the way I understand it, insist that the Bible and its stories are the concrete and incontrovertible word of God, I will highlight the problems that are clearly evident in certain biblical/ Christian stories and beliefs, starting with the Adam and Lucifer, and even Christ, factors.

Take the omniscient and omnipotent attributes of God, for instance; was he not in a position to know that the forbidden fruit meant trouble and did not belong in the Garden of Eden? Being omniscient means his foresight is 20/20 and all the crystal ball he needed. Does his not foreseeing this temptation and ensuring that it was not to be, not negate his ascribed omniscient and omnipotent qualities? Of what good was the serpent in the Garden of Eden that God had to create and put it there anyway? What was it about the forbidden fruit that it had to be Eve, the female, who had to be the weak link and the serpent had to succeed in getting Adam through her? Might this fruit, which no botanist or plant biologist to my knowledge has determined what it is, be a metaphor for sex?

As was told and written, the first reaction of Adam and Eve, who hitherto roamed all over the wide earth in the Garden of Eden naked, after they had eaten of the infamous fruit, was to know that they were naked. Further, when God came calling on Adam following their meal of that fruit, Adam's response was said to be, "My Lord, I'm naked;" causing God to ask him: *Have you eaten of that fruit I forbid you from eating*? Doesn't this indicate that the "forbidden fruit" they had eaten was having sex, which husbands and wives routinely and are supposedly entitled to do? If it was about sexual intercourse, does this mean that God forbids sexual intercourse, even between married couples, although he was said to have commanded humans to multiply and fill the world? Could he, God, have meant for multiplying and filling the world to be by artificial insemination? This could not have been the case because artificial insemination is a scientific process that is outside God's realm. What about the facts that the human anatomy and biology underlie human sexuality and sexual acts, and that at puberty the hormones that control sexual arousal are actively in place? What if this was the case with the wife, Eve, and she actively sought to engage in a sexual act with her husband, Adam?

Imagine that because Adam was disobedient by eating whatever fruit he was forbidden to eat; his punishment was visited upon his children through generations to be born indefinitely and including all of mankind today, by a compassionate, loving, just, fair, and forgiving God. Is this not another contradiction that strips him of these qualities?

Not knowing that Lucifer would metamorphose into the devil is another contradiction to God's omniscient and omnipotent qualities. That he lacked this foreknowledge is one thing; that the only way he knew to deal with this his shortcoming was to flush Satan down here on earth where he has since held sway over mortal humans also cancels out his caring, loving, just and fair, and forgiving attributes. This is unconscionable even in the standard of feeble, mortal beings. What father would chase and maneuver a big, poisonous, killer snake from his room after a long and protracted scuffle only to watch that snake head for the room where his five-year-old children are? That father then pries his door open just to warn those children of the big, killer snake headed their way, which they must resist and fight off or be mauled and killed/swallowed by it? This question is relevant even if that snake was acquired as a pet but metamorphosed into a demon. Lucifer was said to have been a loyal, obedient Angel prior to falling out with God. A lot of things have never added up and most likely never will.

What is with this imaginary straw being called Satan or the devil? Like in most things about religion, followers really believe there's a being somewhere out and about called Satan. Is it that hard to figure that both good and evil thoughts and deeds stem from humans and their minds, from their nature? The good or bad in human nature could be triggered and heightened for different reasons. We must not forget that humans and lower animals do what they consider necessary to survive the grind of living and to also thrive. That there is a roaming Satan behind all ills is but a metaphor at best.

Confronted with these puzzles, religious people are quick to state that God is so loving and considerate that he gave man free will; hence the burden is on the person who misuses his or her free-will privilege—falls to the temptation of Satan. In turn, they ask, "Would you rather be made an object?"

"Hell yes!" is my answer to this; if making me an object is what it would have required for that God who never sought my consent to create me needed to make a perfect world just like him. What good is the free will that "he" gave anyway, since the problems of life are, irrationally, being blamed on misused free will by man? A perfect, all-knowing God should have known better.

Other common spins by the faithful to defend God and justify his flaws, in addition to God giving man free will, include: "Would you like not to be given a choice? If you, as a parent, clearly gives your children instructions on how to behave and spell out the dangers of doing the wrong thing, any of them who chooses to err knows what to expect, etc." As they spill out typical rationalizations like this, they never wait to hear you address them and point out that these are but human spins and rationalizations fitting in the human experience realm. They forget that this is about God—the almighty, etc.! With him, what in the world would any of these items and/or similar others be doing in my choice list: need, want, hunger, insufficiency, lack, poverty, risk, homelessness, frustration, sadness, danger, worry, hunger, concern, doubt, fear, stress, anxiety, depression, tiredness, breakdown, sickness, illness, anger, rage, violence, accident, killing, old age, life expectancy, life span, dying, death, and vices like these?

Really, who needs choice when a state of perfection would suffice, or a state of not being, in the face of that choice he is said to give?

A friend, a devout Christian, and I were having some discussions on life in general a few days ago, in late June 2008, with the topic of God featuring in it. My friend had to point out that God deserves lots of thanks for providing free air (oxygen) that humans may live. As I found that ludicrous, my friend did not give me a chance to address that, as he moved and carried on.

Here we go again. Does creating life without oxygen not amount to building an engine that would require one form of "fuel" (energy) or another without that energy being available anywhere, or a four-wall shelter without a roof, for lack of a better analogy? That an almighty God would, out of whim, create life, configuring it in a way that it requires external energy to be and would not necessarily provide for that energy in some way would mean that he never really did create life. That he then deserves some special thanks and praise for doing so is mind-boggling.

Does sending Jesus Christ to earth to rescue and redeem humans, albeit believers, not clearly demonstrate an attempt to correct a mistake by an infallible, perfect God? Either he was capable of creating a perfect, infallible world from the get-go, needing no afterthought remediation of sending down Jesus Christ, or he was not. Optionally, sending Jesus Christ at the same time he was creating the world as a guarantee for a problem-free world might have sufficed. Yet, even with the afterthought of sending him down, God was incapable of having this acclaimed one redeemer, through whom any one of all "his beloved children" would be saved and stand a chance to inherit his kingdom of heaven, appear simultaneously to all his children all over the earth. It is interesting to note the way through which Jesus Christ was sent down to earth—born by the "virgin" Mary. Does this, again, not show that this God has an issue with sexual intercourse? As if this was not clear in the case of Adam and Eve, punished and cursed for sexual intercourse, apparently, he had to choose a virgin for the "holy spirit" to impregnate with Jesus Christ. The question here is, what chance do all humans conceived through male-female, husband-and-wife sexual intercourse have with him anyway? What really is it about women that God, who "created" them also, seems to saddle them with a *lion share* of the burden and blame for the "sins" of humanity? Here is one hint from the Bible:

"What is man, that he could be pure? And he who is born of a woman, that he could be righteous? (Job 15:14-16).

With God, sex must be suppressed and repressed; an impossibility considering that humans did not make themselves and their sexual nature.

That Mary, a married woman, was a virgin opens the door for other stories and speculations. Could it be that the all-knowing God knew that Mary was a virgin before Joseph married her? Then, did he, God, further decided to make Joseph impotent while stifling the libido in Mary, so Mary had no sexual drives and would not resort to sexual intercourse with another man, as Joseph was incapable of such? In essence, this means that Joseph and Mary never consummated their marriage by then. So, God preserved Mary's virginity for the Holy Ghost to savor and cherish while impregnating her with Jesus? The twists and the bizarre about this God get more intriguing.

Typical with Biblical/Scriptural texts, fathoming which account/story of Joseph, Mary, and Jesus is correct is a daunting, insurmountable task. The Christian and Islamic faiths both seem to agree that Jesus is the son of

Mary. In Islam, Jesus is known as *Isa bin Maryam;* Jesus the son of Mary, in English language. The two faiths disagree on his relationship to God, with Islam seeing him just as a prophet of God. Here are some differing accounts of the marital status of Joseph and Mary, and the birth of Jesus.

The variations of these accounts have been mainly attributed to some of the sources being apocryphal—not canonized, therefore unauthenticated and not told in the Bible. Yet, even within the books of the Bible, the accounts do differ. For instance, Matthew 1: 18 - 25, has it that Mary was married to Joseph: "… fear not to take unto thee Mary thy wife;" clear here that Mary was Joseph's wife at the time. But in Luke 2: 1 – 7, this is found: "…To be taxed with Mary his espoused wife, being great with child;" espoused here meaning to take or be taken as a spouse—as wife; to give in marriage. Essentially, this suggests That Joseph was yet to take Mary formally as his wife before she was pregnant with Jesus. One account is that Mary was only engaged to Joseph. Yet another is that Joseph had actually married Mary, but was yet to her take into his home, because he was to build a house, as culturally required, before he could take him into his house. Joseph was said to have completed the house building in a year, has taken Mary in, or was about to, at the time she was pregnant with Jesus. The *hair-splitting* explanations here have to do with whether or not Mary was actually a virgin before and at the time she was pregnant with Jesus. On how Joseph accepted Mary's pregnancy with Jesus that was not by him; one source says Mary has convinced him and her parents with the story of her vision in which the Holy Ghost was to impregnate her. Another states that God/Holy Spirit has actually told Joseph to accept her wife Mary and the pregnancy because it was by the Holy Ghost.

Some other angles to the story of Joseph (St. Joseph), which are attributed to the apocryphal sources, include that he was married to Mescha/Escha/Salome, and that they had six children—two girls and four boys; the youngest of whom was James. Joseph was said to be 40 years old before marrying Mescha; that they were married for 49 years before Mescha died. That one year after the death of Mescha, Joseph married Mary. This means that Joseph was 90 years old when he married Mary, who was between 14 and 16 years old. Joseph and Mary were said to have other children, about 4, after Jesus.

On that cultural requirement that a man builds a house before taking his/a wife in; one could understand this with a young and upcoming man. That this also applies with, or applied to, an old, matured 90 years, accomplished grand (probably great-grand) father, Joseph, is yet another stretch.

Mary was also said to, in her vision in which the Holy Spirit told her she will be pregnant with Jesus, also was told that her cousin or niece, Elizbeth the wife of Zachary who was childless and advanced in age, will be pregnant through the miracle of God as well. Elizabeth, as told, did become pregnant; giving birth to John, identified to be John the Baptist. All these are available in electronic, on-line source; there to be seen and read upon search.

It seems that, like the adult human male, the Holy Spirit who fathered Jesus is also more sexually attracted to younger females than older ones. And for 90 years old Joseph having other children with Mary, who was so young as to be his grand-daughter; he must have been a busy old man, who apparently was endowed with sexual prowess.

Pre-Christ virgin birth of God figures

It's not just probable, but very evident that teaming Christians of today are clueless of other God figures and human embodiment of gods conceived of super gods and delivered by virgin mothers over a thousand years before that of their Christ God. They are so passionate with their belief and faith that they are "sure" Jesus Christ is the son and the equal-God of the one and only God that nothing else gets to them. Whether or not they'll ever get it, here is a noted fact of pre-Christ/Christian historic virgin birth of" God" figure:

1. The Annunciation: the god Taht announcing to the virgin Queen that she is about to become a mother.
2. The Immaculate Conception: the god Kneph (the Holy Spirit) mystically impregnating the virgin by holding a Cross, the symbol of life, to her mouth.
3. The Birth of the Man-god.
4. The Adoration of the newly born infant by gods and men, including three kings(or Magi ?), who are offering him gifts. In this sculpture the cross again appears as a symbol (http//englishaetheist.org/indexd.shtml).

The (4) above sounds all too familiar with the three-wise men visiting upon the virgin birth of Jesus Christ and presenting him with their gifts of Gold Myrrh, and Frankincense hundreds of years before the birth of god That by his virgin mother Queen.

There are more from the same source:

"In another Egyptian temple, one dedicated to Hathor, at Denderah, one of the chambers was called "The Hall of the Child in his Cradle"; and in a painting which was once on the walls of that temple, and is now in Paris, we can see represented the Holy Virgin Mother with her Divine Child in her arms. The temple and the painting are undoubtedly pre-Christian. Thus we find that long before the Christian era there were already pictured in pagan places of worship virgin mothers and their divine children, and that such pictures included scenes of an Annunciation, an Incarnation, and a Birth and Adoration, just as the Gospels written in the second century A.D. describe them, and that these events were in some way connected with the God Taht, who was identified by Gnostics with the Logos."

God	Virgin mother/Queen	Place
Horus	Isis	Egypt
Krishna	Devaki	India
Hercules	Venus	Ancient Greek (Carthage)
Dionysos (The Grecian God)	Persephone	Greece (Cyprus)
Apis ("The son of the god")	The cow ("The mother of the sacred beast.")	Egypt
Ra (The Sun)	Net (or Neith)	Egypt
Attis (The Phrygian god)	Nana	Turkey (Anatolia in ancient times)

While this pre-Christian, historic, god figures appear to be traced to Egypt in the Arabic/Middle eastern geographic zone of the world that is associated with the "Abrahamic" religions, it also resonated in the Eastern zone of China, Japan, India, and elsewhere, as captured in this below quote, also from the same source:

"At the time when Christianity arose all these gods were worshipped in various parts of the Roman empire. Attis, Adonis, Dionysos, Osiris, and Mithra were the principal gods in their respective countries; and those countries together formed the greater part of the Eastern provinces of the Roman empire, and of its great rival, the Persian empire. Classical mythology is full of kindred stories, and the idea of a virgin birth was familiar to all men of that time. Of Plato it was related that his mother Perictione was a virgin who conceived him immaculately by the god Apollo. Apollo himself revealed the circumstances of this conception to Ariston, the affianced husband of the virgin. Virginity, perhaps on account of its rarity in those days among women of a marriageable age, had always a halo of sanctity cast over it by barbaric and semi-civilized tribes; and even in civilized Rome itself the Vestal Virgins were looked upon as peculiarly sacred. This reverence for virginity seems to have sometimes been contemporaneous with the institution of religious prostitution on a large scale. There is, indeed, no reason why this should not have been the case, incongruous though it seems to us, as such religious prostitution was looked upon very differently from the way in which it would now be regarded."

The Tower of Babel story is one that supposedly explains the language diversity in the world, as God was said to have sent down his destructive force to destroy the tower that "his children" on earth were building. The tower was to be used to rise/ascend close to heaven to enable them get a glimpse into the home and abode of God, their father. With the tower's destruction, God, also twisted and varied their hitherto one language, resulting in confusion instead of communication. With this act, rebuilding the tower was impossible; as a request by one builder to another for water, for instance, yielded a hammer, saw, anything but water. Somehow, those storytellers forgot to concoct one to explain racial, skin pigmentation, and size difference the way the human genome does. So heaven and earth were that close together, and God had to pull heaven farther away from earth following that close encounter, that any human with brains would embark on such a tower project to reach heaven could spy and eavesdrop on God? To paraphrase Bill Maher, *I understand enough that there are many things about life that I may never know. What I resent is people making up stories to fill in the blanks in this puzzle called life.*

While on highlighting the stark contradictions in the biblical stories, how about this one with Abraham, the father of the faithful? For a God that is all-knowing, it had to take trying Abraham with sacrificing his only son, Isaac, born when his wife Sarah was ninety and Isaac one hundred years old, to confirm his faith in him. As the story went, with his knife secure in a holster at his waist, Abraham had Isaac carry a tied bunch of firewood and asked him to walk along with him. As he asked his father where they were headed, Abraham's response was that they were going to make a sacrifice to God. "But where is the lamb for the sacrifice?" Isaac was said to have asked his father. In response, Abraham told him that God would provide the lamb. The poor, defenseless child, Isaac, got a rude awakening when his father tied him on the heap of firewood and drew the knife to slaughter him before the all-knowing God realized that Abraham was going through with the killing of Isaac and therefore was faithful to him and sent a sacrificial lamb through some magic. He then commanded Abraham not to go through with killing Isaac.

In today's world, shackled up, Abraham would have wound up first in jail en route to a criminal court; his criminal charges: endangering the welfare and attempted murder of a child. From the criminal court, his next stop would be a hospital psychiatric ward—his diagnosis: auditory hallucination. This would illustrate a clear case of mental illness and not proof of faith, as was intended with this story. Here again, I am reminded of Bill Maher's response, while on CNN's *Larry King Live*, to a caller who had asked him what he would do if he found that God was speaking to him, to which Bill responded, paraphrasing, "I will check myself into a psych ward, and I suggest you do the same, if you think God is speaking to you."

Another thing that is clear in this story is that while Christians condemn and belittle the ritual of sacrificing animals, for religious or other spiritual rites, in the cultures that they went about to convert to Christianity, their God is a bloodsucker to whom animals and humans were also sacrificed.

The notion that my forbears are not welcome to the abode of heaven, the home of God and his righteous children, if that were to hold, as Christianity showed up in their shores way after their time, and one only enters heaven through Christ, ends this one, almighty God conspiracy for me.

Historically, humans have been emotional with their religious faith, and they still are. They kill and die for it as a result. While it is known that religious doctrines and faith do not lend themselves to logic and reasoning, lately, some religious professionals make statements of claims to logic and rationale about their faith. Below is an excerpt from stories by Garrett Toren, a Christian and an editor, apparently telling an anecdotal story to prove there is a God.

Is There a God?

No one can prove to you the existence of God, as in a mathematical proof. But you still will be able to be certain of His existence:

There are many good, rational arguments. We will make them in a moment. But if you do not want to believe in God, you never will. There can be no scientific proof, simply because God is not physical or material, He is spiritual and infinite. Science is the observation of material phenomena in this universe, and then applying our reason and logic to understand and control them.

By definition, God cannot exist as part of this universe, cannot be composed of matter, and cannot even exist in time. We will explain why later on this page. But even things in this world cannot really be proven with 100% certainty. Entire books have been written about how the U.S. space program has been faked by the government. All you have to do is set the standards of proof high enough, and absolutely nothing can be proven. Proof is a tricky subject. As the old Greeks like Euclid discovered, all proofs have to rely on at least several assumptions (which they called postulates) which cannot themselves be proven. So a person who demands hard proofs is doomed to failure. It is a doctrine of the Church that faith does not come to us through reason alone, but by the grace of God. If a person opposes even the possibility of God's existence, then any arguments or evidence can be rationalized away.

Since it is impossible to "prove" with absolute certainty, any amount of belief in God has to come from your own spirit, from within your own heart, because it is the spirit of God that we are trying to find. The paradox is, you will only find this faith if God gives you the grace to find it.

A person of faith already knows why they believe. It is not for any selfish reason, or because they want to be "saved." It is because they know they are a true child of God, and that we naturally seek Him and know Him as only a child can know their parents. It is a completion of our lonely existence. It is a feeling of coming home. And it is a certainty that goes far beyond all efforts at "proof." Our faith is a pure gift from God. It is the result of our having accepted the gift of his grace. The following is from a newspaper obituary of a twenty-year-old girl, written by her parents:

After four years, our cancer warrior Alice has left her earthly bounds and gone to heaven, where her body is healthy again, where the wind can blow through her hair, and where she can finally ride a horse on the beach and

swim with dolphins. She was embraced in heaven by all
the inspiring teens and children with cancer she met along
the way.

My question to atheists is: if her parents asked you for your true beliefs,
would you really take that away from them? Could you really tell them that
their daughter was just unlucky, and suffered heroically for years only to
go out like a candle and be nothing more than dirt in the ground?

If beautiful, loving Alice had been your daughter, would you really
take that away from yourself? Would you really believe it? And don't say
that people have to face facts: atheism is *not* a fact, because no one can
"prove" there is not a God any more than we can "prove" to you—by your
earthly, material standards—that there is one (http://www.meaning-of-life.
info/IsThereaGod.html).

How about that for a proof that there is a God? First, I will comment
on this statement in quotes from the cancer warrior Alice story:
"If beautiful, loving Alice had been your daughter, would you really
take that away from yourself? Would you really believe it?"

Toren had started out leading his reader to believe he was making a
factual argument to prove the existence of God. However, he concluded
as shown in his words in quotes above with what religion and preachers
do best: stroking and agitating the emotions of their audience. Of course,
death, particularly of a girl that age, is very much an emotional thing. So
is religion, and Toren had to go there. As if he needed an answer to that
rhetorical question, I'll give him an answer: No, I do not have to take that
away from them. If that would help them cope, I would not take that away
from them, of course. I know enough about coping and the mechanisms for
it to understand that they are not to be taken away when people need them
the most; no matter what they are. I could help them deal with the loss in
some other ways. Now, here's a critical look at this "proof."

Here are Garret Toren's own words as he made a point that relying on
proof to believe in his God is impossible:

> All you have to do is set the standards of proof high
> enough, and absolutely nothing can be proven. Proof is a
> tricky subject. As the old Greeks like Euclid discovered,
> all proofs have to rely on at least several assumptions
> (which they called postulates) which cannot themselves be

proven. So a person who demands hard proofs is doomed
to failure.

The irony of Garret Toren possibly being right in his statements
above is that religion may have set these postulates about God too high
to prove: *perfect, omnipotent, omniscient, omnipresent, immortal, kind,
merciful, just, fair, forgiving, and in control of all heavenly and earthly
transactions.*

The simple disproof is that a God with those qualities could not have
made this life that we all, humans, are living and experiencing—snake,
serpent, Satan, Eve, Adam, or not.

How about these words, also by Garret Toren:

> It is a doctrine of the Church that faith does not come to us
> through reason alone, but by the grace of God. If a person
> opposes even the possibility of God's existence, then any
> arguments or evidence can be rationalized away.

Indoctrination, mind control (as in the *doctrine of the church*) is the
problem; it does not lend itself to proof. Indoctrination and demagogy are
twin critical tools of religion.

Here's more:

> Since it is impossible to "prove" with absolute certainty,
> any amount of belief in God has to come from your own
> spirit, from within your own heart, because it is the spirit
> of God that we are trying to find. The paradox is, you will
> only find this faith if God gives you the grace to find it.

Speaking of the real paradox in the above quote, God may choose not to
give one the grace to find the spirit of God—to find him—and yet expects
that, somehow, one would or should have found him. That God may chose
not to give one that spirit would then negate the concept of "free will"/
choice, which the faithful cite for God's considerate nature and in turn is
used to blame man for choosing wrongfully, hence his woes.

Yet, another of those real paradoxes in Garret Toren's words: "Our
faith is a pure gift from God. It is the result of our having accepted the gift
of his grace."

Obviously, the concept of gift implies acceptance or rejection by the
intended recipient. Here, again, the capacity to accept or reject a gift
implies "free will"/choice/freedom. That God is all-knowing, all-able,
caring, and loving are enough for him to make all his children accept him

by giving them all that grace. This, of course, would negate his considerate nature to not impose but give the "free will" to choose. And that he gave this free will and still does not take the responsibility for all the mess and turns around to blame the mortal human to whom he had given the free will to do as he decides is, again, mind-boggling.

Garret Toren started out with statements that appear rational, being sure to cast his dragnet wide by including and making a reference to "the old Greeks like Euclid discovered, all proofs have to rely on at least several assumptions (which they called postulates) which cannot themselves be proven." In the end, all he ended up doing is "spinning" his reader, like I guess some would consider some or all of what I have done here. Because I concede up front that no one holds a lock on truth, and having also stated that *reality is perception, as perception is also reality*, what I have written here might as well be considered spinning. In a way, though, Garrett Toren unwittingly agrees that no one could vouch to a conclusive knowledge of the existence of God and that God is but as perceived by the individual, *perception being reality, as reality is perception*. His words here in quotes illustrate this: "God is not physical or material, He is spiritual and infinite." Because things in the spiritual and infinite realm are not concrete, they are not perceived (or "seen") by all humans the same way. One reason, a physical one, among the psychological ones, is that those born mentally retarded (with chemical damage or deficiencies in certain areas of the brain) may lack the mental capacity or function to rise or relate to the spiritual and the infinite realms ever. Another of the psychological reasons is that what people perceive in that realm may not be universal, as they, perceptions, are also subject to one's experience in the physical realm and the influence of one's heritage and culture. Naturally, therefore, Garret Toren must accept the fact that not everyone would buy into the God notion, let alone his own God.

As if he felt that all the spinning above did not cut it, Garret Toren tried further with this story:

> Still, there are some very persuasive arguments, and we
> will make them just after this:

The following is a true personal account, and I remember it like it was only yesterday. I am sure there is a heaven, and that my Grandpa is there. Here's why:

When I was a boy, my mother gave piano lessons to augment our small income. Our piano was an old upright that was so decrepit that it couldn't be tuned, and had several keys that didn't play at all. We couldn't afford a better one. My grandfather whose name was Joseph Weber came to spend the last few months of his life with us. I don't know what he was suffering from, but he was very ill and couldn't get up from his bed. He would hear Mother talk about how difficult it was to teach on our old piano. Just before he died, he told her that when he got to heaven, the first thing he would do would be to make sure she got a new piano. Mom told him that she had been saving for years, and that all she was able to put aside was $50.00, not nearly enough even then. "Don't worry, Ruthie," he said, "I'll make sure you get one. I'll send it right down from heaven."

A few days after Grandpa died, Mother got a call from someone who was moving out of our small town. It seems that they had a nice grand piano, almost new, and they had seldom used it and did not want to move it. They had heard that she was a piano teacher, and they wanted to know if she would like to purchase it for $50.00. Only after it was all set up in our living room, and Mom sat down to play it for the first time, did she notice the brand name of the piano, written in big gold letters above the keyboard. It was a little known maker, the only one of that make that I have ever seen. Mother sat motionless, staring, before bursting into tears.

It was a Weber. So that is how I know that my Grandpa is in heaven. And that is why I returned to God after a long absence.

Garrett Toren, Editor

> *[If you are thinking that a coincidence about a piano is not a good enough reason to have faith, please know that remembrance of this incident, many years later, only caused me to open up my heart and mind to the possibility of God, after a long and firm denial. My faith is a gift from God.]*

One last word on the cancer warrior Alice:

> After four years, our cancer warrior Alice has left her earthly bounds and gone to heaven, where her body is healthy again, where the wind can blow through her hair, and where she can finally ride a horse on the beach and swim with dolphins. She was embraced in heaven by all the inspiring teens and children with cancer she met along the way.

One thing is clear in the above quote: *delusion—not only of God, but also of heaven (where there is a beach with horseback riding and the wind blowing through her hair, and there are also dolphins for people to swim along with)* just because they died of cancer and their parents wished that for them?

For a God that is only in and of the *"spiritual and infinite"* realm, his residence, the abode of heaven, a place that Garrett cannot vouch to have physically verified, also has some physical attributes. Those include a beach, horses, and dolphins in the water/pool. This is not only bizarre; it speaks to the nature and "reality" of this delusion. It is an irrefutable testimony to the fact that perceptions and realities, and those of God in particular, are but depictions based on experiences and cultures in the physical world. Because not all cultures of the world have horseback riding, parents or other adults of other cultures used in a similar story would not conceive of a heaven with those activities. Again, one does not need to reinforce Alice's parents' belief and statement that their daughter is in heaven because one emotionally empathizes with their loss. While they may be devastated by one saying to them that heaven may only exist in their minds; it does not necessarily justify dishonestly and deceitfully vouching for this imagination of theirs. As an option, one could find soothing words of comfort to say to them that could be helpful.

Nothing could be a weaker proof of God's existence than Garret Toren's Weber piano story. It is good for him that he correctly considered the piano's brand name of Weber a coincidence. Yet he chose to use this coincidence as ironclad proof. This simply implies that all coincidences, based on religious faith, are evidence or proof of the existence of a God or something. It would have been different had he stated also that, *as a kid*, having heard his grandfather making that statement about making sure his mother got a piano when he got to heaven, when a piano sold to his mother also turned out to be a Weber, like his grandfather's name, he saw it as God-sent. Because kids perceive many things magically, it would have been okay.

If a coincidence, such as that in Garrett Toren's story above, is proof of the existence of a God, the coincidence of this story must also be proof of the existence of the God, or some God.

Amaechi: A Hope Fulfilled and a Hope Shattered

An Igbo couple had been childless for about six years of their marriage. In Igbo culture, across the board and particularly at the time this couple lived this experience, having children to continue the family name is not an option; it is a requirement. For this couple, their need to have children was made desperate by the fact that the man and husband was the only male offspring of his father.

Over the years of their childlessness, the couple did all in their power by following up and through with every suggestion they received. Their efforts and perseverance paid off with the birth of a baby boy in their seventh year of marriage. They appropriately named this boy Amaechi, meaning "the lineage will not shut down." It was obvious that the birth of their first and eventually only child after seven years with all hope almost lost brought such relief and happiness to the couple. Naming him Amaechi underscored the point that his birth doubled for fulfilling their lives and marriage as it also assured that the lineage and family would be carried on as their Igbo culture required of them.

When Amaechi became ill at the age of three, his parents did not think it was something to really worry about as they took the necessary steps to seek a cure for his ailment. As his health deteriorated over time despite the treatments, Amaechi's parents became increasingly worried. Unrelenting, his parents desperately tried different ways, conventional and otherwise, to treat him and to save his life. The couple consulted with modern medical experts within their locality and beyond. They also sought out Christian diviners. They decided at a point to work with the Christian "prayer warriors," as they were termed, when they had no luck with modern medicine, but after having stayed with them for a while with no success, the husband attempted unsuccessfully to persuade his wife to go along with trying a renowned local, traditional diviner, popularly known as Dibiaukwu—meaning "the great doctor or healer." His wife considered herself a born-again Christian and saw nothing good in traditional healing. The husband decided to give it a try on his own anyway.

As the consultation progressed, Dibiaukwu shared with the man that the prognosis for their son was very bad and that he, Amaechi, would end up dying. This news predictably devastated Amaechi's father. Making things profoundly hopeless, Dibiaukwu himself felt troubled that he could not help reverse Amaechi's impending death. All he could say was that Amaechi was a troubled and possessed child, who was not destined to live to either bring closure to his parents' yearning or bring them the hope they expected and deserved. In a week, Dibiaukwu's determination came to pass as Amaechi died, even as his mother got deeper in prayers and was told that Amaechi was healing slowly.

As preparations were made for Amaechi's burial, a kinsman was assigned the communal role of buying his coffin. When he returned with one and Amaechi's body was laid in it, his father noticed that the coffin had a tiny sticker with the name Dibia, toward the foot of it.

It turned out that Dibia, as in the doctor/healer, was the maker of the coffin. I point out here that this kinsman who procured this coffin was not privy to Amaechi's father's consultation with Dibiaukwu and did not set out to go looking to procure a name-brand coffin, let alone a Dibia brand.

As in Garett Toren's story, this one also ended in a coincidence. If his logic is followed here, it also means that Dibiaukwu was in touch with someone or thing, as Garrett Toren's grandfather, Weber, was in his story. So, the coincidence here would be taken for a proof of the existence of God, who in this case chose not to grant the wishes and prayers of Amaechi's parents but validate Dibiaukwu's determination, as was spiritually revealed to him the way God divined it. Or is the difference supposed to be that Weber pledged or made a promise of sending help from heaven after he died, whereas Dibiaukwu made no such promise?

Really, coincidences do happen in life. However, they pale in comparison to the ovewhelming number of times that wishes have not come true and are therefore a very poor way of proving the existence of a god. To Garrett Toren, however, this story is proof that God exists, constituting a logical and rational approach to religion to him. If anything, his attempt to attach logic to religion, with this story and other things he recounted in the same source that I don't deem necessary to repeat here but that still fall short, is an indication that many things done in the name of faith alone may no longer hold firm for him.

Chapter 6

Conflict

Conflicts seem to be inherent in life, in the quest to survive, preserve oneself, thrive, achieve, and progress. Basically, disagreements arise when interests or needs collide. The resulting conflict, when not resolved, stifles relationships and charges the atmosphere. This potentially translates to stress and with it poor fulfillment of needs and lack of desirable ends. On the individual, intrapersonal level—the most microcosmic of the levels of conflict—it is evident that conflicts play out as one navigates life, scouring to meet needs. Although conflicts on this level could and do result in negative consequences, they pale in comparison to those from the larger interhuman—the macrocosmic—levels. Using the urban landscape, for instance, the human world community is linked from the individual, the family home, the city block, the city street, the community district, the city, the state, the region of a nation, the nation, the region of a continent, the continent, the region of the world, and then the world. Each of these, a notch up on the ladder/scale, constitutes a subgroup in the scheme of interhuman transactions and relationships. The history of the world is replete with the large-scale negative consequences of conflicts in interhuman group relations: slavery, the Holocaust, Hiroshima, wars—civil, of occupation, and of expansion, to secure and protect interest, to assert authority and control, to exert religious influence, etc.

Some means employed by humans to deal with conflict, beginning from the interpersonal level, are as old as conflict itself. Religion, though significantly about discovering and relating to and with God, which in itself does brew conflict, is known to be used to deal with intrapersonal, interpersonal, and group conflicts. Others are hallucinogens and intoxicants, which have been used and are still being used to take refuge from harsh, unpleasant situations. Whether it is spiritual/psychological, religious, or chemical from substances, the effect is to numb or escape an undesirable state—a dose of opium basically. Even though the use and abuse of mind-altering chemicals in some cultures in recent times, especially by the youth and those not that young, may have started as a learned behavior—an en vogue/in thing of fitting in with a social group, with many becoming addicted—it is established that many use them for the above reasons. Between these two broad means of dealing with conflicts are the tools and skills of the scientific, mental health model. This model is about understanding and dissecting the need and what may have been consciously or unconsciously done to meet that need (the behavior) resulting in the undesirable situation from which relief is sought. Such behavior may have to be changed. That tools and skills are involved and required here underscore the point of this means being more challenging, as it requires more investment and engagement of the mind.

As I have become increasingly self-aware with age, exposure—therefore life experience and skills—I find myself to be generally conflict-shy. For instance, I'd rather not go for or after things when everyone else is doing so or is there. In a graduate social work class in New York University, a course that has an experiential slant, with students/participants being prompted by the professor to kind of self-disclose, I shared this. In that instance, I stated that as a young worker in Lagos, Nigeria, in the 1970s, I did not go shopping on paydays like many workers my age did. Further, while my peers would frequent clubs and hotspots at night, I never did. Even when it came to girls, a prominent feature in the life of boys at that age and human developmental stage, I never was reckless. I did not date more than one girl at a time. The feedback I got from the professor suggested to me then that something was wrong with that. Now, however, I have a different way of interpreting that feedback. That is, that there is something about me and my nature that had me using a coping mechanism that seems not to be the norm at that stage of human development. Raised in a culture and time when reckless sexual behavior constituted defamation, I had witnessed older half sisters slapping young men/boys for daring to ask them out. Contrast these to the "norm" of some cultures where parents help make or encourage matches (boyfriend/girlfriend and vice versa) for their children. Partly or fully due to the fact that I don't like rejection, I am conservative in chasing after women and will not compete for one either.

Actually, I had told my mother at a point when violence characterized late-night events at nightclubs or other events in the city, that she could rest assured that she would get no bad news about me being one of the victims, for

I didn't go clubbing, much less, late at night, and would not. Looking back, it seems it was for people like me that the U.S. baseball legend, Yogi Berra, known for his philosophical sayings had said (an oxymoron), "Nobody goes there anymore; it's too crowded." Also, I am about as gambling-shy as I am conflict-shy. Embarking on goals or objectives, I would want to know as much as there was to the factors I could control to accomplish the goal/objective. I would be careful to manage those and in the process hope to improve my chance at the factors beyond my control. Being this way, I accept the reality that the higher the risk, the higher the return—negative or positive. I am more comfortable with not losing all than with hoping to win all. I know myself well enough that I do not necessarily compete just to do as others are doing. Yes, there's a saying in my ethnic culture that *"Anughi l'ibe (la ibe) ji agu akwa; (adighi ka ibe na'gu akwa)* (in general Igbo). Translated into English, it means, "Not measuring up to one's peers triggers sobbing [self-pity)." Yet, the goals I set for myself, or the standards, are from within and of my conception and imagination. I'm really my own competition and would determine that either for my life stage and/or the efforts that I have put to my goals, I should have certain objects and standards to show for it. There's a difference. My way recognizes the fact that people are gifted differently and people are better off knowing themselves enough to identify where their strengths lie and finding the ways to hone them, than just doing things because others, whose strengths may be in what they excel doing, are doing them.

Dealing with interpersonal conflicts, to resolve or challenge them, as one avoids any and/or all conflicts to the detriment of one's self-preservation, I have also learned of response blocks to conflicts that I or others may have. As one tends in nature to make up (compensate) for some personal attributes needing to be made up for, I find that for my conflict-shy nature, I tend to use *logic*—a response block to conflict all the same—over other bases of dealing with and handling conflict. As I find this basis to be effective for me, this is how I have compensated for my conflict-shy nature.

This nature of mine continues to make me see dealing with intrapersonal and interpersonal conflicts logically as the most appropriate. My resolving conflicts this way may not be a panacea—nothing is—but it has emboldened me to stand up to the threat of demagogy to follow through with these intuitively prompted reflections and discourse, particularly about God, which I share here. One thing that makes logic and common sense such a strong and dependable basis for dealing with phenomena and concepts is that deductions are made from laying out and analyzing reasonably incontrovertible facts, using them to make predictions or reach conclusions.

Although conflict-shy, when in my mind I have analytically considered the facts and other factors that contribute to the issue(s), I may and do find that the time becomes right to face the issue head-on. My experience is that dealing with and resolving conflicts this way has served my life and the human experience in general better.

Given the potentially drawn-out negative consequences of unresolved conflicts, doing nothing about resolving them should not be an option. Yes, some attempts at this may fail. But when the time is right, resolutions, especially splitting the difference—some comprise by the parties to a conflict—do result. As conflicts will always surface, dealing with and resolving them do boost life skills in that domain at least, with the confidence acquired sticking through to a resolution. Speaking for myself, I find this to be true.

Dealing with interhuman conflicts on a larger scale, starting with reaching out to intervene, engage, mediate, and resolve them, certainly requires greater understanding and skills. Some could come from intuition, but most obviously come from experience and development. This could be very challenging, especially where parties to the conflict have to do the resolving without a third party mediating. To effectively deal with and resolve conflicts entails understanding that needs and meeting them drive conflicts. The need could be physical and obvious or at the subconscious level of the mind. It could be psychological and/or subtle and at the unconscious level of the mind, yet there. Even when a need may be obvious or physical, those having identical needs may not see or go about meeting them the same way. This being because the variables of experience and background—the underlying issues—differ.

The point of problem with parties to a conflict seeking to self-resolve stems from the fact that "normal" people may be blinded to (unaware of) how their relative underlying issues contribute to the conflict. Stated above, that experience and development necessary here is introspection—self-awareness. This entails understanding and accepting the strengths and the weaknesses—the insecurity—one may have. Achieving this is not easy because many people are uncomfortable seeing and acknowledging their insecure sides. They carry on operating and relating in ways that mask their insecurities, meeting their need to project strength on the surface, while the interpersonal conflicts they breed endure. When a neutral, unbiased third party mediates conflicts, he/she is likely to be better able to deal on a factual and analytical basis and therefore find a more mutually acceptable outcome.

Many things exacerbate conflicts between individuals, groups, and even nations. Having cultivated and projected a certain persona and image

113

over time, it becomes routine to feel "safe" and fulfilled so that some can neither see what havoc they wreak, their own vulnerability, nor living any other way. Whether done innocently or arrogantly, the consequences do become damaging all the same. Two renowned incidents in ancient Greek mythology which have since become metaphors probably capture, in these cases, the personal vulnerability inherent in this attitude the most: *the Icarus paradox and the Achilles' heel*. In the former, Icarus became too confident in the wings he had invented to escape from an island, losing all sense of caution and bordering on arrogance, to his detriment. He soared so high in the sky that he got too close to the sun, against his father's counseling, and the wax with which he made the wings was melted, causing Icarus to fall and drown in a river. And in the latter; King Achilles' mother wanted to make him immortal by dipping him in the River Styx, the world of the dead, when he was little. As she dipped him, Achilles' mother held him by the heel. This meant that his heel, which was not dipped in the river of the dead, did not get that immunity like the rest of his body. As a feared, warrior king later, his heel, as his only vulnerability, did him in. It was hit by a poisoned arrow from the bow of Paris in a battle at Troy, causing his death.

Returning to my stated competition-shy nature, having noted that I am my own competition, I lately, in many recent months to this day, Saturday, November 15, 2008, have found myself "competing" to keep up with myself, particularly in my job. On July 1, 2007, my requested transfer to an office in the Bronx, in my current employment with the City of New York, became effective. I had asked for the transfer to be closer to my home in Peekskill, Northern Westchester County, having commuted about two and half hours one way to work in downtown Manhattan (New York, New York) for over a year and a half. The commute was taking its toll on me. With this change in location came a change in my job function. For the first time in over fifteen years, I had no staff to supervise and delegate work to, having had to supervise a staff strength ranging from five to over thirty, directly or indirectly, in the past. For one whose job functioning for many years had been comprised mainly of supervision and administration, designing and creating tools to monitor and track productivity, and giving guidelines to accomplish those, this took quite some adjustment. The issue here is not necessarily that I had no staff to supervise, but that the volume of work had suddenly made me struggle to be up-to-date with my work the way I had known myself to be. I was reassured that it was not just me, as my colleagues often shared their frustration with the sheer volume of work and the difficulty they had keeping up. Having started out in the first few months feeling good about this change and having done well with it, my suddenly not measuring up to my own standards seemed to be at the root of an anxiety spree that I came to experience.

Before then, I prided myself that I would do my job, most of the time, before a supervisor hounded me for it, as that would chip away at my self-esteem. In a way, I am insecure about not measuring up and also expressed that feeling in this term as I got to acquire the appropriate expression for it, particularly given my human behavior profession and clinical background. With this feeling, I find myself struggling to go to work on a daily basis, for the first time, as I can recall in my work-life which spans some thirty-plus years. I would point out here that no "real" threat (official sanction or reprimand) known to me was at issue then. As the feeling lingered and also stretched to not feeling excited at even things I had enjoyed doing, as nothing seemed to excite me any longer, I shared my frustration with my wife, my son, and close relatives and friends. A particular sensation I felt in my brain at the height of the feeling made me wonder aloud that some brain chemicals might have been triggered and were keeping the "heat" up.

I used the term "crazy" earlier in the "Rhetorical Dialogues" segment of this discourse to describe certain human behaviors that life imposes or conditions people to. This has also led to human endeavors and expertise coming up with insight and understanding. This endeavor in the human behavior field has resulted in the categorizing, diagnosing, and treatment of conditions like the one I am experiencing now even as I am documenting this. It is possible that I am going through some stress related to adapting to my current job functions, although there are likely other contributory factors. In acute cases, stress does manifest even in physical ailments and has biological (biochemical), psychological, and social (biopsychosocial) components to it. I could not, therefore, but think that if this experience that I have does not rise to the level of a neurotic state, then anxiety might capture what I feel. Indeed, craziness is embedded in life.

Per Wikipedia-on-line, Carl Jung, "an influential thinker and the founder of analytical psychology," had a theory for neurosis. This theory is said to be "particularly fitting for people who are successfully adjusted by normal social standards, but who nevertheless have issues with the meaning of their life." While I thought this came close enough to applying to me, particularly on having issues with life, I ruled it out. Doing so, I'm clear that the trigger for this discourse is mostly the religious-based morals that the ubiquitous, self-righteous religion ideologues persistently work to impose on people and judge them by. For me here, the issue is not necessarily with the meaning of my personal life, but with life in general, and I have been clear about this. If ever neurosis were to apply, it would be more based on the theory of the ideal and the real selves, which is rooted in the conflict of surviving and living life.

With conflict a norm in life, the mental health field, psychology in particular, in some ways validates the central theme of this discourse—that the world and life are flawed. In *Understanding*, psychologist Ozodi Thomas Osuji (2007) writes:

> Our physical world requires strength to adapt to it; our society is competitive; the physically challenged child may feel unable to meet these challenges. The physically challenged child uses his thinking and imagination to construct an idealized self image, a self he thinks is able to overcome the exigencies of living on this uncaring world.

Osuji in the above quote is essentially addressing the onset of sense of self, said to occur at or before age six, as humans start the lifelong journey of preparing themselves to adapt to and cope with the harsh realities of the conflict-ridden life. This reality includes the standards and expectations to which society squeezes one to conform, by which one is also judged, and to which inherent biological traits may not equip one to measure up.

This, then, requires some balancing acts, beginning in the mind of the individual. This "necessary" balancing act is said to be at the core of neurosis that, if pervasive, constitutes mental illness in the psychoanalytic theory.

If Osuji's articulation above captures the essence of neurosis—the emergence of idealized self (in a way, the rejection of an inadequately equipped real self) early in life to strive at measuring up to culturally and socially imposed standards—then just about everyone in life is neurotic. This is because those culturally and socially imposed standards were not tailor-made to fit any one person's standards. This being the case, therefore, neurosis would be a norm, and not an abnormality. It would only be a mental illness when pervasive.

Personally, I could in some ways relate to or identify with the concept of the real versus the ideal self in striving to measure up to some standards. I became aware early in life that I did not achieve or attain the motor/locomotion skill of walking at the "standard" age of development when this is attained, having not been so endowed. I knew this after I had attained that milestone from the mockery and derogatory names that I was called growing up. It was not clear to me how long it took me to attain that milestone until 2008, when I brought it up with my mother in a general discussion. She told me that I did that at age two.

Having turned out more cerebral as I have since known that I did, I could say that this is the way I made up (compensated) for a conflict-shy nature. About aspiring to conform to culturally/socially set standards, I know myself to have done all I could early in my life to not be a disappointment. In this "dog-eat-dog world," some of those who identify with the traits that I have articulated here may have experienced, in a job or other environment, that some other people may see their even-keel nature as an invitation to pile and dump on them. It is my sense that those who think they have seen an opportunity to "get one over" on an even-keel person are typically shallow and erratic. The typical bully comes to mind here. To a point, they do "get one over" on the nonabrasive colleague who also may not have gotten a grip on the dynamics of the personalities at play, including his. However, when the game is attempted on the discerning easygoer, the abrasive player does get stunned into a rude awakening that even burns him. Personally, I'd take steps to not only stop him dead in his tracks, but to also put him on notice not to venture my way ever with any attempt to get one over on me. No, playing fair for me is never an invitation to dump or pile on a person; it's rather a challenge to the other to evolve beyond the crude, lower animal level of relating.

Overall, I have been very much a conformist for most of my life, even in religious faith, till recent years when I grew to intellectually question it. A metaphor that I use to describe my imagined community expectation of the behavior of offspring is that there is a record kept and maintained back home in which one's acts, no matter where on earth one might be, are chronicled. That metaphoric "record" here symbolizes the socially and culturally imposed standard. I alluded in the preface of this discourse to my having achieved success despite not-so-good fortune in my teens. I also came up with another expression to capture this, vis-à-vis those others, including my peers, who are seen to not have done well despite having better opportunities than I had, for instance. This is how I have communicated it in discussions on life, destiny, endowed skills, and achievement with others: There are those who found themselves in a deep ditch, but managed to dig and maneuver themselves out of it. And there are those others who, although they found themselves on a reasonably high ladder rung, jumped and pounced on that ladder until they broke it, fell, and found themselves in a ditch.

I had started working in the early 1970s immediately after the Nigerian Civil—Nigeria-Biafra—War ahead of most of my peers who, having fought in that war as teenagers like I did, had returned to finish their high school education, which was interrupted by the war. While on my first job with the Nigerian Hotels Ltd. as a cleaner, I took advantage of correspondence education to enhance my chances to move to better job opportunities. A breakthrough came my way when Paul Ogwuma (De Paul) referred me to a German businessman, Joerg Holger Viereck. At the time, Mr. Viereck, in partnership with Nigerian business entrepreneurs, was starting an industrial gas and welding material business, Gas & Welding Nigeria Ltd. in Lagos. Just about the first Nigerian employee of that company, my duties were broad, and included handling and moving large amounts of cash, as Nigeria was and still may be a cash-based transactions economy. My salary was more than I had imagined and was motivating.

In that position, I worked closely with other German and Dutch officials of the company, including Rudolph Hentschel and Dieter Weiss. After a while, Rudolph Hentschel left Gas & Welding and became involved with another company, also a Nigerian-German partnership, G.E.R.I. Nigeria Ltd. Not long after, Rudolph Hentschel, with whom I did not quite get along at Gas & Welding, made overtures to hire me. When I left to join him, I heard from a former colleague at Gas & Welding that Mr. Viereck, the managing director, had expressed surprise that Rudolph Hentschel had pulled me from his company, despite the known differences he and I had. I joined Mr. Hentschel at G.E.R.I., and he more than doubled the salary I earned at Gas & Welding. He also offered me a company car and paid my house rent. With this job, I earned enough, over time, to pay for one year of school and boarding fees upon securing college admission in the United States and to be issued a student visa, before migrating to the United States in January 1982.

When I informed Mr. Hentschel of my plans, he understandably felt a sense of loss but still was very supportive. He paid for my airfare with Lufthansa, round-trip, as he had asked me to return to Nigeria in the summer to work for the company. Also, based on the trust he had in me, he asked me to recommend a relative of mine to take my position. Interestingly, at about the time I was preparing to leave Nigeria, Dieter Weiss, who had also left Gas & Welding for another Nigerian-German partnership, Horicon Nigeria Ltd. approached me to work for a Northern Nigerian arm of Horicon—Hocon, with benefits slightly higher than those I enjoyed with G.E.R.I. I had to turn down that offer to follow through with my plan for a university education overseas. Both G.E.R.I. and Horicon/Hocon had their parent corporations in Frankfurt, Germany, with Horicon/Hocon's parent company being Philipp Holzmann AG, and that of G.E.R.I., G.E.R.I. Gmbh. Horicon meant Holzmann-Rivers Construction of Nigeria, with its head office in Port Harcourt, Rivers State, Nigeria, and Hocon, Holzmann Construction of Nigeria. I had asked for some financial assistance from Mr. Weiss to help enhance my available fund for my U.S. adventure, and he obliged me with the sum of N500.00 (five hundred naira). At the time, one naira exchanged for one dollar and eighty cents. I owe a lot of my success to the Germans that I worked for and with, with a particular place in my heart for Rudolph Hentschel. He and I were about two years apart in age.

My processing these details here brings context to the factors of family heritage, being at the right place at the right time (luck factor), and personal natural endowments in my life's history. First, I had De Paul, who in his illustrious career as a banker and economist, peaking as the governor of the Central Bank of Nigeria, became the most known of the Ogwuma clan, one of the largest and most accomplished families in Ngwa; my grandfather, Ogwuma Nwagbaghi, having been accomplished in his life and time. Also, Ngwa, arguably, is the largest subgroup of the Igbo ethnicity of Nigeria. I used my access to De Paul to appeal to him to meet my need and desire for a job change. Then there was De Paul's contact with Joerg Holger Viereck. I later learned he, Joerg Holger Viereck, was the managing director of a large German company in Nigeria, Moneer Construction Company (MCC), at a time when Samuel Mbakwe, who eventually became the first governor of the Imo State of Nigeria, was the company's chairman. I had to have performed to earn that level of trust and the goodwill of my German immigrant bosses. Holding up my end of the deal, I had been sure to control the things I could, resulting in my having earned this trust and goodwill, of which I continue to be proud, looking back more than twenty-six years. It is very possible that another person in an identical situation and given the same or identical opportunities would not have performed in such a way to earn the trust and goodwill that I did.

As far as conflict goes, I know that intrapersonally it played out as I grappled with my life and faced my future. For one, the fear of failure, particularly given the stark threat of a bleak future that stared me in the face with the loss of my father and with it the opportunity for higher education, nudged me on. Subconsciously, I worried about not living up to the Ogwuma name. And as one whose father and mother were among the few in their generation to have some education of note, I felt too privileged to underachieve. These account for the factors of parental heritage, luck, and natural endowments in my success.

One way I look at this is through the Freudian theory of *psychic determinism*, observed behaviors being driven by unconscious underlying factors (needs) and not by chance as it would seem.

I tend, therefore, to buy the notion and concept of the real self, imposed standards, the idealized self, intrapersonal conflict, and a resulting neurosis, as articulated and argued by Ozodi Thomas Osuji. One other way to look at this is by examining actors who have become "movie stars/celebrities" in societies where movies are a serious part of the culture. Some of those celebrities are known to have eventually led some lifestyles, including drug/substance abuse, which caused them to self-destroy. Addressing the drastic and dramatic bad turns in their lives, they are known to state that at the height of their success, they had begun to see themselves as the "star/celebrity" they had become (the ideal self) and no longer as who they really were (the real self). In trying to maintain that ideal self to continue to be on that pedestal, they got involved in the habit of drug/substance use and then abuse to help them feel numb or escape the pressure of reality. Doing so, they ended up destroying that pedestal, tumbling to the bottom in a hurry, as it is unrealistic to sustain and maintain that exaggerated and glorified ideal self over a long period of time. Tying this directly to the theme of this discourse, by bracing self to come up to some standard to live life, like conjuring an idealized self, the individual plays God here also. If God had not failed to eliminate the need for this, there would be no need to invest energy into this conflict-inducing task, and therefore, there would be no resulting neurosis.

Still on the conflict that competition entails, it's my sense that finding themselves in a life they didn't choose that will ultimately fall on them to survive and live in, growing children need to acquire the skills to achieve these survival and living goals. To do so, therefore, demands that some competitive impetus is proper earlier in life. With age, experience, and knowledge, however, competition for competition sake should not be a virtue. Life as a game of winner-takes-all or a zero-sum game is delusive and paranoid; as a learned behavior, it is dysfunctional. This is a fact that should begin to take hold at some point in a dynamic and multidimensional mind.

For what I have described that I'm going through in my life now, with particular emphasis on my work volume and my thinking that I am not measuring up to a standard of job performance acceptable to me, here is why I think anxiety is more applicable.

According to Wikipedia online,

> Anxiety is a physiological and psychological state characterized by cognitive, somatic, emotional, and behavioral components. These components combine to create the painful feelings that are typically recognized as uneasiness, apprehension, or worry. Anxiety is a normal reaction to stress. It may help a person to deal with a difficult situation, for example at work or at school, by prompting one to cope with it.

Chapter 7

Intra-World Relations and Politics

Humans must have started out confined in the earthly locale in which they found themselves, adapting and surviving in whatever way they could. Over time, for true survival, curiosity, or other reasons, they linked up with neighboring communities. Somewhere along this line, beyond intruding and trampling upon others, they must have discovered the benefit of collaborative efforts and the place of common interest and mutual benefit in a human community on a level that lower animals may not be equipped to. The synergy from collaborating may be the idea behind humans formally organizing into groups and the concept of private and public corporations of the modern world that result in huge material profits, among other benefits.

The trend of linking up with other communities continued with humans venturing way beyond the bounds of their geographic locales of origin. And as the humans' innate thinking and creative attributes evolved, they came up with the means of traveling to make forays into areas not just in their regions of the world but other continents also, having delineated the world into nations, regions, and continents accordingly. It is also nothing short of humans playing God that their ingenuity has led to their breaking and conquering the natural barriers of space, time, sight, and hearing through the rapid and large transportation modes of the automobile (cars), train, ship, and airplane; the television and satellite; and the telephone and two-way radios respectively. Apparently, the also innate greed component of human nature, not necessarily just survival instincts as that was no longer enough, may have prompted these intercontinental incursions. It appears also that the common characteristics that humans share notwithstanding, some people from certain parts of the world must be more curious and/or greedier than those from certain other parts, making them the ones that initiated the transregional and transcontinental incursions.

Whether or not race is a factor may be a conclusion that may have been reached by some, many, or humanity. Here are some thoughts on this. Something in the nature of humans gets them drawn to, or positively excited by, things seen as attractive. Some observed behavior seems to indicate that there is more attraction to the light/lighter-skinned person than the other way around; whether it is sexually, for the consideration of some favor, or some other reasons. A few years ago, a U.S. television network showed a study or an experiment featuring toddlers and crawlers before whom were held pictures of a black and white person side by side. Most, if not all, of the children were drawn to the "white" picture, as shown by their reaching to it and touching it, even when that of the "black" was closer. Among those who also watched that broadcast is a friend, Lawrence Ahuruonyne, who with his family had relocated back to Atlanta, Georgia, from New York City in 2001. Although he and I did not watch it together, he shared this with me when he and I engaged in a general discussion on life, with that subject and broadcast also featuring.

In some black societies, including Nigeria, I know that in the 1970s many young women; and some men also, were bleaching their skin to look lighter. It is possible that this goes on there and elsewhere still. That psychologically, the low self-esteem of the individual who bleached may be a factor, or all there is behind it, is noted. It is my experience also that in Nigeria back then; and some say it still happens, a lighter-skinned person, mostly foreign and Caucasian, was esteemed higher than the natives. In service lines, they were attended to before the natives, even when they were back and behind in the line. Foreign whites, who had held lower jobs and had low or no status in their native countries, saw their position and esteem boosted and bumped way up in Nigeria, certainly above those of natives who rightfully would rank in their class or even higher. Those foreigners would reap many benefits that came with their newfound status. They were housed in an exclusive section of the city in sprawling, manicured estates. They had company or government vehicles free, with a chauffeur. They also had gardeners, night watchmen, and cooks/stewards. In the rural setting, some natives would even follow them around, gazing at them in admiration. In turn, they could have almost anything they wanted just for the asking. Taking these points into consideration, it is difficult not to look into whether race, a clear discrepancy/difference, is a factor when the fortunes and misfortunes in life are at issue.

Some form of documentation and/or acknowledgement is that early ideas and "developments" that have served humanity on planet earth originated in Africa. And if people started out in their geographic locale of the earth, could those ideas and developments not have been by Africans themselves? As one of many whose life experience spans more than one continent, I could not conclude this discourse without posing this question. If the answer to this question is certainly or probably a yes, how come then the trend of development and its derivative fortune in the modern world favor the West, instead? Could this be attributable to the incursion and intrusion of the people of the Western world who, upon sizing up what they saw in the land and of the people of Africa, vis-à-vis what they desired, decided to colonize Africa? There is evidence that, by design and/ or default, colonization leaves the colonized and his culture subdued as they imbibe the values of and adopt the culture of the colonizer, potentially leaving the colonized unable to grow and evolve in his naturally given ways, as his mind seem to be stifled, repressed, and stunted, except to mimic, parrot, or mirror that of his master/colonizer. My thinking is that humans, irrespective of race and geography, have comparable innate intellectual potentials. If that thought process is correct, then what is it that makes some people susceptible, vulnerable, and gullible to be lorded over by others and those others confident, bold, and brave enough to make far incursions and forays into the land of those others to lord it over them? Could this be attributable to their respective environments, in terms of surviving in them, and certain other demands of those environments to which they must adapt?

It is evident that the Western world is both a major benefactor and beneficiary of the ideas and development of the modern world. If early Africans were that innovative, should their succeeding generations then not have inherited the ability to replicate and continue that innovativeness, as Africa is synonymous with poverty and misery in the world of today? Could science, hard or social, adduce or proffer any answers to these questions?

Industrialization and Agrarianism; Intellectual and Natural Material Endowments; Affluence and Poverty

The modern world has been shaped along the lines of the industrialized/ affluent and the less-industrialized or generally agrarian/poorer worlds. It would be difficult to ponder this fact without reminiscing on what intellectual endowment (capital) has to do with it. Natural material endowment or capital also comes into focus here for the purpose of assessing any relationship between it, intellectual endowment, and affluence and poverty.

As with nearly every convoluted and complex issue about and with life, some explanation of why Africa, the symbol of backwardness and poverty in the modern world, is in this precarious situation has been attributed to organized religion. That explanation is rooted in the biblical story of Esau and Jacob. Among the many other biblical references on this issue found in Wikipedia online, here's one:

Question: "Why Did God Love Jacob and Hate Esau?" (Malachi 1:3; Romans 9:13)

Answer: Malachi 1:2–3 declares,

> "I have loved you," says the Lord.

> But you ask, "How have you loved us? Was not Esau Jacob's brother?"

The LORD says, "Yet I have loved Jacob, but Esau I have hated, and I have turned his mountains into a wasteland and left his inheritance to the desert jackals."

Malachi 1:2–3 is quoted and alluded to in Romans 9:10–13,

> Not only that, but Rebekah's children had one and the same father, our father Isaac. Yet, before the twins were born or had done anything good or bad—in order that God's purpose in election might stand: not by works but by him who calls—she was told, "The older will serve the younger." Just as it is written: "Jacob I loved, but Esau I hated."

Why did God love Jacob and hate Esau? If God is love (1 John 4:8), how could he hate anyone?

When studying the Bible, it is critically important to always study the context of a particular Bible verse or passage. In these instances, the prophet Malachi and the apostle Paul are using the name "Esau" to refer to the Edomites, who were the descendants of Esau. Isaac and Rebekah had two sons, Esau and Jacob. God chose Jacob (whom He later renamed Israel) to be the father of His chosen people, the Israelites. God rejected Esau (who was also called Edom) and did not choose him to be the father of His chosen people. Esau and his descendants, the Edomites, were in many ways blessed by God (Genesis 33:9; Genesis 36).

So, considering the context, God loving Jacob and hating Esau has nothing to do with the human emotions of love and hate. It has everything to do with God choosing one man and his descendants and rejecting another man and his descendants. God chose Abraham out of all the men in the world. The Bible very well could say, "Abraham I loved, and every other man I hated." God chose Abraham's son Isaac instead of Abraham's son Ishmael. The Bible very well could say, "Isaac I loved, and Ishmael I hated." Romans 9 makes it abundantly clear that loving Jacob and hating Esau was entirely related to which of them God chose. Hundreds of years after Jacob and Esau had died, the Israelites and Edomites became bitter enemies. The Edomites often aided Israel's enemies in attacks on Israel. Esau's descendants brought God's curse upon themselves. Genesis 27:29 tells us,

> May nations serve you and peoples bow down to you. Be lord over your brothers, and may the sons of your mother bow down to you. May those who curse you be cursed and those who bless you be blessed.

Despite all efforts at spin and rationalization, the above story is still what it is and should be to a rational mind—ludicrous!

Out and away from the world in the days of the Bible, I have heard insinuations and even Christian preachers of the "real" world state or imply that Esau represents the black race, and Jacob, the white. Even if this above fairy tale and others of the like are correct, why would I, a black man of African origin, descent, and culture, acknowledge, embrace, respect, or even fear that God?

Back to this "real" world, there is a preponderance of factual evidence to rule out the direct relationship between endowment of material natural resources and affluence. Conversely, the case for such a relationship between intellectual endowment and affluence could be made, as that is very evident. Supporting the latter is the fact that the Western (and in recent years the Eastern) world, known for its affluence in materials and power is not known to be overly endowed with natural, material resources and has neither capitalized on nor commercialized whatever little they may have. Also, the facts support the former scenario of the nations of Africa and the Middle East, bountifully endowed naturally with materials highly demanded worldwide that have remained generally poor, materially or otherwise. Certainly, they are dominated and controlled by the Western world, which with intellect-based ingenuity, has not only come up with the technology to tap and process the material endowment of Africa and the Middle East, but also come up with concepts that make them pay for those resources to the net benefit of intellect. This fact really rubbishes the acclaimed affluence of nations like Saudi Arabia, with per-capita material income that doubtfully would equal or trump that of the United States, for instance.

As the Western world, apparently greedier in their value and in their nature, set out to change and control the world, they, among other things, conceptualized the nation-state and also imposed it on their "third-world" target territories, which they colonized. Then with their economic mercantilism, they aggressively expanded and added to their colonies with a central goal of achieving massive wealth in comparison to their competitors. With this, they sapped and bilked the resources of their territories and helped plunder them further into poverty.

As a drive for freedom and independence from colonial overlords eventually developed, started by the elites/nationalists of the colonies, colonial entities, put together and created by the colonial lords, eventually were allowed some independence. In Africa, this began in the 1950s. Inheriting a nation-state, a creation of the Western (European) world, the post-colonial African leader has since struggled and stumbled in keeping up with this inheritance. In the scheme of human societies, the nation-state is a relatively new concept. Seen in the context of organizing to enhance societal advantages, this concept serves some adaptive purpose. This has come to mean that in today's world of the animal species that include humans, societies that fail to adapt will not survive, but may, sooner or later, become extinct and only committed to the fossils of time and history. Before the advent of colonialism, the African seemed to have a grip on his natural way of life but may perhaps have lagged in growing wealth. Whatever wealth they may have produced, the Western world, steps ahead in scheming, has found ways to suck it from Africa and transfer it over to their home territories. To achieve this, they have their accomplices—the corrupt leaders of the poor nations, who on the one hand, aid in this, and on the other, loot the treasuries of their nations and stash them away in the Western countries' economies where they help boost those economies, and with the urging and support of those nations. One of the ways through which this is done is the International Monetary Fund (the IMF); it loans to "poor nations" and requires repayment with interest. It does seem that Africa and the rest of the so-called "third world" are but fish out of water still gasping for air, having been dislocated from the world of ethnicity. Although being granted some notion of independence by the colonial masters of their respective nations may have slowed down their demise as "free" nations somewhat, their "extinction" as nations and people will come if they continue to not evolve by moving along the line of embracing and mastering the skills and tools for running a nation-state in the current world reality.

Nigeria

To illustrate the point of facing extinction if they do not evolve and become adept at mastering the skills to run a modern nation-state, I bring Nigeria into some focus here. In my ethnic nation of origin, the Igbo societies were organized in subcommunities where all are related to one another in the kinship line. There is no intermarriage in this kinship community, like Umuawala, Abayi Ngwa-ukwu, where I was born and raised. There are no formal laws, as the norms are automatically lived, passed along the generational line, and known to and embraced by all. The norms and tenets of the community are generally conformed to by all but about 2 or 3 percent of the population, who would not so conform. As there are also no formal but known consequences and punishments that served to deter a breakdown of the social order, the deviants were vigorously and consistently punished. This really was effective and accomplished the desired and intended goal of deterrence. It was also that successful despite not being formally written because of the homogeneity of the shared values, norms, and culture of the people.

In contrast to the experience and environment above, there are cities, like Aba, the large and sprawling Ngwa urban area, where people of different experiences, culture, values, and background have settled for the purpose of finding a better life. Imagine then a big nation like Nigeria with its diversity of people, cultures, and values. Would it be realistic to expect the same unwritten norms of a homogenous, kinship community like Umuawala to enforce and bring about compliance and conformity? It would be beyond naiveté to so expect; it would be idiotic really. This then speaks to some of the reasons that the Nigerian nation, a country of about 130 million people, is failing. It would take written laws and accountability through the enforcement of those laws to manage law, order, and decorum and make citizens feel safe. Nigeria has not evolved a mechanism to enforce any of the written laws she may have. As a result, anyone, particularly political leaders of any level, can practically rob and loot the national treasury and other resources with impunity. Job offers and contract awards are not premised on screening from a pool of people with competing credentials, skills, and track records to determine who from that pool would meet the standard required to perform, produce, and deliver. Instead, offers are made to those who fit in the corrupt mold of what I call CNS—Cronyism, Nepotism, and Sexual favors. Crime runs wild and rampant, and it goes unchecked.

I feel bad for the beautiful but educated, skilled, and talented women who would rather compete fairly for positions and/or contracts based on their qualifications and would also prefer integrity and respect. Those who would hold on to these esteemed values confront a mounting pressure to put out or lose out, which they cannot ignore indefinitely.

This is enough to cause some to give in, becoming the sex objects they so dreaded and succumbing to a fate they wished would not be theirs. This culture gets more bizarre with the story of Dr. Gbenga Obasanjo, the first son of Nigeria's immediate past president, Olusegun Obasanjo, accusing his father of sleeping with his wife Mojisola before she was awarded contracts with the Nigerian National Petroleum Corporation (NNPC). According to the news story in the *U.S. Immigration News* (published by Nigerian natives in the United States; Dr. Obasanjo made the allegation in a fifty-paragraph affidavit in his divorce suit filed with the Lagos High Court. The tenth paragraph of said affidavit of his lawsuit seeking to dissolve the couple's seven-year marriage is said to state the following:

> The Petitioner (Dr. Gbenga Obasanjo) further avers that he knows for a fact that the Respondent (Mojisola Obasanjo) committed adultery and had intimate, sexual relationship with his own father, Olusegun Obasanjo, due to her greed for favors and contracts from him in his capacity as the President of the federal Republic of Nigeria. The Respondent (Mojisola) got rewarded for her adulterous acts with several oil contracts with NNPC.

Nepotism is bad enough, and this had to include what could be classified as incestuous adultery. Although that the notarized charges of the son here are but allegations that may yet be proved, this is still disturbing all the same.

Making decisions on matters as critical as employment and contract awards on the CNS formula could only produce mediocrity and a legacy of failed structures and institutions, depriving society, the nation, and her future generations the coveted place of sound and solid institutions.

The sexual favors component of the CNS model reminds me here of a cartoon in Nigeria's *Daily Times* newspaper or its weekend edition, *Lagos Weekend*, several years ago that featured an employment office. The employment manager approached a female applicant who was waiting in the reception area and beckoned her into his office. Back in his office, that official asked, "Your credentials, Miss?"

The lady got up, unbuttoned her blouse, and unhooked her bra, popping her front credentials out bare and letting them hang. Flaunting the rather elaborate pair, she said to the manager, "This is but the introduction."

Accountability is not an attribute or a factor of governance in Nigeria, which is now renowned worldwide for corruption. Public leaders are neither subjected to nor held to any standard of morality or ethics, to the extent that holding them to some standard of such could give a clue or hint to the possibility that they would model and promote the reduction of corruption in society. In a nation that is largely paternalistic, married public and political leaders having mistresses whom they support and make rich with public resources is but a benefit that inures to their power, wealth, and high profile. In this culture, public resources are not seen as meant to serve public good but also as a right that inures to whoever finds a way to access them. Some may question the relevance of a possibly immoral or unethical act of infidelity to corruption; the answer would be that when some vices that appear to have little or nothing to do with political and public leadership are acquiesced to, it should be expected that the morally compromised could, consciously or not, bring that to undermine and corrode public trust and the public good.

Contrast the ethically challenged governance in Nigeria to these two instances here in the United States. A few months ago, the comptroller of New York State, Alan Havesi, lost his job. The issue was that he had a state driver drive has wife who is paralyzed with a state vehicle. As this "corruption" and ethical problem surfaced, Havesi in the process wrote personal checks to the tune of tens of thousands of dollars to reimburse the state for the cost associated with that. Yet, he, Havesi, lost his job as he had to resign solely on this issue.

The second of the two instances involved the governor, also of New York State, Elliot Spitzer, who has since been replaced by the lieutenant governor, David Paterson, earlier this year, 2008. What led to the disgraceful fall from office of the bold, strong, and generally considered effective governor was that the monitoring of the transactions in his personal bank account, as this monitoring is the norm here in the United States, especially after September 11, 2001, revealed a higher-than-usual activity. As those activities were traced further, it was indicated that some monetary payments were made to an "escort" service, a "middleman" for prostitutes. Plainly, the governor had had an affair with a particular young prostitute, prostitution and interstate money transfers of certain natures being illegal. Therefore, the governor had violated the law, plus the fact that married public officeholders in the United States, and a governor for that matter, having an extramarital affair, committing an act of infidelity, is a serious ethical issue that has ended even some of the most revered public servants' careers. This was the case for Governor Spitzer, who had to resign within a week of this becoming public.

A good number of Nigeria's politicians, some of them governors, who claimed (and was also rumored) to have been in some shadowy business before they conned their way into political office have seen their wealth explode while in office. One is known to float an airline, a shipping line, and other huge businesses while in office. As this went on, questions were being raised openly by many, including those who were in a position to know, about huge sums of the state funds running into billions, being stolen, misappropriated, and unaccounted for. All this attention to the probability of the state's resources being stolen as the gaping needs in the state requiring the use of those resources were very evident received no attention due to the prevalent culture of corruption that was helped by the constitutional immunity from prosecution of governors and the president.

While politicians bilk their governments there, some of the political leaders in the United States, known to have made fortunes legitimately in business or the private sector, choose to serve the public freely—with no salary. One is Mayor Michael Bloomberg, now in his second four-year term as the mayor of New York City. Michael Bloomberg is the multibillionaire who founded and built up the Bloomberg business conglomerate. When his daughter offered to serve voluntarily also in her father's first term, there were even cries of nepotism. One other political leader who has since followed in the footsteps of Mayor Bloomberg is Governor Jon Corzine of the state of New Jersey. Starting first as a senator from the state of New Jersey, this former chairman of the investment company, Goldman Sachs, volunteered his public services both as a senator and now as the governor of the state of New Jersey.

Nigeria, Your Other and More Fitting Name Must Be Corruption

An encounter I had with the police in May of this year, 2008, while on vacation in Nigeria triggered the thought captioned above. Nigeria may not be the most corrupt nation on the earth, as there are many others, but she certainly has more than her fair share of corruption and continues to pay dearly for it, including a diminished status and the potential for her to fizzle and break up as one nation as a result. As I went about my daily business during my "working vacation," tripping from the city of Aba to my village, in the company of a younger cousin and another young man, the police would randomly stop vehicles—nearly all vehicles. This is nothing new in Nigeria and has been going on for years. The only thing new about this practice, as I have just learned, is that it is said to be mostly in the eastern part of the country, rarely occurring in the west and almost nonexistent in the north, even though policing is federally controlled. It is also widely known that this random stopping of vehicles on the road is just to demand and extort money from the traveling victims. It needs no effort or investigation to confirm, as the police have collected and pocketed cash in the glaring view of anyone over the years.

My disappointment this time came probably from assuming that Umar Abubakar's federal government might have started changing things for the better and would have brought the brutal and bizarre victimization and extortion by the police into check. So, when the police, in what eventually was a ruse to extort money from us, abducted and took my young cousin to their station because he dared to ask why one of them had to pry open and dig his hand into my briefcase just after I had opened and showed it to them when they insisted on knowing what was inside, it had to be a rude awakening for me that Nigeria and corruption are synonymous. In that experience, about six policemen armed with A-K rifles jerked my cousin about, roughing him up and bruising him with their rifle muzzles (the tip/opening end of a gun/rifle barrel) before stuffing him into a small, non-police minivan, with no plate number. And because I had pleaded with them to let him go, one of them insulted and threatened me, saying, "Look at this fat, old man. Get away from here, fat, old man." Twice, he added, in broken English, "If na armed robber, they for scatter you now." Translated, it means, "Had we been armed robbers, we would have wasted you [shot you to death] here." The parallel to armed robbery in this statement by the so-called policeman speaks volumes about policing and its complicity in crime in Nigeria. This drama and near-tragic encounter ended when they collected about N2,000.00 (two thousand naira) from my young cousin in a back room of the Osisioma police station to which they had hauled him.

Frustrated and angered, I wanted to do something about this, beginning with a telephone call to a lawyer nephew and a demand to speak with the divisional police officer (DPO) of the Osisioma police station. I was discouraged by my victimized cousin and my younger brother whom I had also contacted by phone; both told me that I would be wasting my time. They said the DPOs were known to be behind planting these police thugs, who had to account for their daily hauls to them, from those strategic spots on the road. Turning around at the premises of the police station, I noticed a woman in plainclothes coming out of the police station. I approached her, asking her if she was a police officer or a civilian working with the police.

She responded that she was a police inspector, which is a ranking police officer in Nigeria. She then asked, "Is anything the matter?"

I explained our ordeal with her men to her and described the shenanigans that had since unfolded. I asked her whether speaking with the DPO was the way to handle this as a formal report.

First, she spoke to the demand by the policemen at the roadblock to see the inside of my briefcase, justifying it obviously by rhetorically asking, "Suppose there was a gun or guns in it?"

To that I responded, "But I had just opened it, and they had taken a good look inside; what else could justify their going back to dig into it, having not indicated that they had not seen the entire interior when, at their demand, I had opened it wide to their clear view?"

Then the inspector said, "If you want to see the DPO, go ahead."

I heeded the advice of my brother and cousin and did not follow through.

One has to ask why the proliferation of police checkpoints and the whimsical stopping of vehicles are still allowed to go on. What I call intelligible policing might include that stopping vehicles, which should not be the norm, would require that there be a profile—information—of either a criminal or stolen property. The police, carrying out a legitimate official duty, would only stop and/or search vehicles and people fitting the profile of the wanted. In Nigeria, one only needs to be plying the roads to be entrapped and victimized by the police. With all the police menace, crime is still at its peak, with the latest craze of kidnapping people at gunpoint for money, also said to be mostly in the east, a new and booming "enterprise." In this criminal activity, many individuals, some in their eighties and nineties, who are considered well-to-do or who have children or grandchildren seen as doing well or residing in the United States or elsewhere overseas, are abducted at gunpoint, from their homes or elsewhere. This is followed by phone calls to those relatives of the abducted to extort money, beginning with a price set so high, in the millions of the local currency—the naira. Through a back-and-forth haggling and bargaining process, some compromise in the price is reached and delivery made to a location and spot that the abductors identify, before the release of the victim. Yet, not one of these known incidents is solved by the police.

It was back in 1981, when my company-issued Volkswagen beetle was stolen that I got a glimpse into official police institutional corruption in Nigeria. I had gone to a police station in Ikoyi, Lagos, to report the theft. The police officer, or constable as they were termed in Nigeria then, asked me to provide cash for the purchase of the paper to use in writing the report. I had already seen firsthand that the corruption of bribery was rampant in the civil service from working as the liaison of my company with different government departments. I did also know that individual policemen took bribes routinely from citizens while out on assignment. With that bizarre extortion within the police station, however, I was worried even then that in the front-line law enforcement arm of the federal government, it felt "normal" in the office, the police station, to extort bribery.

Given the way in which corruption is embedded in the culture in Nigeria, any thought of empowering women, for instance, would never see the light of day, as that would deprive the corrupt, powerful men in the still predominantly paternalistic system of their "entitlement" of exploiting women sexually. Empowering the citizens by educating them of their civil and human rights would also never see the light of day, it seems, as that could translate to the police and the well connected and powerful being deprived of their power to intimidate, abuse, victimize, and extort money and material. In Nigeria, policing is naively organized on a national (federal) level and not even on the level of her current thirty states structure, let alone on the level of the hundreds (if not thousands) of local or city governments. Insecurity is a given and almost an accepted norm, as people are robbed, maimed, and killed openly and randomly with no arrests ever made, with no talk of prosecution, punishment, and/ or restitution. Even as so organized, it appears that the police force is not properly oriented and may be ill-trained. Known to be poorly compensated as far as salary and benefits go; they are clearly ill-equipped to realistically and effectively police a criminal world that is increasingly becoming daring and sophisticated.

There is no question that humans in any society would tend to overstep their bounds and encroach on the territory and personal lives of others if not deterred. Here in the United States, for instance, in about 97 percent (that's my guess) of criminal and other activities and infringements, the criminal/culprit is apprehended and prosecuted, punished, and restitution where applicable is enforced. With this also, the facts and circumstances of the crime or incident are known. This includes whether they were random or pervasive and whether the victims were targeted to settle personal scores. Are the incidents random or pervasive? If either, how much so? Furthermore, the additional information helps victims of crimes and citizens make informed decisions on how to behave—in certain neighborhoods, at certain times, and/or around some people, ending speculation and irrational fear. Citizens, seeing how responsive and effective the law enforcement is, will not only appreciate and respect the law enforcement system; they will have more confidence and trust.

Understanding the place of the youth in the life of a nation, as they constitute any nation's future, apparently does not factor into what governance and the running of a nation-state is about for the Nigerian politician. The youth line up outside the gates of higher education institutions for hours and for weeks hoping to be admitted into the institutions and still end up unsuccessful. Admissions are corruptly bought through the back door for those whose parents have the money and the contacts, or based on sexual favors, even if the applicant does not have the academic qualifications. Coupled with the lack of jobs for most of those who graduate, the youth not only have become frustrated, they have also become discouraged about choosing education, especially seeing that their peers forced into the world of fraud and crime seem to have something to show for it, while those who would embrace the right values lose out. The Nigerian public and political leadership clearly have no clue about anticipating trends to come up with effective ways, like legislation, programs, and the structures to manage them. As the country went through a massive rural-to-urban population migration, nothing was done to expand the infrastructure in the urban areas to deal with the trend and reality. The urban areas are littered with homeless people. The roads are not only overcrowded; they are damaged beyond recognition as many constitute water pools and lakes and garbage dumps. Hospitals are but jokes and apologies; the list goes on.

One sad thing about all this is that things have not always been this bad as far as the neglect of the youth and job opportunities in particular go. As a young man, I had the opportunity to be employed in my first job in the early 1970s in a Lagos hotel, Bristol Hotel, after the civil war that ended in 1970. I recall here that one Mr. Eke, who I learned was a pre-war employee of that hotel chain and became an amputee from fighting on the Biafra side of that war, was rehired for a desk job as a room service clerk when he returned to Lagos seeking employment. This just gives me a sense of nostalgia of how much better things were. Such accommodation and opportunity is but a dream in the Nigeria of today. Among other benefits, my first job paid for me to acquire some more education that made it possible for me to explore the opportunity for and be able to switch to a better and different line of work. It was because of such opportunities (to change jobs also) that I was able to earn and save enough money to pursue university level education outside of Nigeria, as there has hardly been enough room in the universities and other higher education institutions of Nigeria to absorb all applicants/candidates. That the reality of today is that the Nigerian youth do not have the opportunities that I had back then to pursue their dreams as I was able to mine is nothing short of saddening.

With such a gaping leadership vacuum, the society that has hardly embraced and moved into the world of science and its role in addressing humans' needs more than anything else has slipped further into a world shrouded more in the mystery of the spirits and the guessing and con games that come with it. In significant numbers, couples desperately needing to have baby boys in a society that still values having them so highly, for instance, still seek the help of the so-called Christian prayer warriors and the traditional healers/doctors to divine that even eight-month pregnancies turn out to be boys. Instead of seeing the direct relationship between corruption and crime, lack of law enforcement and accountability, and the absence of planning by a badly compromised leadership on one side and the misery that is all over the place on the other, people blame poverty, joblessness, illnesses, and their other attendant vices on witches and their powers and ill will. The drama is so bad that a witch hunt and trials, like the one documented to have taken place on a large scale in Salem, Massachussets, United States, in the 1600s, became prevalent in a particular area of the Igbo ethnic group in 2006 and 2007, with the Christian religion behind most of it. The saga of this ignorance is such that many people were lynched publicly and some were considered lucky to have been only banished from their communities, by a mob of frustrated, jobless youth, manipulated to take out their disappointments on the imaginary cause and source of their misfortunes—the unfortunate victims actually.

The Prevalence of the World of Deities
While Salem, Massachusetts and the advanced world have since evolved beyond that antiquated mind-set and "reality" of dealing with the phenomena of life and moved away and on from it, having been there and done that, in many ways, Nigeria still lives in the 1400s. A deity known as *Ogwugwu Okija*, with a shrine in Anambra State, a southeastern Igbo state, exploded in popularity recently when it became known that deeply corrupt political and other prominent people consult, make bonds, pay allegiance, and make binding contracts with it and its priests. To point out again, that Nigeria is still mired in the dark ages, hence her dismal future, the *Ogwugwu Okija* shrine is a reminder of the Apollo oracle of classical Greece, located in Delphi, considered in its heyday by the ancient Greeks to be the center of the world. The Oracle was consulted through its priestess and Pythias; the business of Delphi also boomed with the ever-flowing consultation and the patronage it enjoyed. While it is the *Ogwugwu Okija* today, it has been the oracle *Igwekala*, another renowned Igbo deity, in Umunoha in Mbaitoli, today's Imo state, and not of a distant proximity to *Ogwugwu Okija*. The Greek may have moved beyond and away from seeing Delphi as the center

of the universe. Nigeria shows no sign of the capacity to get a grip with what it would take to be in sync with the modern world and the future.

The amalgamation of Nigeria into one country in 1918 by her colonial master and lord, Britain, which hitherto ran her as the Northern and Southern protectorates, has meant that Nigeria is the largest single concentration of black people anywhere on earth. In the context of modern nation-states and in the scheme of world politics, this means that Nigeria would have considerable advantage, especially considering that she is also bountifully endowed with natural material resources. To actually realize and achieve this potential synergy and its benefit would require finding ways to bring about some necessary commonality among the vastly different values, cultures, and ways of life of the ethnic and the sub-ethnic groups that constitute the Nigerian nation-state. If, on the other hand, it is determined that the differences are so ingrained that they could not be overcome and constitute a setback, as it appears through the years, then going separate along some acceptable lines should considered. The challenge here would be for a leadership astute enough to manage the separation process to see that it goes as smooth as possible. What appears to have prevailed are vestiges of the ethnic system.

A clear vestige of colonialism that undoubtedly plays a role in setting Nigeria back as a modern nation-state is feudalism, which although historically confined to the north and southwest of Nigeria, has proliferated into the southeast where the colonial master had appointed tax collectors and agents for the colonial government whom they termed *chiefs*. While the feudal systems of the southwest and the north were headed by the Oba and the Emir respectively, the Igbo of the southeast had a community-group head, the Eze or Obi, who in no way enjoyed an influence level over the people like that the Oba and the Emir were known to have. In modern times, the chief of the Igbo in particular has metamorphosed into some social status symbol and enjoys a hierarchy of a superlative structure of chiefs, more chiefs, high chiefs, superior chiefs, ultimate chiefs, ultimate high chiefs, etc., all ranking next to the Eze, whose number has equally mushroomed in geographic areas of the Igbo nation.

An Eze is the equivalent of the head (monarch) of a kingdom. The Eze has been so trivialized and replicated that one Eze is lucky to have a kingdom of one-half of a village. In the days past, when an Eze had some clout, his kingdom was a sprawling area of several village groups. The mind-set and the psyche today is that one feels unfulfilled, unacknowledged, unaccomplished, disrespected, and even "naked" without the title "chief" before his name, resulting in the mushrooming of chiefs. Anyone from any region of the country who has acquired one title or another in the too-fashionable chase and craze for titles is practically above the law and cannot be subjected to any kind of investigation, let alone be prosecuted and held accountable for any crime or other infraction in society. The immunity from any prosecution that the Nigerian constitution gives to the governors of the thirty states and the president of the federation compounds the woes of the society and of the nation. Imagine then that there are multitudes of people in the titled persons "class" and what that adds to the problems of Nigeria. The landscape in social occasions is a littering of individuals decked out in elaborately decorated, beaded, and shiny outfits in the name of titled persons' robes that rightfully trigger the thought: *All fluff and gloss, no substance.*

The ego-feeding frenzy constitutes a near epidemic in the society in which a disproportionate number of the population seeks titles and accolades to fill the voids in their egos. The current Lagos state governor and notably some other high-profile individuals, for instance, were recently found to have acquired fake and illegitimate doctoral degrees and were appending "Dr." before their names. Again, in Nigeria, titles and "Drs." open doors, as they also propel one's profile.

One has to pause and wonder why the colonial master had to call their tax-collecting agents in their African colonies chiefs, considering that in their home societies, chiefs were but ranking officials of the uniformed crew—the army, the police, the fire service, the prison wardens or guards, the customs services, the immigration services, and the like. One thing in common for all the identified governmental services here is force or quasi-force, and a common characteristic or slogan across the uniformed gangs is "Obey the last order." Clearly, this is how they operate. Members of the force are not supposed to question their authorities but must do as ordered. So, as enforcers, the tax-collector chiefs were supposed to treat citizens from whom they must squeeze taxes as programmed tools that should neither have brains nor the right to any opinion, just like the uniformed gangs really were. Forget that many are branded heroes for fighting in mostly unjustified wars. This is a clear case of taxation without opinion or representation, for which the United States, beginning with the Boston Tea Party, revolted and eventually fought Britain for her independence.

The system of governance in Nigeria in recent years is unfriendly to, and unwelcoming of, anyone who would espouse and promote some ideals. Nigeria's government has been characterized by changes of government by military coup d'états. That has presently been replaced by an equally brutal alternative system that has been dominated by former military dictators and leaders who have managed to establish and nurture a crony system that promotes, supports, and helps sustain them. Anyone who is not part of it and who would dare to partake in the polity to bring about a transparent change ventures in at his or her risk. Many have been killed, rendered useless, or forced out of the country for attempting. Only the like-minded are welcome and "succeed."

How about this total lag in putting together and nurturing a functional system helping to make the unevolving Nigerian nation-state extinct and the lynching of people literally so?

The United States of America (USA)

There is no question that the United States of America is one country that has not only revolutionized government and governance, but has also been on the leading edge of the changes that continue to benefit life and living. For me, the USA symbolizes experimentation—going where none has been in ideas, concepts, and prototypes; developing and actually bringing practical tools and solutions to life; practically constituting an incubation of ideas. Invention of the automobile is but one clear instance. Considered a young nation, relative to her European counterparts, including her historic colonial overlord, Britain, the United States has a lot to gloat about and to be proud of. With republicanism and democracy as the bedrock of her government, the United States is not considered an empire. Idealism is one principle that tends to underscore America's vision and drive her success. Again, in so many and different ways, America remains a model. I have been so taken by her tremendous ability to structure and establish an authority for just about every facet and issue that impacts life, ensuring responsibility and accountability across the board. Practically nothing is left to just chance. One instance, still very fresh in my memory, is the rescue of all 155 people—passengers and crew—of U.S. Airways Flight 1549 from the Hudson River in New York City by the city's emergency response team on Thursday, January 15, 2009, as that plane was landed on the Hudson River by its pilot following a catastrophic accident. Dubbed by the New York State governor, David Paterson, as the "Miracle on the Hudson," in most other places, this rescue feat would definitely not have been accomplished.

While humane ideals and principles seem to have fuelled the American Revolution and independence from Britain, as a nation, she has also tended to clothe herself in supernatural drapes, at least in words and expressions. For clarification, humane ideals are about empathy and compassion for the human, his desire for self-fulfillment and dignity in a way that does not necessarily infringe upon those of others, and consciously and conscientiously creating an environment conducive for him to realize these. Supernaturalism, conversely, implies deferring to a supreme authority in life, implying humility and submission to that supreme authority and also touching the conscience of a human-controlling authority, as one's claim, and justifying one's right to not give in or up in the pursuit of that to which one is entitled. In attempting to play in the two worlds of humane ideals and supernaturalism, the United States wished to cover all bases, hoping not to lose out in either realm.

Capping the humane ideal sense is the metaphor of a "melting pot"— the ideal republic where peoples of different nations, races, backgrounds, creeds, and cultures are "melted" into one—that has been associated with the United States for about as long as she has been independent of Britain. And as for the supernaturalism sense, here are a few facts that at least substantiate its embracement, albeit rhetorically, in American public life:

- "We hold these truths to be self-evident, that all men are created equal, that they are endowed by their creator with certain unalienable rights, that among these are life, Liberty, and the pursuit of Happiness ..."—culled from the United States Declaration of Independence (this feeds both the humane ideal and the supernaturalism).
- There is the (oath) Pledge of Allegiance to the flag of the United States, the version with the two words—"under God"—approved and added to the pledge in 1954 by the U.S. congress, making it controversial and subject to lawsuits over the years: "I pledge allegiance to the flag of the United States of America, and to the republic for which it stands: one nation under God, indivisible, with liberty and justice for all."
- And then there is "In God We Trust" eminently inscribed on United States currencies and coins.
- Lastly, it is customary for political leaders in the United States, from the president down, to conclude speeches and addresses with "God bless America."

One thing that stands out from this leaning toward supernaturalism is that for a nation that by constitution/law has no and should not have a state-established religion, like Britain from which she broke free, it's like déjà vu all over again. Religion has made its way into American public life, playing out subtly, and sometimes almost overtly, in political campaigns and elections—local ones for the most part, but also for national offices sometimes. It's not just rhetoric.

One way to look at this, though, is that the American nation wants to make prominent the idea that she is indeed humane, not arrogant, and is different in her pursuit of building a country of free people. The practical American experience shows that she has not always lived up to the ideals that she has set for herself, though. This may not be the critical point to underscore, for there is hardly such a thing as always living up to the ideal. Rather, it is whether America is self-reflective enough and has the humility, or even the capacity, for introspection, given the success and power she has come to command and enjoy. The notion of all humans being created equal, which is an acclaimed and prominent feature in the Declaration of the Independence of the United States from the Britain, at a time when she saw herself at the receiving end of injustice, apparently means little, in the context of the hype, since she became independent of Britain. One clear fact of this is the United States' history of and role in slavery and the attendant unequal acceptance and treatment of the races even several decades after the end of official and formal slavery.

Domestically and internationally, evidence is littered that the United States has an airtight compartment for the dual positions illustrated above that she has set for herself, as her history is replete with shortcomings, making her rhetorical ideals sheer utopia. If this were to play out in the life and world of an individual, s/he may meet the criteria to be diagnosed with a DSM axis II, personality disorder, like narcissistic personality disorder and paranoid personality disorder—narcissism for preoccupation with self, seeking attention and notice, wanting to be number one at almost any cost, and tending to show no capacity for empathy in her dealings with other cultures and values, and paranoia for preoccupation with "enemies and haters" always lurking to take away her freedom, tending to lack the capacity to trust, and therefore to dictate terms to engagements.

Domestically, only a few instances would highlight the hypocrisy in the ideal and the actual lives, the most prominent and notorious of which is slavery. Whether for economic and/or racial reasons, the *melting pot* had a compartment, frozen and heatproof, for the black race, which had to be isolated as subhuman property of the superior race. These words in the Declaration of Independence, "We hold these truths to be self-evident, that all men are created equal, that they are endowed by their creator with certain unalienable rights, that among these are life, liberty, and the pursuit of happiness," did not make it from the idealism compartment to that of practical American society. Blacks, seemingly, were created less than equal in the latter compartment. Also, "In God We Trust" turned out not to be true, as he, God, was neither trusted nor respected for creating the humans whose skin he made black. Even though ended formally in 1865 with the

Thirteenth Amendment to the U.S. Constitution at the end of her—the United States'—civil war, vestiges of slavery still linger about a century and half (exactly 144 years) after.

Also, within the chosen and superior race is the WASP (White Anglo-Saxon Protestant), the crème of the crop whose natural right it was to occupy the positions of power and run the nation. Said to originate "in reference to White Americans of Anglo-Saxon descent, who were Protestant in religious affiliation," as found in Wkipedia on line, the term *WASP* is also said to initially apply "to people with histories in the upper Northeastern United States establishment, who were alleged to form a powerful elite." And like the wasp, the flying, stinging insect that predatorily stings other insects out of its way, to take control of the territory; being a WASP was a requirement, though not constitutionally, to be president of the United States.

It took the groundbreaking election of John F. Kennedy, the thirty-fifth president in 1961—the first and only Catholic and the youngest to be elected at age forty-three (though second youngest to serve after Theodore Roosevelt, the twenty-sixth president, who at age forty-two, as vice president to William McKinley, succeeded him in 1901 following McKinley's assassination)—to break that WASP grip somewhat. Forty-seven years and eight other presidents later, the election of Barack Obama, a black man, although of Caucasian heritage on his mother's side, as the forty-fourth president in 2008, an earthshaking event of notable seismic proportions, seems to have sealed the casket of the WASP-hold on the presidency. Yes, America has made progress, particularly with the election of Barack Obama, but the long history shows a pattern of disconnect between the ideal and the practice.

The pattern goes on as patriotism is used to trump freedom of speech and expression. Recognized and adopted by many and varying entities, the earlier of which include the British *Magna Carta* (1215) and the Declaration of the Rights of Man (1789), "a key document of the French revolution," (Wikipedia online), freedom of speech is also enshrined in the First Amendment to the United States Constitution:

> Congress shall make no law respecting an establishment of religion, or prohibiting the free exercise thereof; or abridging the freedom of speech, or of the press; or the right of the people peaceably to assemble, and to petition the government for a redress of grievances (Amendment I).

Although the amendment is addressed to Congress, it is generally and widely accepted that this freedom applies and holds, period. While restrictions to this right and efforts to apply such may not have been initiated with formal congressional acts; some of them have either enjoyed the tacit approval of Congress and/or have been encouraged by it or its individual members. McCarthyism, the Communist-era witch hunt that targeted, terrorized, and punished certain American citizens, fits as an example of patriotism running amok and stifling individual rights and freedom. From this mold come expressions like: "My country, May she always be right; but right or wrong, my country" (adapted from this toast at a dinner in Norfolk, Virginia (April 1816), by the American patriot Commodore Stephen Decatur:

> Our country! In her intercourse with foreign nations may she always be in the right; but our country, right or wrong.

Obviously made in the context of U.S. foreign relations, this patriotic fervor continues to be used to repress and stifle citizens' expression of opposition or disagreement with certain U.S. policies. It is also true that the freedom and right of expression is not absolute, as even the courts have weighed in on some cases to interpret, particularly when that "freedom/ right" potentially puts those of others in jeopardy, like in the "harm or offense principles." Hence, your freedom/right to swing your hands stops where my nose begins.

The fairness and balance in this immediately preceding statement is what someone like President Jimmy Carter, the thirty-ninth U.S. president, stands for. A peace-maker and non-warmonger who also was awarded the Nobel Peace Prize, President Carter is a vilified figure in American history for his stance. I recall watching President Carter in a TV interview years ago answering a question which I paraphrase here: What do you consider your biggest accomplishment as president? President Carter responded, and I paraphrase here also: Not having sent one American youth to die in a war. In yet another TV program that I watched, an anchor termed President Carter America's greatest ex-president, apparently in reference to the numerous humanitarian works he performed and the very good life he has lived and led since leaving the presidency. Implied in this also is that he was not a great president while in office. To be a great American president requires asserting American authority and power and fighting wars to put in their place other nations who may want to demonstrate their interest and will. It became clearer to me that Jimmy Carter is indeed a good person and a man of justice and peace when I read up on his background. Doing this, I noted the second sentence in his televised speech on April 18, 1997, on his proposed energy policy: "With the exception of preventing war, this [the energy crisis] is the greatest challenge our country will face during our lifetime."

The challenge of the energy crisis, foreseen by Jimmy Carter, has now manifested, beginning in 2008, if not before.

Certain groups and individuals would rather allot the right of "unabridged freedom of expression" differently, or have it abridged, for some segments of society. One group that this sentimental bias does target is naturalized, non-native-born Americans or others legally here but yet to naturalize. This sentimental bias becomes pronounced if anyone/group fitting that segment holds/and or expresses disagreement with certain U.S. foreign polices or actions. The implication is that those in that category should be seen and not heard. Further, they should settle for appreciating America for giving them a better opportunity in life, as they have not earned the patriotic standing to voice an opposing opinion on that level.

An instance that illustrates this point above involved Martina Navratilova, either in the 1980s or 1990s during the administration of President Reagan or President George Bush—Bush I, (George H. W.). Martina Navratilova, the number-one women's tennis player in the world for an extended period during her time, had spoken out against one of the U.S. incursions into a foreign country at that time and triggered a barrage of criticisms. Then a recent defector to the United States from her native Czechoslovakia, as accomplished foreigners in different fields from certain parts of the world or nations were encouraged and lured into defecting to the United States to score cheap political points on those nations, Martina had spoken out against that U.S. intrusion. Responding to her critics, Ms. Navratilova said that she did not leave one dictatorship for another.

I am also reminded here of an encounter with a fellow worker last year, 2008, as the U.S. presidential election narrowed down to Senators McCain and Obama, the Republican and Democratic party nominees respectively. The fellow worker, a retired New York City police officer, one of many providing services to my city agency as an investigative consultant, was discussing the chances of the candidates with a few colleagues. The consultant obviously was favoring Senator McCain. Certainly not wishing that Senator McCain emerge the winner, I had chipped in that this would be bad and another step backwards for America. Then the consultant cut in: "Have you been in war?" I responded by asking him why it was that serving in the military, and especially fighting in a war, inured and entitled one to a public office, with nothing else mattering, even for an office as important as that of the president. As I made that assertion, he, in a cheap shot, accused me of being loud. From my standpoint, this was a manipulative reaction to a superior argument from me, as it may have started dawning on him that he had nothing effective to counter the point I had made.

I made the determination not to vote for Senator McCain, having heard his all-consuming militarism and his reasons why the United States should continue to do what she does militarily, even more aggressively, all over the world. Clearly, McCain and his supporters see his military service and record as a war captive and prisoner in Vietnam as the utmost qualification for the presidency. For me, what unfolded about him was a bunker mentality. It is well known that McCain spent so much time in captivity in Vietnam (in a bunker practically), for which he should be thankful that he was not killed in his role as a member of a military force that invaded a sovereign nation. The dent, it appears, that the experience left on him is that he appeared to still be in the bunker mentally, even after several years of having left it physically.

Before that encounter with the quasi-military man/ex-police officer; he and I had not really had a significant interaction as I had just transferred to that office months earlier. Therefore, he had no idea what I could bring to discussions. I had paused, following his manipulative accusation that I was being loud, to hear his counterargument. But he quickly, in a dismissive manner, redirected his focus to doing what I have often overheard him do: loudly cracking jokes with female workers. This was why I had said to myself: *Of all people,* he *accuses me of being loud.* This is a guy for whom being loud and telling abrasive jokes to the female staff is the norm. Women are the overwhelming majority in my job; they come to consult with him in the course of their jobs. I had also noticed that the women seemed to enjoy his jokes, and he seemed to get attention that made him feel good and validated, like a "hero" also, in his mind. So he had to return there, where he was comfortable and felt appreciated and fulfilled.

Unbeknownst to this "hero," however, I had been in a war, as if he was expecting an answer. He had asked that question to reduce me and push me aside. That was why he had dismissed me the way he had originally intended when he saw an opening to do so. Even if he had expected an answer and had gotten one, that I was in a war—in the Nigerian civil war in the 1960s as a teenager, on the side of Eastern Nigeria when the region attempted to secede as the Republic of Biafra. This, of course, would have meant nothing to him. For one thing, it was not a war for the United States and did not qualify me as a hero who put his life on the line to save America's freedom from the legion of evil enemies always lurking to pounce and take her freedom away. And I had the effrontery to opine that an American, a military and war hero of John McCain's caliber, draped and wrapped in the American flag, should not be the next president. This translates to not knowing my place in his America and staying it, in his mid-set.

On the world stage and in the global arena, many—nations and individuals—have felt the brunt of the United States' might. An avowed republic and non-empire, the United States has actually turned out to be one looming and large empire and has done just about everything to guard against the demise of its empire like those before it in history. Using alliances is one way the United States has connived and worked to sustain her imperial instincts and interests. The alliances the United States has either started or currently leads include the North Atlantic Treaty Organization (NATO), a military alliance which has gone from being comprised mainly of the Western world to lately including non-Western states, especially in the post-Union of Soviet Socialist Republics (USSR) era. This expansion lately, in 2009, triggered a reaction by Russia, causing her to invade Georgia, a former USSR block state. Another is the Organization of American States (OAS), a regional alliance of the nation-states of the North and South American continents. The South East Asian Treaty organization (SEATO), with the United States clearly a non-South Asian nation member state, is another. There is the group of seven, or eight (the G-7/8), an alliance of the so-called leading economic powers of the world. The G-20 (the world's richest nations or something close) has also been added to the list. The imperial stance or advantage of the United States through these alliances may not be clear to the non-discerning or closed mind, but the need to get a lock on power and influence on the world and sustain it cannot be denied. While the United States has not gone about her imperial ways chiefly the ways of the empires before—the Roman, the British, etc.—by physical occupation and military conquest—she has also engaged in these to some degree. The invasions of Granada, Panama—to scoop her head of state—and Iraq and its occupation are examples in recent history.

In the OAS and SEATO alliances, it should be clear that the enticing factor to the smaller, poorer, and less powerful members is the big-brother protection from some imaginary or real threats that the United States dangles before them. Any such member dares question or disagree with the "dictates" of the United States to her detriment. Many other nations around the world that fall into no formal alliance with the United States but are considered friends of the United States, have some enticements dangled before them. One is that a United States military/naval base on their territory/coastal waters would make them feel safe from, again, imaginary or real threats of "enemies." As for other states/nations, the United States considers unfriendly or hostile to her or her interests, she still stations military/combat vessels off their coastal waters, with the "justification" that they are "international waters," the objection of such nations notwithstanding. The United States gets away with it because it is indeed a conventional military superpower. Any other nation dares attempt to station her own military base close to United States coastal waters using the same "justification" of "international waters" to her peril. This is but one instance of many double standards that characterize the poise, stance, and persona of the United States.

Poor Mexico

Any "enemy" closely located to the United States or not is not immune to her wrath. Also, smaller and/or poorer neighboring but independent nations get trampled upon by the United States at whim. Often termed the American backyard (like President Ronald Reagan did in making his case for "stopping of a communist beach-head in *our backyard*" in order to invade the island of Grenada in the 1980s), these nations are often caught in the American crossfire. Having years ago read a caption or headline in a U.S. daily newspaper that read something close to: "Poor Mexico, So Far From God, So Close to the United States," I decided to Google it, documenting this discourse. Doing so, I found the caption with an article that includes the excerpt below, by Sandy Goodman, a retired producer for *NBC Nightly News* and a freelance writer.

> Back in civilian life, I next visited Mexico in 1962. I was still a young man when one of my heroes, John F. Kennedy, was president, and as far as I was concerned, my country could do no wrong. Until a tour guide named George Lugo drove me around Mexico City and took me to Chapultepec Palace. There, he told me, six teenage Mexican military cadets made a heroic, fatal last stand against an overwhelming force of U.S. marines in 1847, during the Mexican War. In that war and, earlier, by annexing Texas, he reminded me, the U.S. snatched away half of his country. He later took me to the rundown cemetery where, he said, Santa Anna, the Mexican leader who lost Texas, was buried.

That caption essentially captures the frustration that in run-ins and face-offs between God and the Devil, the devil, the United States in such face-offs, seems to have the edge and does prevail. For Mexico, this dates back to 1847, during the U.S.-Mexican war, or even before. This was but one of such consequences for "poor" nations bordering the United States. Driven to fulfill her "destiny," which was "divinely manifested" to her, the United States went about it accordingly.

On the current (2009) issue of the influx of illegal drugs saturating the news, Mexico is said to be the source of most illegal drugs entering the United States. It would be laudable if the laws of Mexico which were enacted to address and curb whatever problems the nation of Mexico objectively has determined to be detrimental to Mexican society were the basis of her war on drugs. It is very probable; however, that Mexico is fighting the drug war because the "big boss man" across the border demands it. As it is clear from this side of the United States-Mexican divide, illegal drug use and abuse is a major problem and concern. But rather than Mexico being nudged into and accepting the incursion of the United States into her territory to stake and wage this drug war, should the United States not be figuring out a more effective way to wage the war by focusing on the insatiable appetite for illegal drugs in her own territory instead? Doing so should start with looking into the reason there is such an appetite for illegal drugs in the United States and addressing it. Until a better, more efficient way is determined, what could make an impact on putting an undesirable industry out of business? Would it be drug in-flow in this case, rather than curbing the demand for it? This is unlikely here because the underlying social and environmental factors in the appetite (huge demand) for illegal drugs in the United States, to soothe an extreme capitalism-induced stress probably, is "as American as apple pie." Why else would America be the world's largest consumer of illegal drugs?

And for Mexico, the supplier, unless there is something in it that is inherently bad for the Mexican society, why must she fight a major source of income into her economy? Who better to understand the law of supply and demand than the United States, the world's strongest proponent of unfettered capitalism? On the U.S. side, there is history of criticism that the drug laws have a built-in big business bias, with the "consumer," the average street user, getting the short end of the stick here too. This is because prison sentences and terms are determined to be worse for the user, compared to that for the bulk distributor—big business. From news accounts, too close to America, Mexico, the supplier here, is already being decimated by battles between government forces and the suppliers. Unless Mexico shows how the "hard currency" the drug business pulls into her economy from her big, powerful, and strong neighbor hurts her, she is probably just being bullied into inflicting these injuries upon herself. While this may be the case for Mexico, on this, the U.S. side of the border, pro-business bias stacks the odds against the consumer. With business possibly in favor of Mexico here, had the shoe been on the other foot, it would be Mexico that would have been challenged and pushed to address her problem of a high demand for and consumption of illegal drugs.

Almost nothing could capture the United States' double standard and hypocrisy in her dealings with other nations, vis-à-vis her "interests," better than this statement in 1948 by the U.S. president Franklin Roosevelt, as the United States was supporting and arming Nicaraguan president Anastasio Somoza, a known corrupt figure, "Somoza may be a son of a bitch, but he is our son of a bitch."

The history of the United States' involvement in subverting the popular interest of Nicaraguans is extensive, with documented incidents that range from arming and supporting corrupt, criminal leaders/leadership to planting dissent and active military incursions/intrusions. The "beat" was on and continued in the 1980s, on Daniel Ortega, a Sandinistas leader and the president of Nicaragua, in the "hands" of President Ronald Reagan of the United States, culminating in the Iran-Contra scandal. President Ortega's crime was that he shunned being the United States' son of a bitch that the Contra, the domestic Sandinistas opposition, propped, financed, and armed by the United States was, and for daring to do what was known to be good for his country, Nicaragua, instead. Nicaragua's fate in the hands of the United States probably rivals that of the United States' stifling of the independent island nation of Cuba.

Capitalism versus Socialism/Communism
The United States' history is littered with wars, some of them of ideology. One war of ideology that she is very proud to fight in perpetuity is the war to limit, eliminate, or eradicate Communism. Convinced that Capitalism is superior to Communism, the United States sees Communism almost as a crime and/or sin, or even a deadly affliction, for which anyone or nation embracing and/or practicing it deserves to be punished even by death, or some dose of *the mother-of-all antidotes*. The question is: should it come to this in a so diverse world? In a nation built on the foundation and principle of freedom and civil rights, the scourge of *McCarthyism* rubbished those ideals. *McCarthyism* is a term that described the intense anti-Communist suspicion in the United States in a period that lasted roughly from the late 1940s to the late 1950s. In a spell of Communist paranoia, *McCarthyism* was coined after U.S. Senator Joseph McCarthy who started the campaign of aggressive investigations. Many Americans— perceived to be agents or sympathizers of Communism were intesley

terrorized and pesecuted. Despite the shaky basis of the accusations and the lack of evidence to substantiate them, many of the accused were visited with punishments ranging from loss of employment and destruction of careers to imprisonment. The intense fear, shenanigans, and the crippling blow dealt on citizens warrant asking: whatever happened to the freedom to conceive and/or embrace ideas, put them to the test, and allow them to thrive or fall flat on their face on their merits or demerits, the way Communism is said to have failed in the Eastern bloc nations? While *McCarthyism* may have occurred decades ago, it still does today, and hardly subtly. If arrogance and myopia does not explain this "war," what else does? In this arrogation of moral fortitude and superiority, many have been victimized, including nations, when just minding one's business should have sufficed.

Fighting injustice and for the freedom of a people is one mantra the United States has always used to "justify" her actions of minding the business of the diverse world. The United States will cite that she spends very hefty sums of money and more in materials helping the poor nations of the world. This would be commendable and encouraged if doing this was indeed not self-serving and to impose influence and control. The point of minding the business of the world here makes me recall the words of a one-time boss, a United States citizen of Haitian heritage, in the 1990s when the United States engaged in a military incursion in Haiti: "The United States is all over the place minding other people's business."

The fact is: no matter how much the United States pretends to liberate or pull others out of poverty, she simply cannot impose or create one standard, economically or otherwise, in the world. Further, neither the United States nor any other nation could rid the entire world of poverty ever, as the world is just what it is: an imperfect manifestation.

For starters, the United States has no intention of having every citizen of the world become citizens of one nation—that of the United States—that all would, for instance, have access to whatever privileges and benefits that come with it. Even if the entire world was known to try beating down the United States' borders to migrate to it to access all the perceived advantages she has to offer, there are always those—nations and individuals—who would never join that bandwagon. Also, the United States, no matter how much she has done to live up to her image as a nation of immigrants, would neither allow nor cope with that ideal. This is a reality that the United States should understand, appreciate, and accept.

It is in the dragnet of her war to eradicate Communism that Cuba, an island just ninety miles off the coast of the state of Florida, is caught. Since Cuba's Castro, a leader of the revolution that adopted Socialism for the island nation, emerged as Cuba's president, the United States has resolved to not see Cuba survive or thrive as a nation. Considered by the United States as her "beachhead" and "backyard," Cuba's sin is daring to be a Socialist state. Although history is clear that prior to the revolution, the United States' Capitalist interest had dominated Cuba, promoting all kinds of vices there, including prostitution and drug dealing, with Cuba not faring well for it, the United States would never see that she had a hand in pushing Cuba into that revolution, resulting in her embracing Socialism instead. The United States would turn around and blame Fidel Castro for being in office as the president of Cuba for as long as he was, labeling and calling him a dictator anytime official U.S. institutions had to mention his name. My sense is that Fidel Castro hanging on to power for as long as he did before transferring power lately to his younger brother, Raul, has to do with the fear that the United States would return to controlling Cuba if a non-patriotic, weak stooge emerged as president. It is my sense also that had the United States not lurked around to pounce and return to control Cuba when an opportunity presented itself, Fidel Castro would have vacated power much earlier.

Elian Gonzales

The story and drama of Elian Gonzales, a little boy who had to endure tremendous abuse in the process, captures also the United States' disdain and disrespect for Cuba's independence as a sovereign nation. With the United States encouraging Cuba's citizens to flee the island nation to the United States as a way to spite Cuba as a dictatorship, Elian Gonzalez's mother had drowned in her attempt to so flee. This caused Elian Gonzales's father to seek to get custody of his son who survived that attempted flight that occurred without his father's knowledge or approval. Instead of honoring the father's request, elements in the United States, encouraged and prodded by other Cuban relocated citizens in Florida, chose to use Elian Gonzalez as a pawn in their Capitalism-Socialism war. Eventually, Elian Gonzales's father was allowed to come to the United States to see his son, not necessarily to get custody of him and return to Cuba, as he had intended. Believing in the temptation and attraction of materialism prevailing, the enticement game to lure Mr. Gonzales into deflecting to the United States was on.

The enticement included a house, car, and all. In the end, Mr. Gonzalez did not fall for all the gimmickry and propaganda and chose to take his son and return to Cuba instead.

Notably, the administration of President Bill Clinton, comparatively progressive by the U.S. standard, led by its attorney general, Janet Reno, helped to rescue Elian and delivered him to his father. That Elian's father chose to turn down the "heaven" that is the United States and return to the "hell" of Cuba was another demonstration of people choosing self-determination over material handouts, rubbishing the notion that human satisfaction would always be measured materially.

Selfish, materialistic, and altruistic acts to smaller and poorer nations designed to pacify them will prevail for a while but will not endure indefinitely. It might buy the loyalty of the leadership in an era or generation but will dissipate and fizzle as a new generation that is more informed and patriotic emerges in the scene of leadership. Why this is hard to see defies reasoning, except that power and privilege are addictive and blinding.

That an individual trapped in poverty and the lack of opportunity, which will always be around on earth for as long as there is life, would welcome gifts, even with strings attached and place immeasurable value on them, is understood. That another person would, conversely, value self-determination over altruistic, material acts with a self-serving, ulterior motive, to the point of preferring death instead, should also be understood and respected. It would help if nations would simply mind their business and let others be.

The above said; if it's true that there is indeed selfless giving, with only caveats of psychological personal redemption and feeling good and hoping a beneficiary is empowered to help make a desired difference for self and society, by all means, let the floodgates of altruism swing wide open. Again, because there will always be poverty, deprivation, and absence of opportunities for as long as there is life; selfish altruism has nothing to be appreciated in the contextual scheme of eliminating poverty. The lopsided landscape of life said to be a creation of some god cannot be made even by imperfect, mortal beings, themselves an inseparable part of that inherently flawed creation.

Control of the World

The desire and ambition of the United States to control the world is as elaborate as her schemes to actualize them; the negative consequences for the target nations and their citizens are not given consideration. What, otherwise, could explain the fact that the United States has repeatedly carried on accordingly. From plotting and inciting dissents and poisonings to make targets debilitatingly sick, to assassinations through intermediaries and directly, the United States has done it all, employing the tools of her Central Intelligence Agency (CIA) and related operatives. Certain of the CIA's complicities internationally, and even domestically, suspected or reasonably known, have been brought to light and confirmed from different sources. One such source is a publication, *The Militant*, of December

22, 2008, which highlighted the documentary film, *Cuba, An African Odyssey,* and the United States'/CIA's complicity in the death of Patrice Lumumba. Lumumba, of course, was the renowned anti-colonial leader of Congo in the 1960s. The fact of the United States' complicity in the assassination of Lumumba is reasonably known since. Among the light shed in the documentary are a series of interviews with Lawrence Devlin, identified as the head of the CIA station in Congo then. In one interview, Lawrence Devlin quoted from the message he received from President Dwight Eisenhower ordering the CIA to eliminate Lumumba "physically." The plot was said to include Devlin being provided by a CIA operative with poisoned toothpaste to do the job.

The following excerpts from *The New Nation* (*Bangladesh's Independent News Source*), posted on Wikipedia online, adds details and clarity on the nature of these "clandestine" activities:

> AFP adds: The CIA offered 150,000 dollars to mafia figures to kill Cuban leader Fidel Castro, just one of several CIA plots against foreign leaders detailed in 693 pages of classified US documents released Tuesday. Other targets of CIA, long alleged but only now revealed in the intelligence agency's own documents, included Congo independence leader Patrice Lumumba as well as Dominican Republic dictator Rafael Trujillo.

> The documents also detail apparently illegal government spying on US citizens opposed to the Vietnam War and on prominent journalists in the 1970s, as well as experiments using drugs on unsuspecting subjects.

Among the released CIA files is a lengthy memo which exposes the agency's recruitment of top mafia figures already wanted for crimes in order to assassinate Cuba's communist leader. "The mission target was Fidel Castro," said the 1973 document. According to the memo, the man chosen for the "sensitive mission requiring gangster-type action" was one Johnny Roselli—in reality Santos Trafficant, head of mafia Cuba operations. He recruited a second man for the mission called Sam Gold, whom the CIA discovered was actually Salvatore "Momo" Giancana, head of the Chicago mob and "successor to Al Capone." Both were on the US attorney general's ten most-wanted fugitives list, according to the memo.

"It was to be made clear to Roselli that the United States Government was not, and should not, become aware of this operation," it said.

The Mafiosi recommended against the use of firearms to kill Castro, it said, and suggested instead "some type of potent pill that could be placed in Castro's food or drink."

"Sam indicated that he had a prospective nominee in the person of Juan Orta, a Cuban *official* who had been receiving kick-back payments from the gambling interests, who still had access to Castro, and was in a financial bind," the memo said. Roselli gave Orta the pills, but "After several weeks of reported attempts, Orta apparently got cold feet and asked out of the assignment."

"Roselli made it clear he did not want any more for his part and believed Sam would feel the same way. Neither of these individuals was ever paid out of Agency funds," the document said. The assassination was meant as a prelude to the disastrous invasion of Cuba's Bay of Pigs. The documents declassified Tuesday were dubbed the CIA's "family jewels," denoting the importance of their secrecy. They detail surveillance of Americans who opposed the Vietnam War; opening personal mail to and from China and the Soviet Union, including four letters to actress Jane Fonda; break-ins on the properties of former CIA employees; wiretapping of journalists' telephones and experiments using drugs on people who weren't informed about it. These acts were all part of the CIA's snooping in the 1970s, even though the agency is forbidden to conduct intelligence gathering on US soil. Also revealed are plans to assassinate the Congo's anti-colonial leader Lumumba, who was overthrown in a 1960 coup long believed backed by the CIA, and Dominican Republic strongman Trujillo, who was shot dead by political opponents in 1961.

On the South African front and the capture of Nelson Mandela by the Apartheid regime of South Africa; a publication, *JNN, in* an article, *Truth Commission Spotlights CIA Role—Our Man in South Africa,* by Jeff Stein, identified as a former deputy foreign news editor for United Press International (UPI), and a teacher of Investigative Reporting in South Africa on a U.S. government grant in the past, detailed the role of one Millard Shirley in it. Described as a long time "African hand" with the Central Intelligence Agency and a senior covert action specialist who lived and worked in South Africa for a quarter of a century, Millard Shirley is said to be the one who tipped off the South African police to Mandela's whereabouts, prompting the roadblock and his capture in 1962. A source in the article only identified as Ludi spoke of a high-ranking informant, and an associate of Shirley, who was close to Mandela shortly before his capture, as the one that gave detailed information on Mandela's whereabouts while on the run, as America was said to have interest in having Mandela out of the way. An article, "CIA releases declassified documents," by Xinhua;

dated Wednesday, June 27, also chronicles some information, known since the 1970s. CIA released those documents in compliance with the order of its director James Schlesinger that "all senior operating officials of this agency to report to me immediately on any activities now going on, or that have gone on in the past, which might be construed to be outside the legislative charter of the agency."

Among the information in those released documents are on CIA's involvements in attempts to assassinate president Fidel Castro of Cuba and also in a plot to assassinate Patrice Lumumba of Congo.

As if the above facts were in any doubt, the U.S. Congress recently (sometimes in late June 2008) passed a bill, quickly signed into law by President George W. Bush, removing Mandela from the U.S. terrorist list, shortly before Mandela's ninetieth birthday. The terrorist watch list was established in the Ronald Reagan era, in the 1980s. Ludicrous and obviously laughable, Mandela leading the fight against the injustice of the apartheid government and system in his home country was until recently against the U.S. interest, apparently; hence, the United States branded him a terrorist and blacklisted him. It is probably for legacies like this that some American conservative nuts (revisionist rear fringe) to whom Reagan was god have done just about anything to hoist and engrave him in the shrine of America's greatest heroes. In the "mind-set" of the revisionists' rear fringe, Ronald was a great hero for restoring America's pride and prestige and making the men and women who wear America's military uniforms proud again following the Carter presidency. Reagan did so by his military adventures and incursions in places like Grenada and others, which he had proclaimed accordingly. This was their way of repudiating the Carter presidency for being respectful of others and for President Carter's humane ways and decency. There are real knowledgeable people who see the buffed-up image of President Ronald Reagan as myth.

All these do is really show that the United States has hardly risen to her expressed and public ideals. It is also one of the many things that validate the questioning of the existence of that god who is not only attributed with perfection, but who also supposedly put all the lopsidedness in place. This obsession with world control in the modern era to which the United States has evolved has risen to the point of paranoia. As with paranoia in an individual, the paranoid nation lives with fear and distrust and always sees danger, mostly imagined. Devoid of insight and the ability to see reality, it does not let its guard down for fear that doing so translates to ominous danger. They operate in a manner that victimizes others, and if the paranoia goes unaddressed for a long time, it results in self-inflicted damage also.

The Icarus paradox, when one's egotistic perfection and arrogance limits one's ability for insight and realization of changing and shifting trends, fits here.

With so much credit claimed by and attributed to the Western world and the United States for intelligence; that they have either failed or refused to understand and/or accept that the diversity in the world and of life is such that the world does not see everything the same way speaks volumes. Perspectives in and views of life are as diverse as the peoples and cultures of the world. That the United States has set for herself a goal of knocking and muscling the world into seeing and imbibing her values defies logic. This must be why her history is immersed in wars—active, "hot," or "cold."

There are other facts to support that even if the United States were to be willing to absorb all seekers of entry into her shores; there would always be those who would not so seek. It really takes a lot for immigrants to the United States, and I guess to other countries, to adapt, cope, and survive in their host culture. One exception, in my experience, was that a Westerner residing and working in Nigeria when I lived there got the luxury of being availed of the money it would take to buy and bring him his culture to make him comfortable. Besides, natives would mimic him before he even considered learning any or some of the ways of the natives.

I recall here an instance when my German immigrant boss and I were at a Lagos, Nigeria, airport in the 1970s to pick up another European staff member of our company arriving in Lagos from Port Harcourt. As passengers from that flight were making their way to the arrival hall, my German boss noticed a Caucasian, probably from that arriving flight. As the man approached the arrival hall from a distance, my boss fixed and gazed his eyes on him, as if to make sure that what he was seeing was correct and that his eyes were not deceiving him. Closer and with a clearer view, it was clear that that Caucasian had obviously spent some time in the sun and the tan on his skin showed, suggesting he was on a job site/fieldwork. Also, that individual, a male, wore native Nigerian attire. Gesturing in the direction of the man, my boss remarked, "Bushman proper." I understood his joke well. The "norm" is for Africans to mimic the Westerners. This, of course, includes in clothing choices. In that instance, however, the reverse was the case; a Westerner was wearing African attire. Doing so, the Westerner "dumbed" himself down to the level of a "bushman."

As a United States citizen of African origin, my sense is that the bar of adaptation is higher for the immigrant of non-Eurocentric background. That the native Nigerian or African gets to serve a Western immigrant in the native's home country warrants imagining the depth of servitude from which the African has to dig himself as an immigrant in a Western country. There is indeed something in the native-born American that, I believe, makes him come across with an attitude of superiority, making him condescending to the people of African origin, at least.

Brown is my first name, given to me by my father who worked in the Nigerian court system under the British colonial authorities; it is clear that my name was influenced by that experience. Having learned since that in America, Brown is only a last name; here's how I give my name in exchanges/communications in which I have to give it: "First name: Brown, as in color. Last name, I'll spell; O-g-w-u-m-a, Ogwuma."

Between specifying my name as I did and the foreign accent which seems to be always noticed and also constitutes a hindrance, there could and should be enough clues, if not clarity, about my name. Still not convinced that Brown is my first name, I have been asked in different ways, "Are you sure Brown is the first name and not the last?"

This has prompted me to respond, "Yes, I am sure. It is my name; I would know. Don't you think so?"

In my culture of origin, last names were someone's first name—a father, grandfather, great-grandfather, and great-great-grandfather, down the generational line. Certain names were not picked and just meant to be last names.

A few days ago, Friday, October 16, 2009, to be exact, I initiated telephone contact with an employee of an agency regarding a client, an African, and his family. After giving the name of the client to that agency's staff, who had made me respell each of the first and last names of the client, she said, "Let me spell back this thing you spelled to me."

To that, I responded, "This 'thing' is somebody's name; a client/family you [the agency] will work with."

Language Accent as an Impediment

With verbal/oral communication, for example, the native-born American finds African names and accents unintelligible. Nothing, apparently, has clued him in to the typical African alphabet and Afro-centric pronunciations and that linguistically, the African is different from the American. The American easily gives up on African names, making up his own names for the African with whom he has had to deal, even as he easily makes out Eurocentric names, including those made up of only consonants. Conversely, the African, though he had to learn the English language, would master unique American and European words and names and attempt also to master Eurocentric and Americentric accents.

Averagely ignorant on this subject, a U.S. native-born does not know that there is such a thing as American accents and would easily say to one who does not sound like he does, "I cannot understand you; you have an accent."

Getting tired of having to cope and adapt on this level still after over twenty-six years, I came close to flipping on two incidents of this recently. In one incident, I had made a job-related telephone call to a New York State employee in Albany, the state capital. I identified myself and followed up with a question. The person at the other end of the phone, a man, said, "I cannot understand a word you said."

To that, I asked, "Why not?" And there was silence, as he did not respond. Continuing, I asked, "Sir, are you there?"

And he responded, "Yes."

Then I said to him, "You understood me this time, didn't you?"

He did not respond again. I then unloaded on him with these statements, "Your initial statement that you cannot understand a word of what I said implies that I am at fault by being unable to communicate. But to me, it tells me that you understand only those residing in the same block with you, who probably share the same cultural background with you. That you had to take my call from New York City tells me that your job requires you to communicate with callers from New York, about the most cosmopolitan city in the world, where diverse nationalities and cultures are represented. Because your understanding verbal communications appears to be limited to understanding the accent of your block of residence, I would not assign you to a job that requires that you communicate with the public, particularly from the New York City region of the state. Until you adequately train your hearing or grew up to this reality, you would not be qualified to hold that position. And if I were your supervisor, I would make sure this was so." Concluding, I added, "Thank you, sir, and try to have a nice day."

I handled the second incident with a woman who actually used that infamous line, "You have an accent; I cannot understand you," about the same way. It is like an accent is a deadly disease that one catches. Although good knowledge of the English language may have little or nothing to do with the accent with which it is spoken, I would still point out here that the professor in of one of my English classes, Professor Ursula Garrison, gave me an award for being the best in the class in my sophomore year in college, here in the United States of course.

I have met some individuals who have arrived in the United States and upon coming face-to-face with the reality, and not just the rosy, lofty picture always painted, came to realize and appreciate what they had in their native homes and decided to return to work with it. Others have

157

broken down mentally by the draining toll of surviving in a "superior" culture. As the U.S.-born carries on as if programmed into an automatic mode, one could decipher from his verbal response and non-verbal cues in reaction to one's effort to communicate verbally with him that he implies that one's non-American accent is an indication of one's low intelligence.

It may be my fault that I chose to migrate to the United States and to remain there as a naturalized citizen who has "failed" to fully melt my accent; must I also be blamed that the average native-born American is only able to understand the accent of his block of residence in the "melting pot" that is America? I don't think so.

Here's a recent exchange that inspired me to be a little more elaborative on this issue than I had initially intended. A female colleague of mine and I, among others, had interviewed (a group interview) for a manager-level position with a program area in our agency of the City of New York. Months after the interview, having heard nothing as to a whether a decision had been made, I already concluded that I was not accepted for the position; there were only a few slots to be filled as we were told during the interview. The thoughts that a decision may not have been made would occasionally cross my mind, based on the fact that the city was downsizing and restructuring many agencies and programs in the wake of the economic downturn. With this as the case, I would think, holding back on promotions and/or not filling in certain vacant positions might be one way to start.

Then, in a telephone conversation with this colleague (the first contact between us since the interview) who is in a different office in a different borough of New York City, that interview came up. I asked her whether she had had any word, and she responded, "No." I asked her whether she knew if any offers had been made, and she said that offers had been made. Then she added that she never really expected she would be offered a position. I asked her the basis for that statement. She responded, "With my accent, I didn't think so." Although I already knew that limitations have been set on the career paths of people based on their accents, with me possibly one, I did not expect that would factor in with her. Originally from the Caribbean, I believe, I thought her accent was no longer that "strange" in New York City, with a considerably large population of Caribbeans, many of whom migrated here as children. This colleague of mine has worked in the City for about 25 to 30 years, therefore has considerable experience to go by. With her statement, the impediments around accents that I have always felt existed were validated for me. It made me feel some good mentally that others do indeed walk in my shoes. It does feel good that it is not just in one's mind, and that one is not alone here.

Fresh from completing my second master's degree back in 1996, I was invited to interview for a position with a human services agency in Westchester County, New York, in response to my application. I interviewed with Jerry, the program director, a Caucasian male; one thing he asked me was, "Don't you think your accent will be a problem for your clients?" I do give him credit for coming out and saying it.

In response, I said that I was aware that I spoke with a foreign accent and looked for cues from clients, verbal and nonverbal, to manage communicating with my clients well. Continuing, I said that I also know myself enough to have confidence that I bring skills and knowledge of resources and the experience to help clients and their families. Further, I explained that when I had engaged clients and formed working relationships with them and earned their trust based on what I bring to help them, they do look beyond my non-American accent and worked well with me. I was offered that position. When I arrived at the unit to start working, the unit supervisor, Janet, a Caucasian female, told me she would accompany me to a number of fieldwork appointments initially. Fieldwork entailed visiting with client families in their homes. I had done these a few years and had become a unit supervisor prior. After just one visit, Janet decided it was not necessary and informed me. In a one-on-one supervision, she told me how much confidence she had in me just from that one fieldwork experience with me. This was validating for me.

Having interviewed for a professional clinical position with a mental health agency in Manhattan that had a job fair at New York University prior to my accepting the job with the Westchester County-based agency, I received a call offering me that position. When I got the offer in writing days later, I put in a written notice of resignation with the Westchester County-based agency. Then, my supervisor, Janet, invited me to meet with her. In the meeting, she asked me to reconsider my resignation, letting me know I had a future with her agency. I probably would have, had the new offer not meant more to me, in terms of its clinical core, which I thought was better for my career. Also, the salary was more, and my commute to work shorter.

If I could make anything of my experience with that agency and those two administrative staff members, it is that stereotypes and personal biases do not always prove anything.

The seeming focus or obsession around "accent" in this culture is something I don't think plays out that much in every culture. I'll admit I have not lived in many cultures. However, going by my experience in Nigeria, my nation of origin, I found that although it was clear and known that accents differed and varied, I did not see it used to impede people.

First, within the many ethnicities of Nigeria, English, the official language, was spoken with accents that differed with the ethnic groups. Then, the many foreigners that lived and worked in Nigeria from the 1970s to 1981, where I lived and worked in Lagos, the nation's capital for most of those years, spoke the English language with accents that varied also with their nationalities and ethnic backgrounds. These included citizens of other African nations, Europeans, Americans, and others. Personally, I worked with Europeans from Germany, Czechoslovakia, Holland, and Austria. I'm sure they too would attest that in their interactions with either members of the Nigerian public, individual agents of the Nigerian government, or representatives of other corporations in Nigeria, they were not put down, dismissed, ignored, or rejected because they did not speak a Nigerian language or the English language with a Nigerian accent. Could this be because, as a "third-world" nation, Nigeria and Nigerians know no better? After all, it takes a science-inclined "first-world" nation to figure out and understand good, evil, and limitations. Or, as a poor, backward, "third-world" nation, must Nigeria adapt to whatever "standard" citizens of the "first world" bring with them? After all, they are there for Nigeria's benefit. If this is the case, what about the Africans from that continent's other nations who also resided and worked in Nigeria?

Here's a little more on bias in the United States and its implication on accent. Take the Middle-Eastern nations of Israel, Iran, and Iraq; all three of the so-called Abrahamic heritage in religious terms, for instance. The American will pronounce Israel correctly, with the "I" in Israel as in the Middle-Eastern phonetic, "I." But coming to Iran and Iraq, he pronounces them Eyeran (or I ran) and Eyeraq (or I rack), with the "I" becoming eye, Anglicizing or Americanizing it. This would have meant that Israel, too, is pronounced Eyesrael, but that is not the case. One way one could explain the discrepancies in pronunciation here is the prejudice of friendly Israel and the enmity/hatred toward Iran and Iraq.

For a "know-it-all power"—the United States—that is up and about and in everybody else's world and business, who also gives signals and the impression that the world is welcome to her fold, would it not make sense that it is about time that she "educates" her native-born about the fact the entire world does not speak America's very contracted, fancy English? They, the others, for the most part, pronounce English words fully, according to the alphabets. Even for the third-world-born who learns and speaks English as a second language; while in the United States, s/he does understand that to many Americans, the letter "t" could be "d," "r," or totally discarded when some worlds are pronounced. Katie could and does become Kayddie/*Kaddie*. Water is pronounced *warer*, and *moun'n* is said for mountain; *accoun'ning* for accounting; *fighding* or *fi'n'* for fighting; *eading* or *ea'n* for eating; *shooding* or *shoo'n* for shooting. Then there is *Some'n like'at* for the phrase "something like that," *Innernet*, for Internet. That there is an Innernet does suggest that there is Outernet also. The list goes on. If one person says *fin'lly* for finally; what stops another from hearing or thinking a word like *finelly*; excepting that the other, and/or both, is/are capable of incorporating context in their communication?

Here's an instance that underscores the place of context in communication. In it, the word artistic is confused with another, autistic; because of the inability to incorporate context in a scenario that had art in the background of it. In my job, I was facilitating a conference for and with a client and other service providers. A little earlier in the conference, the client, a male American of African descent (African-American) had shared that he is an artist. He emphasized that he writes poetry, draws, and paints; and uses art to express himself and gets some relief with stress and other issues. At some other point when this client had to speak again, he made a statement beginning with "Being that I am artistic, ..." Then a female participant; an American of Hispanic descent' asked him: "You mean you are autistic; really?" Visibly agitated by that question, the client responded with his own question to her: "What, what do you mean?: gazing steadily at her in a confrontational manner. As the facilitator, I had to step in to try redirecting the process. I said to the female, as he had said earlier: that he is an artist, you may have sought his clarification by asking, you mean your art skills (the context), for instance; if you were not sure he meant artistic or autistic. As I said that, the client nodded repeatedly in agreement. With the nods, the tension that had enveloped his demeanor began to dissipate simultaneously. The conference came back on track, and eventually successfully concluded.

One does not have to live, or have lived, in Australia to understand and comprehend that *mo'o* means motor as in *mo'ocycle* for motorcycle. The burden to adapt and acculturate clearly is on the immigrant, of course. It is clear, nonetheless, that after a certain age, most people cannot totally "dissolve" their origin so as to "perfectly" fit into a new culture. In the new world of "global society," isn't it time that world citizens become more understanding, knowledgeable, and empathic?

It's true that one common identity that all people share is world "citizenship." This may be where the common identity stops, and it has never inured common or identical laws, protection, benefits, or privileges to all. Other and diverse identities that people are identified by are race, ethnicity/tribe, region, continent, nation, etc. For any nation to "front" as being in the business of rescuing poorer and/or needier nations, it is not only disingenuous; it is also hypocritical. The fact, crystallized by the renowned Maslow's hierarchy of needs, is that self-preservation dictates that the primary and most basic of human needs including food, shelter, clothing, etc., are paramount and must be met before higher needs like self-esteem and self-actualization come into focus and are pursued. This fact has become routinely exploited for selfish ends. Exploitation of this fact fits what the powerful nations have been doing to perpetuate their selfish interests by fronting and faking "altruistic" acts. These are but ruses to expand their influence, power, and dominion of the world.

The cold war in which the United States and the now-defunct USSR engaged for decades was nothing but a contest of whose power and influence held sway in most parts of the world. As the power players engage in their schemes, they lose sight of the fact that those nations over which influence and control are sought might over time have reasonably moved beyond focusing on the primary needs of food, shelter, and the like. They may also have grown to have a notable number of individuals who are intellectually endowed to place a premium value on self-determination. Where either or both of these are correct, those nations would be inclined to recognize and resist gimmicks from external forces to impose upon and to control them. Trapped in their delusive myopia, the power players would always believe that they are seen and accepted as messiahs by all—the poorer peoples of the world, in particular—and would always be eagerly welcomed and embraced.

The essence of self-determination and of perspectives in and views toward life are succinctly captured by Patrick Henry, hailed as an American patriot, in his speech to a pre-independence United States Congress, from which I quote here:

> But different men often see the same subject in different lights; and, therefore, I hope it will not be thought disrespectful to those gentlemen if, entertaining as I do opinions of a character very opposite to theirs, I shall speak forth my sentiments freely and without reserve.

Emphasizing his value and his preference for liberty, Henry concluded his speech with these words: "I know not what course others may take; but as for me, give me liberty or give me death." Like Patrick Henry, patriots of respective nations have rights too to choose to die of poverty over mortgaging their lives and sense of pride for material handouts. Those nations and their citizens should be respected if they would rather die than acquiesce to or accept those "altruisms," having seen through them for what they really are—a ruse for influence and control. A concept and context that would also apply here is "taxation without representation," which culminated in the Boston Tea Party on December 16, 1773—an attack on vessels in the Boston Harbor carrying shipments of tea from Britain, by citizens of then British America, who had become American patriots. The protest became symbolic and iconic and has been attributed with culminating in the revolutionary war to liberate the United States from the British Empire. I am reminded here also of a statement by Gerry Adams, the erstwhile leader of Sinn Féin, the military arm of the Irish Republican Army: "If I am a terrorist, then George Washington was a terrorist."

The point in the above is clear: one person's terrorist is another's patriot. Gerry Adams had stated this in response to a question from a U.S. network TV anchor to a question casting him as, or implying he was, a terrorist for fighting to liberate Ireland from British control. At the time, Gerry Adams was on a tour of the United States to promote a book he had written. In the protracted British-Irish conflict, the United States' position has been to ally with Britain, even to the point of supporting and colluding with her when and where it should be clear that Britain is wrong.

Must the powerful carry a big stick and scold the powerless, hitting the latter with his big stick as he fancies? In the lower animal world, this could be understood. But when the powerful also arrogates to himself a higher intelligence, then something does not add up. The power of respectful mutual engagement and relating, as a more effective way to accomplishing goals, both among individuals and groups, has been demonstrated enough in the human experience. This is captured in this expression:

> There's a way that one could shape one's mouth (diplomatically) to tell another to go to hell, and the other packs up, gets ready, and looks forward to going to hell.

There is always room to extend help to and be a change agent for those for whom change is necessary. However, until one for whom change is necessary is ready for that change, it will not happen, no matter what is thrown at and forced on him. In the mental health field, the professional helper understands that it is his/her role to help promote the awareness of the need to change in the one being helped. Doing this entails skillfully taking the receiver of the help from his current undesirable situation (presenting problem) by engaging him in seeing how it is indeed problematic for his life and well-being. From there, the discomfort of his current situation is heightened for him. This sets the stage to getting him to envisage an alternative, preferable future situation for him. With this accomplished, the desire for change, coming from within, is ignited in the individual, or group, for that matter. As should be clear, it is not easy or simple. Frustration could build for the helper who is not perceptive, triggering unprofessional responses to the receiver, including treating him in ways that make him feel less worthy or less than human. On the part of the helper, this may come out of his own need to be a "curer" or "healer." When he, unconsciously, perceives that he is unable to meet that need, at least in the time he had hoped to, such a reaction is triggered. And when the unperceptive helper does not see this to know when to stop but continues with the squeeze instead, the receiver, unable to tolerate being dumped and piled on as less than human, could and does flip, striking back and lashing out.

Granted, the nations of the world are not in the mental health field and do not play in it. Being this as it may, it takes those mental health field dynamics to constructively engage in any level of human transactions. Suffice it to say, that even in international relations, the above principles should be expected to play out. They therefore should be given due thought when engaging. In the lexicon of that arena, this is called *diplomacy*. In addition to requiring skill, it takes mutual respect. Considering also that the powerful sees his intrusions as rescuing the poor, downtrodden, and repressed, then accepting resistance and refusal is in order. Elian Gonzalez's father refused. Except that the intruded upon is still seen as either not in a position to know or considered incapable of knowing what is good for him. Still in the mind of the powerful; double standards—respect and engagement when the shoes are on his feet and scolding and kicking the unworthy poor when he is wearing the shoes—may be the forgone conclusion and only way. One other thing that the big and powerful should know is that independent nations, their citizens and leadership, are not subject to the jurisdiction of her civil and criminal laws and therefore should not be prosecuted, judged, or punished accordingly. Clearly, appropriate engagement is not only time-consuming; it also demands tremendous skill and the investment of other resources, plus a certain temperament to deal intelligently with others.

But where this is considered wasteful and where the poor are seen as "unequal," then there is no chance that this will become an option. In business—at the core of Capitalism—massive returns is a factor driving the automation mode; hence the approach of a one-glove-fits-all approach of a broad cell of the "consumer market." It is therefore wasteful to factor in or respect individual intelligence or taste. This is the reason human touch in the "modern" business and services arena has practically become extinct. In the context of the big and powerful, and the poor, with the poor, the less worthy; that this factor may be at play cannot be ruled out. Used to having his way and reaping huge returns, the big and powerful can ill afford to waste much factoring in individuality in his dealings with one, who, instead of being appreciative that he is being reached out to, dares to have the audacity to question and even resist him. If common sense were to be given a chance, and considering that the publicly articulated reason behind these incursions is to help and salvage, the big and the powerful should be open to acknowledging and accepting that he does not have what it takes to solve the myriads of the world's problems. No matter the intensity of his desire and good intent, it would help if he had the humility to know that for as long as this life is manifested the way it is, human misery will be a fact of this life for as long as there is life. All one does is one's best, leaving the rest.

The United States and Proclaimed Manifest Destiny
Just like religious doctrines drive the faithful, controlling them mentally, spiritually, and in many ways physically, while disrespecting and nipping their intelligence, Manifest Destiny seems to be one doctrine that drives the United States to assert and force her will globally. Assuming some natural and moral superiority, the United States feels justified to stick it to others, even when nothing demonstrates her overtures are welcome. The following are explanations of Manifest Destiny, found in Wikipedia-on-line:

> Manifest destiny, belief held by many Americans in the 1840s that the United States was destined to expand across the continent, by force, as used against Native Americans, if necessary. The controversy over slavery further fueled expansionism, as the North and South each wanted the nation to admit new states that supported its section's economic, political, and slave policies. By the end of the 19th century, this belief was used to support expansion in the Caribbean and the Pacific.

> Manifest Destiny is a term that was used in the nineteenth century to designate the belief that the United States was destined, even divinely ordained, to expand across the North American continent, from the Atlantic seaboard to the Pacific Ocean. Sometimes Manifest Destiny was interpreted so broadly as to include the eventual absorption of all North America: Canada, Mexico, Cuba and Central America. Advocates of Manifest Destiny believed that

expansion was not only ethical but that it was readily apparent ("manifest") and inexorable ("destiny").

Of the theories forming the basis of Manifest Destiny, three seem to stand out:

1. That divine providence had given the United States a mission to spread republican democracy ("the great experiment of liberty") throughout North America, prompting her to embark upon a special experiment in freedom and democracy—and a rejection of Old World monarchy in favor of republicanism. The United States would then use her calling to spread democracy beyond her immediate geographic territory and continent to liberate the world.
2. A defensive stance to check European powers, especially Great Britain, who were seeking to acquire colonies or greater influence in North America.
3. A justification of actions that were motivated by chauvinism and self-interest, driven by a belief in the natural superiority of the "Anglo-Saxon race."

Whatever the true reason, the third in order above; a justification of actions that were motivated by chauvinism and self-interest, driven by a belief in the natural superiority of the "Anglo-Saxon race," seems to have endured, as the actions of the United States around the world even today suggest. This divine providence, as a doctrine, has the fingerprints of religion all over it. As stated in Wikipedia-on-line, it was initially associated with St. Augustine of Hippo in the Latin West, while "Christian teaching on providence in the high Middle Ages was mostly fully developed by St. Thomas Aquinas in Summa Theological." And just as religion could and does wreak havoc and devastation, the Manifest Destiny of the United States resulted in the decimation of nations bordering her and beyond.

Is it any wonder then that those die-hard supporters of U.S. dominance, like Glenn Beck, who has branded President Obama a racist who hates white people, want the U.S. doctrine of Manifest Destiny/divine providence to run its course in perpetuity? Further, taking a position that the U.S. health-care reform initiative, as proposed by Obama, is a scheme and means by which he can affect reparations for slavery, Beck and his like, very probably in numeric minority now, clearly wish for the continuity of the very egregious ways of the United States. They cannot stand change to them, especially the Obama vision and angle.

9/11

Speaking of lashing out and striking back, could a parallel not be drawn here with the World Trade Center Towers attack in New York City on September 11, 2001, 9/11 for short? At least one person of note is on the record to think so and did so express: Ron Paul, a U.S. Congressman from the state of Texas and a Republican Party candidate for the presidential elections of 2008. Ron Paul is attributed with stating that those attacks were triggered by and were in response to the United States' intrusions in the lives of other nations, the Muslin world in this instance. When I heard this, I was somewhat surprised that someone of that profile was independent thinking and courageous enough to say it publicly in the U.S. political arena.

Congressman/presidential candidate Ron Paul, a patriotic American all the same, did not allow his patriotism to trump his freedom and right, granted him by the United States Constitution, to express this opinion. This information about Ron Paul is an indication of possibilities, possibilities for a balanced perception in the mainstream U.S. discourse, particularly in this new era of President Barack Obama. The president has clearly given indications that he would bring another angle—of mutual interest and mutual respect— to the United States' interactions with other nations.

If America Does not Change the World,
the World Will Change America

Believing as I do that President Obama is sincere, I see institutionalized systemic constraints curtailing and limiting what he can do. I see Ron Paul's take above and President Obama's angle making for a more balanced perception. But for every attempt at a balanced perception, there are tens of others with the same old, distorted ways. Along the latter line is a comment by another U.S. congressman when the lid on the ruse for the invasion of Iraq—that Iraq had nuclear weapons—was being blown open and debunked: "If America does not change the world, the world will change America." Apparently, or obviously, this is the reason for America's endemic mission to change the world, lest she be changed by the world for worse.

Could the invasion of Panama and scooping of her president, Manuel Noriega, who is still stowed away in a U.S. prison, fall within this mission? The official excuse, as I recall it, was that he, Noriega, was aiding the illegal drug trade into the United States and may have been party to other criminal activities. But the real reason, however, was openly noted to be that the people of Panama, under Noriega, refused to renew the Panama Canal treaty with the United States, which would have ended the

U.S. bases, including military, in that independent country. Noted to have been a CIA agent when the first President Bush, in whose administration the nation of Panama was invaded to scoop him up, Noriega, probably a son of a bitch even for Panama then, was no longer America's son of a bitch. Having fallen out of America's favor, he was no longer immune and shielded from America's wrath. The United States visited Noriega with a fate that came close to that she visited on another one-time United States son of a bitch, Iraq's president Saddam Hussein. Propped and armed in his days as America's son of a bitch, Saddam Hussein's Iraqi government was nudged and supported to invade her neighboring nation, Iran, seen by the United States as a thorn in her side even back then. The United States has had hostile relations with Iran dating back several decades to 1953, when the United States orchestrated a coup d'état that toppled the government of Prime Minister Mohammed Mosaddeq. This excerpt from an article "1953 Iranian Coup d'État" , found in Wikipedia-on-line, sums it up:

> This Anglo-American coup d'état was to ensure Western control of Iran's petroleum and to prevent Eastern (USSR) hegemony upon Iran. Moreover, the Iranian motivations for deposing P. M. Mosaddeq included reactionary Clerical dissatisfaction with secular government, fermented with CIA propaganda.

The West-Middle East Tensions

Although material resources are known to play the primary role in the cycle of tensions between the West and the Middle East, as the U.S./ British-backed coup d'état in Iran in 1958 shows, indications also abound that the differing values and cultures of both worlds have a lot to do with it. Predominantly Islamic, Middle Eastern values are engrained in religion, as Islam is said to not just be a religion, but a way of life also. At the core of that culture is a clear distinction of the places and roles of the two sexes, of male and female, with women being limited in a number of ways that include education. As the place and profile of women in the Western world have progressed over time, as all human societies and nations started out male-dominated and progressed overtime in areas like enfranchising women for instance, they have lagged in the Muslim world, by Western standards certainly. That the unequal treatment of women, which most cultures of the world historically shared, may face the most resistance to change in the Islamic world and culture is very much a fact of the dangerous side of organized religion, albeit Islam in this case. This, the perceived mistreatment of women, and children, may just be symptomatic of issues for which Western-influenced interventions beyond to access mineral resources have been targeted at the Middle East.

When they perceive opposition to their values that insult their sensibility, elements of the Muslim religion fall back on their religion to respond or react in manners that include killing. Whether the external intrusion is physical incursion or even literary, the Middle East has shown its resentment all the same. The *Satanic Verses* controversy is but one instance. In the controversy, Ayatollah Ruhollah Khomeini, the religious leader of Iran, issued *fatwa*. *Fatwa* is a religious opinion on Islamic law issued by an Islamic scholar. That issued in 1989 ordered Muslims to kill Salman Rushdie, the author of that novel, because of Muslim anger over the novel. The anger was around:

> The novel's alleged blasphemy or unbelief; with the controversy being notable for being the first time in modern times a government had publicly called for the killing of a private individual in a foreign country. The issue divided "Muslims from Westerners along the fault line of culture" pitting the core Western value of freedom of expression— that no one "should be killed, or face a serious threat of being killed, for what they say or write"—against the core belief of many Muslims—that no one should be free to "insult and malign Muslims" by disparaging the "honor of the Prophet" Muhammad., http://en.wikipedia.org/wiki/ The_Satanic_Verses_controversy - cite_note-3.

Terrorism is a Western-influenced term, coined for and labeling those acts carried out by invoking religion to resent and respond militantly to the military and psychological elements in the Middle Eastern/Arab, albeit Islamic, world seen as threatening to their values and ways of life. It is a very biased and pejorative term designed to conjure negative sentiments in those individuals and groups. As bad or dehumanizing as certain Islamic-based values on the treatment of certain classes or members of their societies are, they have to pale in caparison to the treatment of slaves to warrant the intrusion of some foreign and external moral authority. Although "I wasn't in slavery, I have heard of it. Thinking about it still gives me flashbacks," paraphrasing a joke line of Don "D. C." Curry. To think of slavery is also to think about its feature of the literal tightening of the noose, the hangings, the lynchings, the burnings, and the bombings, as if slavery wasn't dehumanizing enough. Curry is a stand-up comic who featured regularly in seasons of *Comic View* on U.S. Black Entertainment Television (BET). Over the very many and long years slaves had to toast and burn, no external moral powers barged in to their rescue, so should none in the case of the differential Islamic-based values. There must be, and are, preferable ways to address those issues. They may take longer to yield results. Yet, they are preferable alternatives.

The fact is, in life, ugly and even abominable experiences will be around, no matter how hard humans try.

The attacks on 9/11/01, an obviously horrific act, is seen as unprovoked by the United States, having been at the receiving end of that act. If my sense of this is correct here, this is the first foreign attack on United States soil since Pearl Harbor. Conversely, the United States has been fermenting deadly military actions on foreign soils by direct troop invasions, or air and naval operations. For the loss of those human lives plus the material capital that act wreaked on the United States and her psyche, the morality of the perpetrators has been questioned, and rightfully so, by the United States, the Western world, and their allies. Particularly, their religion has been called to question, hence, the terms *radical Islamists* and *Muslim extremists* have become common. In this "war" of opposing values, for their part, the perpetrators of those acts of September 11, 2001, would argue and have always argued that the moral questions surrounding what they did go beyond their actions and the resulting tragedies. They question and condemn the high premium the opposing camp places on material things and state that they are being subjugated and trampled upon even for the natural resources in their national territories. They regard it as being disrespectful of them that the United States would have military bases in their national territories on the basis of what she terms her "national security interests." They also see this as occupation by a powerful nation of "infidels" that snubs their religion, values, and culture.

This, to them, constitutes immorality, and they see no options for fair and effective bilateral or multilateral media to address it; hence, they take it upon themselves to organize and tackle it the way they deem fit, not able to match the monopoly on conventional war machinery of the United States and/or her allies. They would add that the United States supports, sponsors, and funds policies that result in the killing of numerous thousands of their citizens, many of them women and children, directly and indirectly, especially through the United States' ally, Israel. They justify acts like 9/11 and see them as the equivalent of a sucker punch by a power-disadvantaged person on the defenseless child of a menacing, arrogant, and marauding giant, when he is not watching. Their positions do not get the deserved attention and understanding that those of the United States and her allies do because of the power and influence of the latter. Indeed, it has been an endemic cycle and circle of tension and hostility across the world. Inciting and orchestrating it directly or indirectly, the United States has her fingerprints all over it all.

Again, Congressman Dr. Ron Paul, as a presidential candidate, was candid enough to express his views of 9/11 being triggered by the United States' actions around the world. Paul's expression included the recent invasion of Iraq and the resulting ongoing war and the 1953 toppling of Iraqi Prime Minister Mosaddeq by the CIA. He sees this act as a "blowback," the chicken coming home to roost. Shouldn't the United States have enough humility to examine the sense in that? The United States, however, continues with her *modus operandi* of barging into camps opposed to her ambitions with the arrogance of an unmatched power. She would not consider the option of staying in her place, minding only her business. This business, of course, is about learning not to brutally pursue some "interest" wherever it takes her. If she could do so, she may also see if her perceived "hatred of America" does begin to vanish or diminish. But in the mind of the paranoid, this may never have a chance.

To the powerful, the world and parts thereof are but a battleground for influence and control. "Africa Emerges as Strategic Battleground— Challenges for U.S. Include Terrorist Ties, Energy Issues, Countering China's Inroads," an article in *Wall Street*, April 25, 2006, by Frederick Kemp, is an instance that documents how and why. Among other things in the article is this:

> And finally, China made Africa a front line in its pursuit of more global influence, tripling trade with the continent to some $37 billion over the past five years and locking up energy assets, closing trade deals with regimes like Sudan's and educating Africa's future elites at Chinese Universities and military schools. Most telling about Chinese President Hu Jin tao's just-ended trip to the U.S. was where he went afterward: first Saudi Arabia, then three African States: Morocco, Nigeria, and Kenya. Africa plays an increased strategic role militarily, economically, and politically, Gen. (James) Jones says. We have to become more agile in terms of being able to compete in this environment. Africa is a place of unrecognized opportunity. The continent's overall economy expanded by 4.8% last year; and the Council on Foreign Relations recently calculated that 40%

of its countries were electoral democracies, providing a promising base for U.S. influence.

Anyone can glean whatever he or she fancies from the above, what I see and read in it is that, for the powerful and power-driven, countries and regions of the word are not seen as deserving of respect and are therefore not accorded the respect and space they otherwise deserve. They are just resources to be harvested. Not to be outdone, wooing or stumping the battleground (the target country) into submission, outdoing the competition is all that is relevant.

The paradox of America certainly gives rise to this question: how could a nation that has given so much to the world also have distressed and devastated so many? Are the two sides to this paradox mutually inclusive? Put differently, is it impossible to be great and good without being greedy and brutal? Is the product of being greedy and brutal necessary for the great and good part?

It is for the above questions that, considering the United States' renowned economic prosperity, just a piece of her greatness, that I decided to checkout a few things about Switzerland, given her renowned dovish, nonconfrontational stance in the world. The hosts of many international organizations like the Red Cross, the World Trade Organization, and one of the United Nations' two European offices, Switzerland has not been at war since 1815. Known for her humanitarianism, Switzerland is not just the host of the Red Cross, she is the birthplace of the Red Cross; hence, she hosts the United Nations Human Rights Council, one of the two United Nation's European offices.

Although not in competition with the United States for anything, I would imagine, Switzerland is not a large country. For some perspective, here are a few facts from Wikipedia online. A country of 41,285 kilometers (15,940 square miles) with a population of 7,593,500, per 2007 census, and estimated at 7,700,299 in 2008, Switzerland is ranked ninety-fourth in the world in population. Here's more on Switzerland, found in Wikipedia-on-line:

> Switzerland has a stable, modern, and one of the most capitalist economies in the world. It has the 2nd highest European rating after Ireland in the Index of Economic Freedom in 2008, while also providing large coverage through public services. The nominal per capita GDP is higher than those of the larger western European

economies and Japan, ranking 6th behind Luxembourg, Norway, Qatar, Iceland and Ireland.

If adjusted for purchasing power parity, Switzerland ranks 15th in the world for GDP per capita. The World Economic Forum's Global Competitiveness Report currently ranks Switzerland's economy as the most competitive in the world. For much of the 20th century, Switzerland was the wealthiest country in Europe by a considerable margin. In 2005 the median household income in Switzerland was an estimated 95,000 CHF, the equivalent of roughly 90,000 USD (as of December 2009) in nominal terms.

Switzerland is home to several large multinational corporations. The largest Swiss companies by revenue are Glencore, Nestlé, Novartis, Hoffmann-La Roche, ABB and Adecco. Also notable are UBS AG, Zurich Financial Services, Credit Suisse, Swiss Re, and The Swatch Group.

Switzerland is ranked as having one of the most powerful economies in the world. Around 3.8 million people work in Switzerland. Switzerland has a more flexible job market than neighboring countries and the unemployment rate is very low. Unemployment rate increased from a low of 1.7% in June 2000 to a peak of 3.9% in September 2004. Partly because of the economic upturn which started in mid-2003, the unemployment rate is currently 2.8% as of February 2008. Population growth from net immigration is quite high, at 0.52% of population in 2004. Foreign citizen population is 21.8% as of 2004. GDP per hour worked is the world's 17th highest, at 27.44 international dollars in 2006.

Switzerland has an overwhelmingly private-sector economy and low tax rates by Western standards; overall, taxation is one of the smallest of developed countries. Switzerland is an easy place to do business.

Here is an answer to the paradoxical questions around greatness and good and greed and squeezing. Though small, Switzerland is a sound nation, economically and otherwise, clearly doing well and doing a whole lot of good for her rather accommodating society, foreigners constituting 21.85% of the population, and the world. And she has afforded to do these without visiting devastations or even psychological warfare on other people and nations. I had a sense that this would be the case before doing the research on Switzerland.

I am aware of one controversy associated with Switzerland, though—her banking secrecy laws. These laws allow for money from any and all sources, anywhere, to be hidden in Swiss banks with assured protection for the source. The result is that corrupt individuals, groups, and even governments, with access to the treasury and public and other resources, could and do loot those resources knowing they can stash them away in Swiss banks, assured they would be safe and theirs, no matter what. This has disproportionately hurt poorer nations with cultures of poor law enforcement and accountability, as treasury loot of mind-boggling magnitudes from those countries has ended up in Swiss banks. Even at that, as long as the Swiss are not part of the looting process, the blame for the loot squarely falls on the looting "foreigner," and rightfully so. Records and history do show that other Western, capitalist nations do get used to store loot from corrupt sources, particularly from poor, "third-world" nations. The difference may be that Switzerland does have formal banking secrecy laws.

Pharaohdom
One way for me to make any sense of the way the United States carries on is what I call *Pharaohdom*, coined from pharaoh. This thought was inspired by an interview that I watched on the CBS TV network popular news magazine, *60 minutes*, I believe, with Minister Louis Farrakhan of the Nation of Islam a few years ago. Farrakhan had likened the seat of the American president to that of the pharaoh, implying that whoever sits on that "throne" will stick with the "pharaohdom" agenda, the personality of the occupant—the individual pharaoh—making little or no difference. That Minister Farrakhan is forever condemned as controversial in the "mainstream" United States is no surprise in the context of pharaohdom, as speaking up on official modus operandi is tantamount to a crime against the state.

It was for the same reason that excerpts of a sermon by the Reverend Jeremiah Wright condemning certain official U.S. actions in the mold of her *modus operandi* drew swift reactions and attacks, with hopes it would kill Obama's all-but-sure win of the presidency then. It does not matter that Reverend Wright, in his capacity as a minister, lifted that message from the Bible, from the book of Jeremiah, coincidentally, according to another reverend I had also watched in a television interview in the midst of the "controversy." The Bible may not have named the United States in whatever chapter and verse in its book of Jeremiah; however, Reverend Jeremiah Wright understood that certain behaviors of the United States fit into that mold. Ironically, also, those who were up in arms against him, hoping to hurt Obama's chance at the election, feared that the United States fit that billing. Personally, I had found ridiculous those charges that, because Reverend Wright was Obama's church minister, Obama must be a product of his views or he must imbibe them. Looking back at it now, it's really no surprise they did so. If they were not motivated by other factors, they have demonstrated by their mind-set that they are incapable of having understood that the level of intelligence Obama exudes is such that he is beyond anybody's views, even that of a preacher, forming the sole base of his worldview.

With the world seen as a turf to either be conquered or influenced, the U.S. kingdom found itself in stiff competition with other kingdoms and just like the pharaohs, sought to have its pharaohdom prevail. This text from Wikipedia online on historic pharaohs and *divine kingship* sheds more light:

> As each kingdom grew each king had to be as great as the king of his neighbouring state otherwise his followers would defect to the superior king and oust the mortal. No one would want to be governed by an inferior king. So gradually this idea of divine kingship was developed. This was aided by the priests who found it to be in their own interest to support the king, who supported them in return, rather than risk getting the blame and being slaughtered for not propitiating the gods when things went wrong.

The Pharaoh was not only a god-king but was responsible for holding the balance of "ma'at," that was the rule of order over the chaos that was waiting to envelope the world. As long as king and commoner alike honoured the gods and obeyed the laws set down by them the balance was maintained and all would be well. Should the Pharaoh fail all the world would suffer and descend into the unthinkable state of anarchy.

The more powerful kings obviously said that they had the support of the gods so no one could depose them or they would incur the god's displeasure. How the concept of divine-kingship developed is not known but there are two schools of thought. One is that a king, fearful for his position, spread the rumor that he had had a vision and the gods had told him that he was their representative or intermediary on earth where he could guide his successors.

The above on the pharaoh has a striking similarity with the United States' historic Manifest Destiny, to be elaborated upon later. Some elements at the core of the ways the historic pharaohs operated could be found in the *modus operandi* of the U.S. pharaohdom in the modern world. An instance of paranoia in the kingdom of the ancient Pharaoh with a striking similarity with some of the ways of the United States is captured in "... had to be as great as the king of his neighboring state otherwise his followers would defect to the superior king and oust the mortal. No one would want to be governed by an inferior king," and "Should the Pharaoh fail all the world would suffer and descend into the unthinkable state of anarchy." With the United States, it is the enemies and "those who hate us" lurking and waiting to pounce and take away our freedom, against whom we must even take preemptive actions, lest they snatch our freedom and/ or plunge our world into a state of anarchy.

And so it is that as the United States, by her actions also, like the historic kingdoms of the pharaoh, sees her role as the "divine king" of the world and in the process has developed loyal and die-hard priests who must continue the "tradition," not just for the pharaohdom, but for their personal interests equally. This also, at the risk of obvious repetition, is supported by this from the Wikipedia piece above, which I repeat here:

> This was aided by the priests who found it to be in their own interest to support the king, who supported them in return, rather than risk getting the blame and being slaughtered for not propitiating the gods when things went wrong.

From such could only a heavily "conservative" mind-set in the mostly conservative-liberal framework of U.S. politics and economics emerge. For me, a mind-set is just that, a mind-set. It is like concrete mixed in cement with water and cast as in stone, nailed, chained, clamped, locked down to a place, literally concrete and incapable of thinking. This is contrasted with thought process, which implies that one is capable of engaging the mind in assessment and consideration of issues in the context of changing circumstances. Seeing and hearing many of the so-called conservatives talk automatically on issues supposedly being discussed just conjures an image of a literal icon of conservatism the way a "concrete" landmark does. It is like they want to be frozen and installed in a place to remind generations of Americans what conservatism is symbolically. They actually fit the mold of what has been mockingly termed "talking heads" on TV, for they spit the same ideologically driven reaction to whatever is in focus, time and circumstance meaning nothing. For any of them attempting to justify their position, it is like they literally hold on to Murphy's Law, and in their minds, anything that could go wrong will go wrong. They'd rather be a revisionist agent all the time than understand anything progressive and where, when, and why it may be necessary.

Responding to the entrenched mentality over a particular issue at the time, a state governor, I believe of Utah, some years ago likened people in that frame of mind to wing nuts, of the Right and Left wings, that is. I think the terms *front* and *rear* capture the concepts at play better, with pragmatic assessments and positions the front and stagnant and unevolving positions the rear, as revisionism. Positions on the two ends of the spectrum then would fit the label of axis fringe, as in the front fringe and rear fringe. This better communicates the issue of the inability to be responsive to, and in, an ever-changing world. In the games played in the name of discussion, TV programs pitch the "left" against the "right," with an implication that a balanced discussion is the goal. Based on the concept in which the "right" supposedly means core American values and the "left," "un-American," what results is a boring exchange that borders on insulting a thinking mind. Like the "right," many of the "left" discussants take positions in the opposing direction just to be opposite. Turned off by the dramas, I now barely watch these. As if showing a capacity for insight, the "conservative" would sometimes pretend to show reasoning ability, even in his known paranoia; doing so, he would verbalize things along that line, like, "Trust but verify," a line that President Ronald Reagan said one time as he met with President Mikhail Gorbachev of the former USSR.

Operating in the *modus operandi* of pharaohdom, with a locked-down mind-set, significantly contributed to bringing the United States and the world to the brink of a meltdown economically and socially from the immediate past few years to now. It has been like one long journey in a tunnel led by the priests of pharaohdom; the most recent of which include President George W. Bush and his vice president, Dick Cheney. In addition to the legacy of the current global crisis, both are sure to add to it that of invading Iraq, using the ruse of manipulated intelligence to achieve a pre-staged pharaoh agenda. As President George W. Bush prepared to meet with and address the so-called G-7 treasury ministers in Washington DC in the midst of the global financial crisis in October 2008, he made a statement that includes the following: "We, the world, are in this [the financial and economic crisis] together. We'll get out of it together."

This prompted this commentary by Dave Ross of the U.S. WCBS 880 Radio in his routine news commentary, recalling the president's position and attitude just three years earlier in 2005, as the United States took a selfish decision to invade Iraq and carried on willy-nilly in other ways, as he stated that: "The course of this nation does not depend on other nations."

Before her selfish, unilateral actions, including the decision to invade Iraq, got her into a quagmire, the United States needed no input from others. To get out of a mostly self-inflicted problem, however, she suddenly, but selfishly in this case also, considers herself just one in the world stage and invokes/welcomes the passion/commitment of the world to "get out of it together."

The 2008 Presidential Election

The chicken of the economic and political pharaohdom coming home to roost played into and out in the 2008 presidential election. It soon became obvious that both the United States and the world, having been turned off and fed up by conk pharaohdom and the distress it had wreaked, were clamoring for something different—some end to the tunnel and a light with it. This wish manifested in presidential candidate Barack Hussein Obama, the hoped-for light at the end of the tunnel.

As "destiny's child," Obama couldn't have emerged at a better time. Young, intelligent, visionary, and articulate, Obama tapped into the ripe circumstances—mismanaged global politics and economy, the social order, and a clamor for change. Along with his even-keel demeanor and aura, he came across to segments of domestic and international societies as genuine, able, and trustworthy. This became clearer to me when my son asked me whether Obama could emerge as the candidate of the Democratic Party, adding that if he did, he would vote for the first time. My son who was of age to vote in the 2004 presidential election never cared about voting then, even when I invited him to go vote with me. While this was happening and shaping up, the pharaohites, locked and tucked away in their "mind-set," were still clueless. Many people may now get it, but I could honestly state that watching and hearing Obama even earlier in the campaign, I had a sense that so much was coming together in and with Obama that he could make a great impact. Having not directly heard Oprah Winfrey as to why she endorsed Obama when she did, which has been credited with some notable successes Obama achieved, like in North Carolina, I believe that she too identified the unique qualities of Obama.

On the other hand, when I listened to General Colin Powell as he endorsed Obama, I knew he had based that on the grounding and reflective nature/qualities of Obama. As to Obama's rivals, I had decided rather early not to vote for Senator Hilary Clinton, whom I have liked and admired as a person. One reason for my admiration of her, her obvious intelligence and professional accomplishments notwithstanding, was her standing up for her husband and in defiance of his mostly political detractors. The detractors of her husband, President Bill Clinton, operatives of the opposing political party, threw all they had at him to first stop him from being elected, using the "White Water" scandal, and then continuing to invent other antics hoping at least his wife, Hilary Clinton, would abandon him and help drag his legacy into the mud. My decision not to vote for Senator Clinton stemmed from my belief that her support for the Iraqi invasion was to prove to the pharaohites that she has what it takes to be a pharaoh, as that was a primary requirement to occupy that seat. And she knew she had an uphill task fitting that billing, as the first woman to ever come that close to doing so.

Along the way, Obama endured and scaled one obstacle after another thrown in his way. Religion was used, with the Muslim or Islamic-scare, propagating the idea that Obama was a Muslim, to turn the voters against him. Just like a non-Protestant had no place in the American presidency until John F. Kennedy, a Catholic, several decades later, America, the melting pot that established no state religion and has no business in a person's religion, saw religion being used to bias and scare voters.

In the end, and powered by the change-sweeping forces he had mobilized, Obama swept the election, with a huge turnout of young, first-time voters like my son who overwhelmingly voted for him. He achieved the same with the more educated voters, those more prone to thinking independently. These two groups of the electorate, it was learned, had been turned off the most by the old ways of politics until Obama reached them in a unique way that gave them hope for another angle—the Obama angle.

One person who was clearly clueless about the factors driving Obama's surge during the campaign was Senator John McCain. One way that he demonstrated this was stating repeatedly on his campaign stumps and during the debates with Obama, "He [Obama] does not understand." To Senator McCain's credit here, I might add, then Senator Obama was not in a position to "understand" what was going on in his mind, given that his life is mired in the military, culminating in those five years in Hanoi, "bunkered" in the hands of "enemy" troops.

As Senator McCain and/or his staff ridiculed Obama, referring to his short stay in Kenya as his foreign experience that had nothing to add to his foreign policy or international relations credentials, I could relate to where Obama was coming from. As the son of a Kenyan native who obviously was educated and intelligent (I had read up on his father), then candidate Senator Obama could empathize with foreign and distant cultures better than most of his opponents. It was not just his Kenyan experience; his Kenyan heritage, with which I was then convinced he identified and took seriously, is also at the core of his capacity for this empathy. In addition, he was unconventionally raised and brought up in cultures outside the U.S. mainland, like Hawaii and Indonesia. As someone whose upbringing was in a different culture myself and whose experience now spans beyond one culture, I could attest that the average native U.S.-born is not good with empathizing with or respecting many other cultures of the world. Even of those who may have been born outside of the United States to parents serving away from the homeland, any experience they have of those other cultures could not rise to the level of true empathy. The reason is, like their parents, they knew they were just foreign Americans and very probably went about their ways with some "superiority complex." I had no problem, therefore, seeing the genuineness in Obama or his uniqueness that earned him the trust of so many domestically and internationally in a world that was clamoring for some break with the old ways of doing things, largely represented by America. As for Senator McCain's foreign policy experience and credentials, one dares ask: five years in captivity in Hanoi Hilton?

Expecting to be rewarded with the presidency for being an "American (war) hero," of course, Senator McCain remarked that the American president is not a pop star. This had to be his reaction to the huge crowd that turned out at an Obama event in England before the election. Put differently, being fit for the seat of the pharaoh has nothing to do with a popularity contest, Senator McCain was implying. The pharaoh has an agenda, a binding script not subject to popular appeal. As these things played out, it was clear that Senator McCain, a grandson of a naval officer, the son of a naval commander, and a naval pilot himself, who, I repeat, was shot down in Vietnam and was held prisoner for years, was incapable of seeing things in any other way. His life has been all military and war, given his family background for three generations.

Later, after the elections, I watched Joy Behar, a comedienne I believe, on *Larry King Live*, the renowned CNN program, on October 26, 2008, "diagnose" Senator McCain with post-traumatic stress disorder (PTSD), citing the mind-set and the pro-military/war drum he had beat through the campaign. As she did so, Ms. Behar added, humorously, that she is a therapy freak who believes in psychotherapy. She, of course, also alluded to Senator McCain's captivity and being held a war prisoner in the Hanoi Hilton for five years. To his credit, though, I think Senator McCain handled his defeat in the general election maturely and "patriotically."

Still leading a band of pharaohites, who hate the Obama angle in American politics and hope he will fail, is former vice president Dick Cheney. Clueless himself in the changing trend, apparently, among other things, he has said that what America needs is respect, not admiration. Not long after that, he spouted that the United States is now less secure with the Obama angle and not safer. Doing so, he, Mr. Cheney, obviously is seeking to douse the now President Obama's still high popularity domestically and internationally. To Cheney, admiration and respect are mutually exclusive, apparently. The last time I looked up those two words, one could hardly be divorced from the other, as they show up almost as synonymous. In Mr. Dick Cheney's world, respect for America comes from violating others and whacking them to extort and extract respect. This explains why the book on the Iraq invasion was alleged to have been written by him. For one who personifies pharaohdom and grouchiness, Mr. Cheney may be going through a bout of nostalgia and doing so through a wish for the continuation of pharaohism.

Before the recently injected Obama angle, the pharaohists' way was characterized by inflammatory and derogatory terms in defining those with opposing views and interests, such as President Reagan calling the former Soviet Union an "Evil Empire" and President George W. Bush calling a group of nations the "Axis of Evil." Some in the opposing world have reciprocated with their own terms, like leaders of the Muslim world calling the United States "the Great Satan." Recently, in 2008, I believe, President Hugo Chavez of Venezuela, who has been a target of the United States for the same old games and reasons, was to speak at the United Nations after President George W. Bush spoke on the same stage and podium earlier the same day or the day before. President Hugo Chavez used some derogatory terms of his own when making reference to George W. Bush, making a sign-of-the-cross prayer gesture. He called the U.S. president "the devil himself," kind of telling the world that the personification of the devil, George W. Bush, had just appeared on the world stage, on the same podium before him. The U.S. news media reacted to this, that Mr. Chavez had the audacity to so characterize a U.S. president on American soil. In the same vein, Iranian president Mahmoud Ahmedinejad, speaking to some news media, had also spoken and described the "swagger" associated with the way President Bush strutted the world stage, which some said demonstrated his arrogance. To this, President Ahmedinejad said, and I paraphrase, "See how they walk and go about as if they own the world." Does carrying on like this not seem crazy or juvenile at best? In the game of tit-for-tat, an eye-for-an-eye would just leave everyone blind.

In the instance of that comment by the Iranian President, the U.S. news media did not take kindly to it. I recall seeing one news anchor mockingly call the Iranian president "I'm-a-dinner-jack," from Ahmedinejad. If anything, these reactions speak to what it feels like for the shoe to be on the other foot.

Apparently, and some would say obviously, Dick Cheney would rather see the continuous play-out of the above and is so dismissive of President Obama's angle. In that angle, stemming from the ways he obviously carefully processes his thoughts and chooses his words, President Obama, at least rhetorically, speaks in terms of respecting the aspirations of others and engaging them in diplomatic dialogues to reach an understanding and achieve progress. Discontinuing with what core pharaohites like Mr. Cheney are used to is what the change that swept Obama into office is about. And Obama has reminded the likes of Cheney what he was elected to do.

Persuaded as I am that President Obama means to go all the way with changing the old ways as much as is reasonable, there is certainly a limit to how far he can go. One clear reason is that no one gets away with dismantling pharaohdom, not that quickly, not even Obama. There are early signs that many domestic and international supporters would wish he would go rather far. Also, signals that some want to stop him before he even starts sprang up domestically just minutes after it was clear that he had won the presidency. One such was a text message to my Blackberry I received while I was at work on the day after his election, Wednesday, November 5, 2008, which even though clearly racially motivated, I had laughingly dismissed as the ranting and raving of a mindless nuisance. The text read, and I paraphrase: "All white people should report to the cotton fields at 9:00 am for job assignment."

In plain language, the abominable has happened. The role has been reversed; the slave is now the master, and the master, the slave.

I learned later that so many others received the same text message. Working to address the huge economic and other crises in which the United States was mired before he took office, Obama has embarked upon a bold and ambitious plan. Clear as it is that the magnitude of the crisis in different sectors demands a serious plan of action, the pharaohites, knowing not what it means to give plans a chance, has been almost at "war" opposing the president's plan. Yes, the same "mind-sets" that either played a big part in, or supported, driving the nation to the precipice dare not allow time to see whether or not the president's just-initiated plan works before playing the same old and failed ideological games.

Internationally, as President Obama consciously chooses to continue with some old policies of the pharaohdom, like overseas military engagements, albeit modified and refocused, like in Afghanistan, for instance, he also draws opposition. One such opposing voice was that of Miran Khan, an Afghan opposition leader, who appeared on *Fareed Zakaria GPS*, the new CNN TV news magazine, on February 22, 2009. In expressing this opposition, Mr. Kahn used a quote from *Alice in Wonderland* to describe the U.S. policy to boost her military presence in his country, essentially saying that even with Obama, the United States' ways remain unchanged: "When you don't know where you are going, all roads lead to the same place."

Other oppositions in the same vein came in the way of the protests that greeted the otherwise hugely popular President Obama in London, as he attended the G-20 conference, and in France, during the NATO convention, both in 2009. My sense is that those protests are not necessarily about Obama personally, but about what those organizations represent—the institutions of the old ways and, of course, the role of Obama as the leader of those organizations, being the incumbent U.S. president. Only time will tell how much of a difference Obama will make. Whatever materializes, Obama on the United States and world stages is one change of reckon.

Concerned with the racial aspects of President Obama's opposition and/or attacks, there are voices of reason weighing in and speaking up. One is Andrew M. Manis, an associate professor of history at Macon State College, Macon, Georgia, USA, published in the *Macon Telegraph*. The article is solid, sound, well articulated, and speaks for itself, so I decided to insert it here in full:

When Are We Going to Get Over It?

> For much of the last forty years, ever since America "fixed" its race problem in the Civil Rights and Voting Rights Acts, we white people have been impatient with African Americans who continued to blame race for their difficulties. Often we have heard whites ask, "When are African Americans finally going to get over it?" Now I want to ask: "When are we White Americans going to get over our ridiculous obsession with skin color?"
>
> Recent reports that "Election Spurs Hundreds of Race Threats, Crimes" should frighten and infuriate every one of us. Having grown up in "Bombingham," Alabama, in the 1960s, I remember overhearing an avalanche of comments about what many white classmates and their parents wanted to do to John and Bobby Kennedy and Martin Luther King. Eventually, as you may recall, in all three cases, someone decided to do more than "talk the talk." Since our recent presidential election, to our eternal

shame, we are once again hearing the same reprehensible talk I remember from my boyhood.

We white people have controlled political life in the disunited colonies and United States for some 400 years on this continent. Conservative whites have been in power 28 of the last 40 years. Even during the eight Clinton years, conservatives in Congress blocked most of his agenda and pulled him to the right. Yet never in that period did I read any headlines suggesting that anyone was calling for the assassinations of presidents Nixon, Ford, Reagan, or either of the Bushes. Criticize them, yes. Call for their impeachment, perhaps. But there were no bounties on their heads. And even when someone did try to kill Ronald Reagan, the perpetrator was a non-political mental case who wanted merely to impress Jody Foster.

But elect a liberal who happens to be Black and we're back in the sixties again. At this point in our history, we should be proud that we've proven what conservatives are always saying—that in America anything is possible, EVEN electing a black man as president. But instead we now hear that school children from Maine to California are talking about wanting to "assassinate Obama." Fighting the urge to throw up, I can only ask, "How long?" How long before we white people realize we can't make our nation, much less the whole world, look like us? How long until we white people can—once and for all—get over this hell-conceived preoccupation with skin color? How long until we white people get over the demonic conviction that white skin makes us superior? How long before we white people get over our bitter resentments about being demoted to the status of equality with non-whites?

How long before we get over our expectations that we should be at the head of the line merely because of our white skin? How long until we white people end our silence and call out our peers when they share the latest racist jokes in the privacy of our white-only conversations? I believe in free speech, but how long until we white people start making racist loudmouths as socially uncomfortable as we do flag burners? How long until we white people will stop insisting that blacks exercise personal responsibility, build strong families, educate themselves enough to edit the *Harvard Law Review*, and work hard enough to become president of the United States, only to threaten to assassinate them when they do?

How long before we starting "living out the true meaning" of our creeds, both civil and religious, that all men and women are created equal and that "red and yellow, black and white" all are precious in God's sight?

Until this past November 4, I didn't believe this country would ever elect an African American to the presidency. I still don't believe I'll live long enough to see us white people get over our racism problem. But here's my three-point plan: First, every day that Barack Obama lives in the White House that Black Slaves built, I'm going to pray that God (and the Secret Service) will protect him and his family from us white people.

Second, I'm going to report to the FBI any white person I overhear saying, in seriousness or in jest, anything of a threatening nature about President Obama. Third, I'm going to pray to live long enough to see America surprise the world once again, when white people can "in spirit and in truth" sing of our damnable color prejudice, "We HAVE overcome."

It takes a village to protect our president!!!

Old Habits and Ways Die Hard, or Hardly Die
Mad Men

"Mad Men" is the headline and the front-page caption of the New York *Daily News*, September 24, 2009, with the pictures of Iraqi and Libyan presidents, respectively, right beneath it. That headline and picture clearly had a message and that message is that about seven months after the election of Obama as president, it's yet to be seen whether the United States will get aboard "the Obama angle," as far as her old ways of dealing with the world go. Of course, a lot of forces are working against Obama personally, or "the Obama angle," domestically also. Used to and dug in, that old ways are dying hard here was demonstrated by rhetoric at least, in the U.S. print and electronic media—the TV, etc., as free as they come, yes. Still, the U.S. news media is not immune from the encapsulation and bias of the "Psychic Prison" as in Greek Mythology Plato's *Allegory of the Cave*. A metaphor for the lack of capacity to see other sides to issues; *Psychic Prison* captures a warped mindset that seems to stem from being locked or imprisoned, like in a cave for instance. In the case of the above front-page news; it was during the just-concluded United Nations General Assembly session in New York. Things like these would only frustrate President Obama and his effort to deliver on his new engagement nuance. While he works to douse the old ways of inflammatory stances and rhetoric to deescalate and mellow them, incendiary sources continue to reignite and fan them. Those incendiary elements and forces would indeed sabotage Obama's efforts to ensure he fails at any opportunity that presents itself.

In apparent mockery or belittling of Obama's popularity across the world that has endured thus far, the U.S. news media are already questioning what Obama has to show for his popularity. Questioning as they do, they speak particularly about the allegation that Iran is pursuing nuclear weaponry and refusing to give it up and the still intractable Palestine-Israeli conflicts and wars. Does expecting that Obama magically deliver to the United States concessions from her erstwhile "enemies" so soon not demonstrate that the United States neither sees nor respects the intelligence of her "enemy" nations and cultures? Implied further here is that the United States, which hardly trusts anything not aligned with her "interests," expects that those "enemies" will just get sucked in by Obama's popularity without even allowing the necessary time it would require to show whether or not Obama and his envisioned change would take hold in pharaohdom.

From the Louis Farrakhan pharaoh seat of the U.S. president analogy, through the representative, Dr. Ron Paul's blowback to the United States for being over there observation, to the Reverend Jeremiah Wright's "God damn America" sermon, they all could not be wrong. Instead of treating these the same old ways—with the defense mechanism of hostility—it should prompt some introspection and self-search or self-examination.

Obama and the Nobel Peace Prize
The news, on my preparing to leave for work today, Thursday, October 8, 2009, that President Obama has been awarded the Peace Prize by the world-renowned Nobel Foundation caught me off guard but did not surprise me really. In making the announcement for the award, the foundation stated that Obama's articulation for engagement among nations based on mutual interest and respect, among other things, is what the majority of the peoples of the world want. This is what I have said in this discourse in so many ways. I have also been clear with this about Obama in coining and emphasizing "the Obama angle." My being caught off guard at the announcement has to do with the fact that Obama has been in office just barely seven months; therefore, he has yet to see the Obama angle actualized. If I am caught off guard on that basis, I could see analysts, critics, and "experts" rip the

Nobel Foundation for this—Obama's selection for the award. Doing this, they would say that the award, with the prestige and weight accorded it, should be given only to those who have delivered and not just to those with potential. From my perspective, however, that Obama has set a tone for a more mutual engagement of nations that no other major world leader in many years that I could recall has truly attempted warrants giving him the award. This is more so considering the power and influence of the United States in fermenting world conflicts and what she could bring into reversing things for the better. As could be gleaned from the millions of hearts that Obama tapped into in the United States and around the world; the world has waited too long for a change and could afford to wait no longer. The Nobel Foundation, with its history of encouraging positive things in different areas of human endeavor, is not oblivious of this desire of the world. It should surprise no objective mind, therefore, that it made this award to Obama, even if just for his vision.

History will show this to not be the first time the Nobel Foundation has awarded the Peace Prize to encourage the actualization of an idea or aspiration in a positive, desirable direction, particularly as it relates to a more cordial relating of people and nations. Now that a vision along that line is from Obama, the first "black" president of the very powerful United States of America; and with the Nobel Foundation giving him this award, criticism of the foundation may never have been this loud and harsh. Many of these come from Obama's fellow citizens of the United States. Yet some reject that there's a racial undertone in these criticisms. Jimmy Carter, being himself a brave, independent-thinking mind and voice, saw all these and voiced it. All some of those others did was to dismiss it.

Old habits dying hard or hardly dying, it is my hunch also that those incendiary elements in the United States that I have mentioned, who wish and would do anything to see Obama not succeed, may now organize and start a campaign to discredit the Nobel Foundation. To them, anything that boosts Obama, potentially or in reality, is bad for business and identity, particularly of the United States. It would not surprise me, therefore, that those forces may seek to tarnish and diminish the image, stature, and importance of the foundation, digging for and coming up with some unflattering things to tag it.

The United Nations Organization (UNO)

If there was one government of the entire world, it would be the United Nations. It was founded in 1945 after World War II to replace the League of Nations, to stop wars between nations and to promote a platform for dialogue, thereby harmonizing the affairs of the nations of the world. I first learned about the United Nations Organization (UNO) in the 1960s in my elementary "civics" classes. Practically a dictatorship monarchy, emphasizing and enforcing the agenda of the powerful few who constitute the minority of its member nations really, the United Nations has a history of ineffectiveness, unfairness, and imbalance in addressing the issues confronting the nations and regions of the world as it should and could. Wearing "democracy" like a garb, ironically, that powerful minority that preaches "democracy" to the rest of the world's nations is really the force behind the dictatorial stance of the UN. Just like bilateral and multilateral relations amongst nations have been lopsided, so have those handled through the UN medium for the most part.

One reason for the UN's ineffectiveness is all too familiar—might is right and rules. In a world that became divided and polarized between the Western and Eastern bloc, with a big gulf in the middle that some nations that would rather be reasonable and neutral attempted to bridge by terming themselves non-aligned, the power players must have, and continue to have, their way. Caught in the middle, non-powerful nations have no choice but to be left with the "short end of the stick." Any effort at striking a fair balance even on select issues quickly draws the demagoguery and blackmail of the powerful. Overall, it is my sense that the Eastern power bloc has weighed in more in favor of fairness when it comes to factoring in the interest of the non-powerful than her Western power bloc counterpart.

I have watched on TV and read in the print media as the so-called conservatives in the United States, for instance, boldly state that the United States led the formation of the UN to have her control the world "better." The voices would add and/or imply that the United States should not acquiesce to "liberal forces" that push to have her controlled by or be downgraded to the level of poor, third-world nations by relinquishing her influence and controlling posture in the world. Then, those voices play the game of, and make the case for, the financial contribution of the United States to the running of the UN's programs. This, they say, further justifies the United States being in the "driver's seat," driving the poor nations wherever she fancies. This practically says, "He who pays the piper dictates the tune." It is not hard to see that this is never a formula to run a fair, balanced, just, and "democratic" organization of the nations of the world.

The veto power, a controlling tool obviously invented and adopted by the powerful, is the overriding instrument that gives them a full grip on and control of the UN. Even presently, in 2009, over sixty years since the founding of the UN, those powerful few remain unrelenting in calling all the shots. For all their sanctimonious lectures on democracy, freedom, justice, and fair play, it is rather hypocritical that the votes of many, really the majority, of UN member nations amount to nothing because the trump card of one powerful member nation, by the way of her veto power, suppresses and rubbishes the input of the many. In a world where vicissitudes of time and circumstance have always characterized the human experience and old ideas give way to new ones as things evolve to better suit the life and times of the day, the UN remains immune to this as the interest of the powerful continues to hold sway.

As the notion of a world community open to all nations is feigned with the UN, the not-powerful nations and regions of the world are seen by the powerful ones as having nothing to contribute. For all the powerful cares, the not-powerful may be invited to the table, but only to be seen and not to be heard, as their interest is supposedly spoken for. They, the not-powerful, are but window dressing; they all don't even amount to one sidekick.

Nuclear Power/Weapons and the Proliferations Thereof
Since the invention of more potent energy sources and resources, probably beginning with atomic energy, the world has been both privileged by their benefits and subjected to their devastations. They were introduced by the ingenuity and genius of the science inclined, but controlling their proliferation has made it to the forum of the ineffective UN, albeit to be manipulated by the powerful still. Either unilaterally or through some bilateral and group arrangements, the powerful have their way with atomic and now nuclear power. This includes how they are shared and/ or regulated.

Lately, as of April 6, 2009, the focus of the powerful is on Iran and North Korea and their respective quests to develop nuclear energy. With the United States here again leading the way, these two independent nations are being hounded to stop their projects, which the powerful nations and many others—their allies—have and have had for ages. Much as I sense and believe President Obama's sincerity; being human, he is prone to mistakes and would make some. I would caution that he resist casting himself personally as the agitator-in-chief for the campaign against the Iranian and North Korean nuclear programs. This is a role U.S. presidents see themselves "naturally" fitting, as the "the leader" of the "free world," and as the powerful in whose interest it is to pursue her interests wherever she sees them taking her. If this is the logic, Iran and North Korea would have more "legitimacy" claiming and asserting their interests in seeing that no power from a distant region of the world has the right to leading a push to stifle the emergence of nuclear powers or determine who should have one, in their respective parts of the world. Obama has started on a very good note by reaching out to the nations and regions of the world with whom the United States has had a history of strained relations based on conflicting interests, offering a new beginning, favoring dialogue, mutual interest, and respect over ideology and control. Should he allow being the agitator-in-chief to trump his common sense approach, he would fail, with the dissipation of his goodwill leading the way.

The arguments and strategy used to push the agenda of "nuclear non-proliferation" is to tag targeted nations "rogue nations," describing them as unstable and not to be trusted and saying they would belligerently nuke enemy nations. Like with most things in the world's "reality," the objective in this arm-twisting is to maintain the imbalance of power, with the powerful still out to maintain the status quo with monopoly on nuclear energy and weaponry. As to the excuse of belligerent, erratic, and unstable nations nuking their enemies and unfriendly neighbors, history shows that it is not the so-called unstable nations that have gone berserk with attempting to bomb another into oblivion just to prevail in a power tussle. Hiroshima and Nagasaki come to mind here, and this was by the presumed most stable of all nations, the United States. With the same "mind-set" and iron-clad will to be the king of the world, dropping atomic bombs on those two Japanese cities was justified for the Japanese attack on Pearl Harbor, on the Hawaiian island. For whatever reasons that have been adduced for the Japanese attacks on Pearl Harbor (and I have read up on some of those), that the Japanese may have felt threatened by the presence of the U.S. naval fleet in Hawaii, an island in the North Pacific Ocean, about equi-distant from both Japan and the United States mainland, cannot be ruled out. Yes, other nations, Japan in that case, also want to assert rights to their neighborhood and would take actions, destructive but not rising to an annihilation of all lives in cities, to demonstrate it.

Saying this does not mean that I am a fan of mindless killing. Again, considering the "reality" of our world, there may be no end to violence of this nature. In this game, some would rather end life as we know it than cede to another the number-one spot, or even share that spot with another. Going by history, if any nation would bomb the world to oblivion, it is likely to be the United States. She has to win the race. Stopping other nations from developing nuclear weapons, therefore, has to begin with no nation being allowed to have one. This means there has to be sure, verifiable facts to show this. If the problem is that those nations that have them cannot unmake or "unhave" them, then any nation that wants to have them and is ready to do so must go ahead. Any notion that with nuclear weaponry, some nations must have them and some others must not is disrespectful of, and insulting to, those other nations. As naïve as this observation and position seem, it would be more naïve to expect every nation with no nuclear weapons now to roll over and play dead, or fall in line with the order of the powerful, that they not seek to have nuclear energy or weaponry. Believing as I do that today's "nuclear powers" would not let go of them; it should be *nuclear weapons for all, or nuclear weapons for none.*

Even as the United States and her allies characterize certain weapons in the arsenal of their opponents as weapons of mass destruction (WMD), the United States, with pomp and pageantry, unveiled a weapon she tested on Iraq upon her invasion, proudly calling it the "mother of all bombs" (MOAB), never WMB. What else was MOAB designed to do but to maximize killing and destruction of life and property, therefore being a super WMB? Speaking of invading Iraq for no reason but for control, masterminding the killing of her president, Saddam Hussein, and directly killing his two sons plus tens, if not hundreds of thousands of her innocent citizens, should this not qualify President George W. Bush and his pharaohites as war criminals? In the world stage of the UN, it's all a game of double standards and "different strokes for different folks." It was the same UN in recent history that was used to bring war crimes charges against President Slobodan Milosevic of Serbia for his complicity in a war that very probably pales in comparison to what happened to the Iraqi nation. President Milosevic was hauled into jail and allowed to waste there and die of heart failure, if one buys the "official" cause of his death. Who dares haul a pharaoh before any court, let alone bring charges against him and also indict him on those charges?

On the nuclear proliferation arguments, who really loses if the world is blown to oblivion, ending all this drama of life, except "the almighty God" again, I guess. The difference would be that he would lose very big this time, having lost to Satan much earlier in their rivalry shortly after he created a perfect heaven and a perfect earth. Does replenishing the human population through reproduction not simply serve human selfish ends of being fulfilled and having offspring to help keep them human, particularly in old age? Is the other unintended result not to continue having people (victims) to keep perpetuating the turmoil and saga of life? Stepping out from my selfish world momentarily, I visualize that like me, my children would be pummeled by life as they are tugged through it. Would it be bad then if the "conspirators" of the world hatch the "mother of all conspiracies"—in two folds? One, to have every food source spiked with male and female infertility agents, effectively sterilizing both sexes to keep them from reproducing. And the other, to come up with a near-human robot to help care for the aged through their terminal stages of life till they all die out, as no more younger generation of humans replaces them. Ironically, this would be a service to humanity—redeeming and

191

saving it from life's eternal damnation finally. The fact is that when one peels away the beauty of family, including children who are not only fun to watch but also bring out the fascination of family, one gets to the depth of the hurt imprinted in the individual as s/he is tugged through life. While the "conspirators" of the world may be capable of such a feat, they would not do it, because there is nothing in it for them. Actually, having human "victims" in perpetuity to squeeze and milk is to their interest.

As one who despises stressful life, let me be clear, when I expire in this life, I want a place neither in anyone's hell or heaven. And as for that almighty God's heaven, with so many "saints" headed or already there, one never knows who among them and how many would consider themselves so good that they merit and deserve God's throne or to share it with him. And like Lucifer/Satan before them in the original perfect heaven, they would head off another tussle and war. To nip it once and for all, the unstable God, going belligerent, would ensure that all the "saints" pay dearly for it by flushing all down a unique, inextinguishable hell he would create where they would burn, roast, and simmer in perpetuity. Definitely, I would want none of it.

On the world stage of the UN, nothing of African and "third-world" value is seen to be worthy of featuring in that club, it seems—not even the accommodative nature of Africans, that warmly embraces and welcomes strangers and foreigners in their midst, making them feel comfortable, even in instances when they were imposed upon, unfortunately. When not "privileged" to be a passenger in the fast car of the powerful, riding along and not knowing where he is being taken to, the African is encouraged by the powerful to run after that car, on foot of course, tumbling, falling, and breaking apart along the way as he does so. Not given a chance at the table, when elements in the not-powerful nations, so choked and about to be snuffed out of life, lash out in a desperate act of survival, they are still blamed. As they are blamed, some lines used might be that the rich do things to help them. However, as history would tell us, even well-fed slaves never felt contented or fulfilled and never hailed or sang the praises of their master/owner, because there is no substitute for human dignity. Based on their values, some rich nations think every aspect of human satisfaction could be addressed and quantified materially. Nothing could be further from the truth, as history shows.

Chapter 8

The Future Is Now

"The future is now" is a thought I had expressed back in 1987. Never did I realize then that it had registered in the minds of my friends, Sunday Ezeh and Chima Akotaobi. Then, in the course of a discussion about our respective lives at one point, Sunday, who is now deceased, used the line, "The future is now," and reminded me it was an expression of mine. Fast-forward to this year, 2009, about a month ago in May, Chima, also in the course of a discussion of our lives, used the line and also credited me with it. To use this line in this discourse and as a chapter title only occurred to me a few days ago, after I had worked on what I hoped would be the last in it—"Death," which was to be chapter 8. So, with Chima using the line this time, it prompted me to reflect on the context in which I used it back in 1987. As this discourse has been and continues to be on my living experience and reflections on it, I see how *the future is now* fits snugly into it.

Working from 1987 backward, let me explain *the future is now*. I had completed my Master of Business Administration (MBA) degree in 1987 in Alabama, having earned my bachelor's degree from the same university over a year earlier, with a wife (my first marriage) and a four-year-old son. I could not find a job for many reasons, some of which were obvious; I was an immigrant student who had entered the country on a student, F1, visa, with conditions that included that I was not allowed to work, but was to just face my studies as a full-time student every semester, except summer. I then moved to Atlanta, Georgia, and started the process to be allowed to work in the United States, having qualified under a certain Immigration Act program. Not finding the job I was hoping for; through my Friend

Suday Ezeh, who had relocated to Atlanta before me, I got a Job with Domino's Pizza. From that, I switched to working as a bell man with The Stouffer Waverly Hotel at the Galleria, Cobb County, Georgia; combining that with another, as a Building material Warehouse helper. Then I made an adventure of driving from Atlanta to San Jose, California, and back; a journey of about 2,500 miles, at the invitation of a friend and fellow Igbo, William Ibwekwe, who had also graduated from the same university that I had. That adventure was about securing a job in Accounting, as Accounting was the field of my Bachelor's degree. That adventure did not pay off for about one month that I spent there. Being that I had a wife and son in Atlanta, I had to return there. Somewhere in between, as moves and next moves were pondered, I seriously considered returning to Nigeria as I had originally intended upon completing my education. I did travel to Nigeria to explore that option but was discouraged by relatives who pointed out that Nigeria had steadily deteriorated and spiraled down the economic, political, and social slope. It was not until I relocated to the northeast, New York City, in early 1991, and had to complete a second master's degree at New York University, take a professional licensing exam and pass it, both in 1996, and become licensed by the New York State Board in my field, that some career track began and unfolded for me. Thanks to my friend Dennis Agu who provided me with the job information and also helped to submit my resume.

Back in the late 1970s and 1980s, many Nigerians of my generation had made the same educational adventure to the United States that I had made. Many, if not most, of us were on our own—financially and otherwise. All we wanted was an opportunity for an education to which we had no access back home in Nigeria. We were ready to take that chance to access education. So, it was in the thick of figuring out what to do next, following the achievement of that educational goal, that I had made that statement. The reasoning being that many years earlier, I had thoughts and plans for the future. They, the thoughts and plans, were about getting an education, as getting an education was believed by my generation to be the key to succeeding in life. Finding myself, like many of my peers then, still grappling with finding an employment opportunity back in Nigeria or in the United States, I had to remind myself that even before I arrived in the United States in 1982, I had planned that future—in education—that I finally realized in 1987. That future, although realized in education, still had not fulfilled its promise or potential through a commensurate job to earn a living. As one who was ready to live life in that future, I had to find a way to live it, as continuing to plan for the "future" did not make sense and was not gratifying. Who or what is to say that even if I had continued to so plan that I would arrive at that future and even if I did arrive at it, what's the guarantee that my imagination of it would hold? This is how I had come about that expression. The future that I had planned years ago is now; I have to start living it.

Looking further back on the path I had walked in life to that point will help one to understand my thought process then and even now better. I would imagine that most people start out in life charting a course for their future and working at it. Depending on how much an individual has going for him, that path could be long, short, or average.

For those for whom that path turns out to be long, they would have to learn to "hold their breath" much longer if they would "succeed." Some others would be able to "exhale" much earlier as they would succeed much sooner, based also on how much they had going for them earlier in life. Even before I knew myself, it seemed that education was in my future. Education was beginning to take hold as the future in my village and the rest of my rural community. My father and my mother were among the few in their generation to get an education of note. Secondary or high school education was becoming the norm in my time. My mother shared with me that an older cousin, Mark Anyanwu (De Mark), about the first to have a secondary school education in my family, had, upon visiting my mother and me at my birth, made a statement to the effect that he did not see me being a farmer and that education had to be the way for me. Then in 1965, I had the privilege to be exchanging letters with another older cousin, Emmanuel Okebugwu Ogwuma (Dede Oke), who was then in theological college—Adventist College of West Africa (ACWA), later Adventist Seminary of West Africa (ASWA)—in Ilesha Remo, in western state of Nigeria, in those years. To understand the privilege here is to understand the place of age in the Igbo/Ngwa culture. Given the age gap between Dede Oke and I, it was indeed a privilege that he would be exchanging mail with me then. Dede Oke has retired in recent years from his position as a pastor. I have learned since residing here in the United States that ACWA is an affiliate of Andrews College of the Seventh-Day Christian sect in Michigan. Dede Oke had shared with me then that he was amazed at how well I wrote, considering again that all I had had at that time (in my teens) was an elementary education.

At some point later, yet another older cousin, Saul Ogwuma (De Saul), a degreed geologist, politician, businessman, and farmer since, has told me on more than one occasion, that, as a kid, I had said that I would be a doctor. It does appear that this was when I was three years old or before, for there are certain things that happened when I was about three that I could and do recall, but saying that I would be a doctor is not one of them. When I started elementary school, I always came out within the top three in exams and about 90 percent of the time, first. I would never forget Mr. Simeon Okochi (Sir Okochi), my infant one class teacher in 1956, at the College Practicing School of the Seventh-Day Adventist (SDA) Church, Ihie, Ngwa-ukwu, who took such a liking to me that he fondly called me "Brrrrrain" (from my name, Brown), Mr. Okochi would visit my family; I believed for his fondness of me. Then before I could complete my elementary school education, my father's fortune turned downward—economically and in health. This meant that my education and the educations of my siblings and half siblings were stopped or put on hold in 1963, the year my father died. The next year, in 1964, my mother contacted a schoolteacher cousin of hers, Timothy Ọdọ (Dede Ọdọ), and asked him to take me with him, to live with him and do his house chores (a houseboy) so I could complete my last year of elementary school. Dede Ọdọ did, and I had the chance to complete my last year in Ọhanze Isiahia, my mother's village and place of birth.

There was an experience back in 1963, in the midst of the larger Ogwuma family squabbles over land, before my father died. There was a court case in which he was named the key defendant. Too sick to be present at court, my father had asked me to write a note. He struggled to dictate for me, requesting adjournment of the case to a new date when his health would have improved so that he could be present. I had to take it to the *Ngwa-ukwu* "customary court," located in the village of Ahiaba Ubi, to hand it in on his behalf. I was the fourth of my father's seven sons; the first three were not around home then. Of the remaining four, I and my immediate junior, Allwell Atulaegwu (Atu) were around him. The last two were very young. Upon reading the letter, one of the court chiefs, Chief Thomas Akwarandu a contemporary of my father from Amaoji, a neighboring village, openly doubted that I had written that letter, especially as the plaintiff was there insinuating that my father was well. After hearing me repeatedly state that I had written it, he decided to ask me to spell some of the words in it. He and the court heard me spell every one of those words correctly; amazed, he asked whether my mother was from Ntigha, any one of the villages in the neighboring village-Group next to ours, and to the north of ours, Abayi Ngwa-ukwu. Ntigha women, as I recall, are considered industrious and hardworking. When I responded, "No," Chief Akwarandu then asked me which one (of my father's wives) was my mother, and I responded.

Then he said, "Your mother is the one from Ọhanze who had an education (which was rare back then for women of my mother's generation). But for your age, the chief continued, I'm still surprised (apparently that I spelled those words correctly and possibly wrote the note)."

This could be one of the reasons that my father, on his deathbed before he died and knowing he would, expressed these sentiments about me, *"Ibu nwoko; ibe dimpka"* ("You are a man; you are tough"). I do not recall how it was decided, but all my father's children at home then and the others who could return home to see him and be with him were taking turns, in line, saying what turned out to be the last good-bye to him. He would grab on to each one's hand, squeezing and holding it, and offering his blessings. It was in this exercise that he had uttered those words to me. I recount all these experiences because they helped form my positive self-esteem in the early stages of my life. And from that background, I saw myself as one who had what it took to pull through.

Retuning to my village upon completing elementary education, I found that my peers who had the opportunity for secondary school education were already in school and others were still starting. I could not. In the meantime, my older brother, Edward (Dede), who is three years older than I am, even though he had completed his elementary education a little before my father died, could not get a secondary school education either. Out and about trying to find a way to make it himself as a teenager, he was then in Lagos, courtesy of Hart Uche (De Hart), who also helped place him in his first job around 1965. According to my mother, De Hart was visiting the village for the first time since my father had died. At our family's for a condolence visit, he had asked my mother about the child she was pregnant with when, as a student—high school or military academy—he used to spend some of his holidays with my father at his job posts, as did Paul Ogwuma (De Paul) back in their Secondary/High School days. My mother told him of Edward (Dede), the child she was pregnant with then, and her first. She then arranged a meeting between De Hart and Dede. And so it was that in those dark days, De Hart had become a ray of light and lifeline in our lives. As for me, I was in the village in 1965 doing manual labor/jobs to buy clothing and meet some other personal needs. Still, I was hopeful that my doing this manual labor was just for the interim until an opportunity presented itself. Having seen some older males, some of whom were laborers around the village and broader village groups, and others who had left the village temporarily for distant places where they were hired for farm jobs, I did not want a future like that. In my mind, education was the future, and I had to find my way into it.

Dede, who had just started a lower level job, had big dreams, not just for me, but also for my immediate older half brother, Godfrey Chimezie (De Chime), from the second of my father's five wives. He came between Dede and me in seniority order. Dede had planned on sponsoring us both for a commercial school education, one alternative then to regular secondary education for those who could not afford it. He tried it for me first, for one term (semester), but the fees were too high for his income and I could not continue beyond that one term. Then the Nigerian Civil (Nigeria-Biafra) War broke out in 1966. Joining the Biafra Militia as a teenager, I went from there to the army. Luckily for me, unlike the very many who did not, I survived that war.

Soon after the war was over in 1970, Dede, who had returned from Lagos to Biafra (the east) following the breakout of the civil war, luckily, was offered his job again. He was to send for me to join him in Lagos. Through De Hart, I also had started my first job in the Bristol Hotel, one of the hotels in the Nigerian Hotels Ltd. Group then, as a cleaner. With this job, I was able to help Dede pay for the secondary school education of our two younger siblings, my sister Edith, and our youngest, Chidia. For my own educational future, I had heard my mother a few years earlier talk about the General Certificate in Education (GCE). The GCE was an alternative route to secondary education level, mostly pursued through correspondence courses. My mother had particularly mentioned that one Appalos, a brother of his cousin—Benson Erondu's (De Beni) wife, whom she said worked with the United African Company (UAC) then, had gotten his education through GCE. So when I started my job in Lagos, I quickly enrolled in a correspondence course with the School of Careers, London, England, with the goal of earning a GCE, ordinary level. Years later, I passed my GCE, ordinary level, through the West African Examination Council (WAEC). With that behind me, I enrolled in the GCE, advanced level courses, through Exam Success Correspondence College (ESCC), Yaba, Lagos. With a boost from these educational achievements, I got to change jobs and also met the functions and demands of my new job skillfully and in good faith and planned to and went from Lagos to the United States for a university education eventually.

This is the path I had to follow to meet my educational goals. It does seem like one long walk on a journey through a tunnel in search of a ray of light or an exercise in the holding of one's breath and waiting for the time to exhale. I may not have shown it outwardly earlier in the course of my planning for my future, but internally, I was preoccupied with the desire to "succeed" through education the unconventional way. Saying this here reminds me of a statement, a compliment, by Eunice (Da Nsi), my father's second wife and the mother of De Chime in January 2006, as I had helped the family meet a cultural "obligation": "You do your things gradually—as you are able and subtly."

When, therefore, I stated in 1987 that *the future is now*; it was about starting to live the future I had planned and worked for from way back, and I was ready to live it. Another reason that *the future is now* is very relevant for me now in 2009 is the fact that I am more aware now that life ends. Although I have always known this, that reality is clearer now at my age; it might as well have been a theory in my earlier years. With my sense now that the daily routine of life has caught up with me, having taken its toll, I have struggled with a lot of things for many months now. As one who lived his life thus far identifying his needs and issues, dissecting them, and asserting his willpower to take on things that he had control over, I find it difficult that this does not seem to quite get it for me any longer. I still want to get excited by things, events, and daily life, but have difficulty doing so. All this has clued me in to the fact that when life is tough, the individual faces it alone. I could also imagine that this is the case with dying—the individual faces that journey alone, possibly worried and scared. For this reason also, *the future is now* is very fitting here and as a chapter before the very last one and the conclusion of this discourse—death. People should live life, or have the opportunity to do so, when they have arrived in the future they had planned for for so long.

Delayed Gratification
One thing inherent or clear with planning for success in the future is that one has to make choices up front. It should be obvious that choosing between things accordingly is about foregoing certain things now in favor of an expected but enhanced result in the future. In doing so, the individual is essentially dealing with and managing internal and external factors. The external is about the things in the material world and the marketing forces pushing him/her, expecting that consumers, in their typical behavior, could resist but so much, as they would sooner, rather than later, gratify their desires. And indeed, evidence abounds that many, including one's peers, so gratify themselves. These make for additional pressure to join the fray—if for no other reason than to be like others. Then there is the internal factor, one's rational thinking about that better future that could only be achieved if one is disciplined, has self-control, and remains this way over a period of time. To be so able would mean that one not gratify instantly, as doing so taps and saps one's limited resources now that are better utilized to plan and enhance them in the future. This is not a typical consumer behavior, which is supposedly influenced by stimuli and cues. For those who had to go through a long and protracted trail like I did; this is nothing easy. Over time and at a point, it is natural that the individual would want to step out of that "wall," away from "reality," and begin to live. This is about bringing some necessary balancing to one's life. The future should and does get to be now.

Chapter 9

Death

Azumaraọnwu (in the Ngwa dialect of the Igbo language) is "breed/raise well for death," translated in English. Only one of the very many names in Igbo that speak to the frustration that death always lurks and gets its way, *Azumaraọnwu* sums up the acknowledgement and acceptance of the prevalence of death, albeit disappointedly. Indeed, death is always staring people in the face, just like the skull—the symbol of death—above.

Ọnwu is the Igbo word for death; for some perspective, here is a list, by no means exhaustive, of such names that grapple with the reality of death in the Igbo culture:

#	Name	English Translation
1.	Azumaraọnwu	Breed and raise well for death.

2.	Ọnwukanjọ	Death is worse.
3.	ỌnwuzuruIgbo	Death is Igbo-wide.
4.	Ọnwuzuruuwa	Death is universal.
5.	Ọnwuasoanya	Death respects not.
6.	Ọnwueyi	Death makes no schedule.
7.	Ọnwuliri/Ọnwunali	Death reduces (a people).
8.	Ọnwutuebe	Halt, death!
9.	Ọnwusọamaonye	Whose compound does death forbid?
10.	Ọnwuatuegwu	Death fears not.
11.	Ọnwudinjọ	Death is bad.
12.	Eroọnwu (Erọnwu)	Worries of death.
13.	Ọnwukwe	Death permitting.

With death, the damaged goods bound for the dump that a human being constituted in life finally arrive after his involuntary ride on the train at the only stop and destination, his dump—the graveyard. Although it should spell relief, considering the torture it takes to keep up with life, death spells fear to the living and hounds him through his lifelong journey. All the avoidance, the delay, and the agony of living eventually end, as man fulfills the apparent purpose of his life, as scripted in his nature—to enter the sphere of life and exit it through death.

Second Chance at Life

A second chance at life is my way of describing a concept that has been termed *near-death experience* (NDE). This applies to some people known to have died or been considered dead for a certain amount of time before coming back to life. Here is a definition of an NDE by Diane Corcoran:

> NDEs are intense, emotional experiences that occur when a person is close to death or in a clinical compromise such as an accident, illness, combat, surgery, or emotional trauma, and then goes on to have one or more common characteristic of the NDE.

Another definition refers to:

> A broad range of personal experiences associated with impending death, encompassing multiple possible sensations including detachment from the body; feelings of levitation; extreme fear; total serenity, security, or warmth; the experience of absolute dissolution; and the presence of light, which some people interpret as a deity.

Some see NDEs as a paranormal and spiritual glimpse into the afterlife.

In addition to noting characteristics, many of which are identified in the Corcoran list below, this source notes, "Some people have a sense of dread towards the cessation of their life."

It goes on to list five stages of the continuum of the NDE by Kenneth Ring (1980):

1. Feelings of peace and contentment
2. A sense of detachment from the body
3. Entering a transitional world of darkness (rapid movement through a long, dark tunnel; the tunnel experience)
4. Emerging into a bright light
5. Entering the light

On the premise that humans spend most of their lives avoiding death, it would seem that getting a second chance to return to life from being dead is a great thing. This depends on who is asked among those who have experienced an NDE and NDE researchers. As I will touch on shortly, there are thoughts that nothing is better than death, with a documented and published work bearing that title. Corcoran added this in her article, on page 18:

> NDE patients describe being in the most loving and wonderful place they have ever known, but suddenly are hauled out of this peaceful place and sent back to their broken body. Thus, it is easy to understand an angry reaction.

The following is a list of post-NDE characteristics associated with those who have had this experience, irrespective of culture, gender, race, age, religion, and social standing that Corcoran identified:

• Sensing inexpressible peace, comfort, and unconditional love
• Feeling relief from pain
• Separating from the physical body
• A feeling of floating
• Seeing and/or hearing a superior being
• Seeing beautiful scenery
• Hearing beautiful music

- Seeing spiritual beings and communicating with them (often deceased loved ones and unfamiliar relatives)
- Moving through a dark space or tunnel
- Being surrounded by a brilliant light and/or unfamiliar colors
- Possessing unlimited knowledge
- Communicating telepathically
- Coming to a physical boundary

Also, Corcoran and other researchers show an NDE has a tremendous and life-changing impact on those who have had that experience, which translates to some "lingering" change in "basic values, jobs, and life purpose," as they no longer fear death; become less materialistic; change to altruistic jobs; do more service for others; become more spiritual, affectionate, and emotional; possess new knowledge, gifts (e.g. healing, psychic ability), and information; feel sadness, loneliness, and alienation; have difficulty describing the experience; and have increased sensitivity to light.

As is typical with science—medical science in this case—phenomena and concepts are subject to research, tests, and studies to find critical evidence/proof to back positions and/or claims. The NDE is not left out. It seems to be on the basis of debating NDEs and what to make of them that Dr. Sam Panria is attributed, in an interview, with making these statements:

> What they describe is a near-death experience. It's a subjective and dream-like state. I can't say whether your dream is not real or is real. The key point is that no one really in their right mind can deny this experience occurs. The easiest answer is that it must be a trick of the mind, an illusion ...

Because NDEs are the accounts of only the people who have experienced them, since they are subjective, skepticism about them is understandable. After all, there's a saying in the Igbo language (Ngwa dialect) that, translated into English, means, "Whoever wakes from a sleep and claims to have slugged out in a dream with the spirits, who's to be asked to validate?" It's safe to say because there are many NDE experiencers and there are track records of NDE research, they are probably true.

An out-of-body experience is one characteristic of an NDE that I could probably relate to. No, I have not experienced an NDE. But I have had an experience that could fit in that mold. It was in the 1970s in Lagos, Nigeria. I was in my twenties. I used to practice meditation and had a particular weeknight when I routinely did so. I did this for a while until one particular night—I do not recall what I did differently that night, but as I sat, in a relaxed, candlelit room meditating, I felt in a moment a different kind of serene calmness and appeared to be slipping out of my physical body into the twilight, headed to another realm. Then, I became afraid, afraid that I would not return should I slip through. At that point, I awoke and snapped out of it mentally, ending that "journey." I had truly feared I would die if I continued. Only in my twenties then and planning my future, I did not want to die. That experience was the end of my practice of that formal and routine meditation.

An assertion "Nothing better than death," which is also the title of a book by Kevin R. Williams, is as intriguing as it is enticing. I stumbled upon it in the worldwide Web while researching death. Upon reviewing the book though, my take on it could be captured in this statement, which I read years ago, about accounting statements: "Accounting statements are like bikinis; what they reveal is enticing, and what they conceal is intriguing." Williams put a lot of work into the book, doing research on the work of others on NDEs, documenting tens of accounts of NDE, and littering it with biblical quotes and references. Getting to the "Research Conclusions" section of the book, it was like reading the Bible all over again. It seems as if Williams wanted to supplement for what he thinks the Bible did not do, substitute today's people, NDE experiencers, for the biblical figures and names, with the idea they would be more believable because they live in "today's world." On first reading *Nothing Better than Death*, my first thought was if upon reading this book, I had found it plausible, it would have validated for me my position that life, then, has no purpose or meaning, except to live it and die. It would further buttress another point of mine that "the almighty God" deserves all the blame for creating this fundamentally flawed life. In some ironic way, the notion that nothing is better than death buttresses my point that death should spell relief—relief from the "entrapment" that is life.

If one accepts, as Williams apparently does, that NDE teaches the interrelatedness and continuity of life, death, afterlife, and all, with "God" in the center of it all, it still falls short of answers that humans spend their entire lives seeking. Not all humanity has experienced or will experience an NDE. Except, again, Williams' "research" on NDE and its "conclusions" was done with the intention of filling a void the Bible has left gaping open, hoping that by "putting human faces" on "this Bible extension," people would be swayed. At best, *Nothing Better than Death* shows that "God" weaved so many tricks into life. Expectedly, God apologists will remind me here that it's not a trick, but God choosing not to let humans in on what makes him God, lest they be equal with him. If I could make something of the interrelatedness and continuity thought that reading *Nothing Better than Death* provoked in me, it is that humans are only a part of a mystery, in the mystery that is the universe. We read and hear about aliens, or human-like figures or objects from "outer space," either originating from astrology, physics, or other physical sciences. This, in my mind as I write, hints to me that, like us humans, they (whatever they may be if they are "real") are also part of the interrelatedness and continuity of the mystery of the universe. With this, there is a possibility that should they, those "objects," in their world, be as intelligent as humans are here in our world, earth, they too may see us humans as objects from elsewhere. In the preface of *Nothing Better than Death*, I noted that the author quoted one Dianne Morrissey, an NDE experiencer featured in his research, I believe: "If I lived a billion years more, in my body or yours, there's not a single experience on earth that could be ever be as good as being dead." Then I reasoned that the title of this book was influenced by this quote.

Among NDE experiencers (those who got a second chance at life), there are those who were angry that they did not get to die. Conversely, there are people who had expressed a desire/wish for a second chance at life and did not get their wish, ending up dying anyway. Before taking their last breath, some in this category left indications they were disappointed they did not get their wish. Two pre-death wishes of two people close to me—my father in 1963 and my friend Sunday Ezeh in 2005—made it clear to me that there is a stage of disappointment in dying.

In addition to being disappointed when he realized he was dying, my father also appeared to have some regrets, the implication being that if he had had a chance to do certain things over, he would do them differently. I recall him, on his deathbed, recalling a name he said one of his father's (my grandfather) wives used to call him—*Ihemekwa*, short for *Ihemekwa adi ama izu*. This in English means "one learns from happenings/events." My understanding of it is that he had recalled and expressed this in the context of certain conflicts in the larger extended family and community in which he was a key player. Long before the conflict to which I am alluding became full-blown, and also in the context of the culture of the society and community, he had had occasions that made him express a wish to stretch his children with a rope to make them grow, that by some miracle, really, his kids would grow up to be big instantaneously, to be adults actually.

And in the male-dominated culture, with his older kids being girls, this had some implications. Then the only surviving child of his mother, as the younger of his only two sisters had died even before his own children were born, and the other, his older sibling, had died about five years earlier, my father apparently found himself alone in dealing with communal conflicts. Considering this and the fact that he wanted to be around to see his children grow up to become adults, my father was clearly disappointed that his wish to be around longer was not granted, as death had its way. At the time, only two of his daughters (the first two and the oldest of his surviving twenty-three children—Rose Elechi (Adanne Elechi) and Beatrice Ulọaku (Da Ulọaku), who were twenty-seven and twenty-four respectively then) were married. My sense of my father's thoughts then is that he was worried about what would become of his family and still mostly growing children after he was gone.

With my friend Sunday Ezeh, in what was one of the very last telephone discussions I had with him, he had called me from Albuquerque, New Mexico, to inform me he had been diagnosed with liver cancer. He was clear that he was not ready to die, telling me: "I will fight this; I will not do it to Chi [Chinyere, his wife] and I will not do it to Atuọma and Ekeọma [his son and daughter respectively]." When I got to Albuquerque, from New York, about five days later, I was at his bedside at the hospital, in the company of three other members of my community, and he was no longer able to talk, as the doctor was said to have given him about three hours or less to live. Only able to move his head, his eyes were just "glassy," he probably heard things said around him and the prayer vigil we had at his bedside all night. He died hours later. Again, in his case, he affirmed his will to survive the deadly cancer, believing that doing things he thought he had control over—submitting himself and body to whatever treatment was indicated—he would beat it. At whatever time he realized he would not make it, in the stage at which he may still have been conscious but could not express himself any longer, he must have felt disappointed.

It does seem like with living, there is stress with dying; depending on the cause of death—terminal illness, old age, trauma, as in accidents, and other causes. If death from trauma is instant, stress may not feature. With the potential for disappointment and regret I have associated with the death of my father and my friend Sunday Ezeh, I am persuaded to highlight these three points.

First, a stage of disappointment should be addressed when death and dying is at issue. The groundbreaking work of Elisabeth Kubler Ross in the field of thanatology stands out in this area. She laid out her work in a book titled *On Death and Dying: What the Dying Have to Teach Doctors,*

Nurses, Clergy, and Their Own Families. Dr. Kubler Ross identifies the five seminal stages, in progression, of denial, anger, bargaining, depression, and acceptance that a dying person goes through when they are told that they have a terminal illness. Reasonably clear in all the Kubler Ross five stages when one reflects on them is that a stage of disappointment is preceded by bargaining and triggered by losing out in the bargaining. This then is followed by the depression from having lost in the bargaining and realizing that death, the obvious, is the only option, which has to be accepted.

For more perspective, "Disappointment," as defined by Wikipedia online, "is the feeling of dissatisfaction that follows the failure of expectations to manifest."

It went further to distinguish disappointment from regret, thus:

> Similar to regret, it differs in that the individual feeling regret focuses primarily on personal choices contributing to a poor outcome, while the individual feeling disappointment focuses on outcome. It is a source of psychological stress.

I relate this here to the regret I observed to have played out for my father on his deathbed, as he recalled the name *Ihemekwa adi ama izu,* "one learns from happenings/events." He clearly would have made certain choices differently in the same or similar circumstances, had he had his wish to survive to live longer.

The second point is that a person dying from certain terminal diseases, like Huntington's or Alzheimer's, may, ahead of his immediate death stage, choose to die to curtail the stress associated with a long terminal process. So, unlike for others, not all the Kubler Ross five stages of death and dying, or the sixth that I have suggested, play out for them. For the stages that may have played out with them, they did so much earlier; some even as early as when a family member died of the same disease. This is more so if the disease is genetically passed on through the generational line. Upon having witnessed what those relatives went through, other family members inheriting that disease may even prepare and sign a living will that they do not want to live in a certain state.

An instance is the case of Randy Carr, forty-two, and Andy Carr, forty-one, who were shot and killed by their mother, Carol Carr, sixty-four, on June 8, 2002, in a nursing home in Griffin, Georgia, United States. An online publication, *Science & Spirit,* in an article "A Time to Kill," featured the story of the Carrs, who had inherited the terminal neurological disease Huntington's from their father's side of the family. The disease had killed their father, his mother, and his sister. The story also said that their father's brother had taken his own life upon discovering that he had inherited the disease. Having witnessed that before their father died seven years earlier in 1995, he could not move, talk, or swallow, they resolved not to live to experience what their father "lived" through and pleaded with their mother to do what it took to make their wish come true, including killing them herself.

This is the definition of death found in Wikipedia online along with the symbolic face of death above: "Death is the permanent termination of the biological functions that define a living organism. It refers to both a particular event and to the condition that results thereby."

Due to a variety of theories, including scientific ones, and belief systems, Wikipedia online added some clarifications:

> The true nature of the latter has for millennia been a central concern of the world's religious traditions and of philosophical enquiry. Religions, almost without exception, maintain faith in either some kind of afterlife or reincarnation. The effect of physical death on any possible mind or soul remains an open question. Contemporary science regards organismic death as final by definition.

Animals almost without exception (see hydra) die in due course from senescence. Intervening phenomena which commonly bring death earlier include malnutrition, predation, disease, accidents resulting in terminal physical injury, or, in extreme circumstances, grave ecosystem disruption. Intentional human activity causing death includes suicide, homicide, and war. Roughly 150,000 people die each day across the globe. Death in the natural world can also occur as an indirect result of human activity: an increasing cause of species depletion in recent times has been destruction of ecological systems as a consequence of the widening spread of industrial technology.

The chief concern of medical science has been to postpone and avert death. Death in this context is now seen as less an event than a process: conditions once considered indicative of death are now reversible. Where in the process a dividing line is drawn between life and death depends on factors beyond the presence or absence of vital signs. In general, clinical death is neither necessary nor sufficient for a determination of legal death. A patient with working heart and lungs determined to be brain dead can be pronounced legally dead without clinical death occurring. Precise medical definition of death, in other words, becomes more problematic, paradoxically, as scientific knowledge and technology advance. Death remains a central mystery of life.

Whatever other technical terms or definitions of death that certain interests—science, religion, the law, etc.—may grapple with, when a person loses consciousness and cannot make choices or function, he is dead. This gets it for me.

Indeed the end-all, death, however, gets to different people at different times—early, in midlife, later, and/or late in life—and through many different causes. Like my wife would say, death always would have an alibi or a witness—he/she died of an accident, cancer, aneurysm, cardiac arrest, diabetes, hypertension-induced stroke, gunshot, stabbing, etc.

Even if for a graphic and dramatic effect, this chart of causes of death in the United States, 2002;[2]* found online, doubles also for some alibi for death:

FORMAL NAME	INFORMAL NAME	% ALL DEATHS
(1) Diseases of the heart	heart attack (mainly)	28.5%
(2) Malignant neoplasms	cancer	22.8%
(3) Cerebrovascular disease	stroke	6.7%
(4) Chronic lower respiratory disease	emphysema, chronic bronchitis	5.1%
(5) Unintentional injuries	accidents	4.4%
(6) Diabetes mellitus	diabetes	3.0%
(7) Influenza and pneumonia	flu & pneumonia	2.7%
(8) Alzheimer's Disease	Alzheimer's senility	2.4%
(9) Nephritis and Nephrosis	kidney disease	1.7%
(10) Septicemia	systemic infection	1.4%
(11) Intentional self-harm	suicide	1.3%
(12) Chronic Liver/Cirrhosis	liver disease	1.1%
(13) Essential Hypertension	high blood pressure	0.8%
(14) Assault	Homicide	0.7%
(15) All other causes	Other	17.4%

Diseases are just one category of the causes of death, as another category, accidents, has its share, as shown by this chart, from the same source.

Types of Accidental Deaths, USA, 2002

Accident	Percent
(1) Motor vehicle (MVA)	**44.3%**

---

2   * Causes of Death: http://www.benbest.com/lifeex/causes.html
     Causes of Death: http://www.mereck.com/pubs/mmanual_ha/sec1/ch03/ch03e.html
     * Causes of Death: http://www.benbest.com/lifeex/causes.html Causes of Death: http://www.mereck.com/pubs/mmanual_ha/sec1/ch03/ch03e.html

(2) Falls	17.8%
(3) Poison, liq/solid	13.0%
(4) Drowning	3.9%
(5) Fires, Burns, Smoke	3.4%
(6) Medical/Surgical Complication	3.1%
(7) Other land transport	1.5%
(8) Firearms	0.8%
(9) Other (nontransport)	17.8%

Another way to look at these causes of death/death's alibis, in no way an exhaustive list, is that humans are mortals. Mortality/death has to be triggered by something. Even if any of the identified causes of death are targeted and reduced or eliminated by human ingenuity through science or otherwise, death will find a way/cause/alibi with which to prevail.

Although logically, death in old or older age is understood, specific causes are still associated with death in that age. Here's a short chart of such causes of death in elderly Canadians in 2005, found online:

Causes of Death of Elderly Canadians (over 65)[3]*

Cause	*Non-Demented*	*Demented*
Heart disease	**38.5%**	**32.5%**
Cancer	**19.6%**	**6.8%**
Stroke	**10.4%**	**13.1%**
Chronic respiratory	**7.9%**	**4.2%**
Alzheimer's disease	**0.6%**	**7.2%**

When not blamed on one of the categories of accident, disease, or old age above, there are a number of other causes to which death is attributed. One is behavior; as described here by 1993 Carter Center data:

> Behavior greatly influences the likelihood of dying of every one of these causes. That study "estimated that two-thirds of deaths are due to six risk factors subject to influence by the will: tobacco, alcohol, injury risks, high blood pressure, obesity/cholesterol and poor primary care (prenatal/reproductive). (Only 26% of smokers live to age 80—in contrast with 57% of nonsmokers [ADDICTION 97:15–28 (2002)]). [4]♦

---

3   * Causes of Death: http://www.benbest.com/lifeex/causes.html
     (Source: Neuroepidemiology; Chamandy, N: 25: 75-84 (2005).

4   ♦ http://www.benbest.com/lifeex/causes.html

Like many human efforts to help educate and inform in order to help humanity live better and longer, the study includes some figures/statistics on the variables of gender, occupation, and some influence of geography or country, as they impact these "behaviors" that get blamed for death.

The need to self-preserve that is embedded in human nature has meant that humans have done a great deal in every phase of life to improve life from what it is in the state of nature. Take the area of the human body, from the medical to the psychological; they have developed insight to the systematic connections and functioning of the body and the ways one area impacts the other. Listening to and/or watching some of these as they are presented by professionals and "experts," some on public TV channels like NJN, New Jersey, for instance, is nothing short of head-spinning. Some would describe how one mentally engages in delaying or stopping cells from dying so as to be physically and emotionally healthy. The processes are so contoured that mental acrobatics might be one way to portray them. There have been many brave enough to embrace and grasp these tools and skills, as complex as they may be. Between seeing people adopting these pure mental engagements and observing others grind and sweat in gyms/ health clubs, I have come across yet some others in streets at all times of the day running and biking for life and from dying. Many times, this leaves me wondering and thinking that all these too fall short, as some of those so engaged routinely in these "runs for life" are known to die even when so actively "running." It really does not matter in the end what the course of or excuse for it is; the certain end—death—nullifies the significance of the cause of/excuse for it.

At the end of this glamour and fantasy called life, all comes to naught. I invite you, the reader, to just pause and ponder that many, if not most, of your behaviors in life are influenced, shaped, driven, and dictated by the fear of dying; hence you did what you had to and could do to keep living. Still, you could not get away with dying. Yes, you're still living now, but you're aware, however, that you are living on borrowed time; your time will be up someday. I'm sure there's a notion that allowing this to feature more in the consciousness of humanity would make life more miserable. I disagree. Instead, it would help moderate human excesses and bring about humility and therefore more humane relations in the human world community. One way I find this assertion reasonably valid is the mellowing traits identical or common with those who have had near-death experiences, which include the abandoning of, or shying away from, aggression.

Granted, humans have no choice but to make the most that they can of life and hopefully strike a balance as they do so. I am persuaded that life should not be taken too seriously as has been the case. This, the taking of life too seriously, is supported by the facts I have laid out throughout the discourse. Even this late in the discourse, I'm still realistic enough about counter viewpoints, on religious or other bases. There are those who believe or think they know there is an afterlife. Until there is an objective and verifiable proof of this and what it means or it is worth, all I am on it is a skeptic at best. I can only vouch for things I know, based on my experience living this life here and now. For me to believe in a religious-based afterlife has implications that I continue to believe in the God of my childhood. To so believe is for me to also believe in the witches and witchcraft prevalent in my childhood in the rural Umuawala community and beyond. In the same mind-set, I must also believe in the recent lynchings of many innocent people in some Igbo communities who were picked by witch-hunt campaigns and blamed for casting spells and causing people, especially the youth, not to have jobs, get married or progress in life, etc. The phenomenon of mystery and witchcraft was, and may still be, that every sickness, be it heart attack, cardiac arrest, diabetes, hypertension, schizophrenia, depression, etc., and death are the result of spells cast by evil witches who are neighbors or family members. Believing not any of the nonsense, the most I can do about believing in "the God" is doubt.

As famous as Nostradamus was and relatively still is, all that those who study his prophesies do is wallow in guesswork as to what event in history they guess fulfilled or fulfills them. The sciences of logic, reasoning, mathematics, and algorithms, and the study of trends and patterns to fairly predict an outcome trashes all that guesswork. Yes, with some "inspiration," some things could be guessed right or reasonably be predicted. Again, this pales in comparison to science. Otherwise, astrology would have helped humans get a better grip on life and the world before science took hold. An agnostic could and does suspend disbelief. With a religious fundamentalist and an ideologue, conversely, there is no suspending of belief, and no room to be open-minded either. Therefore, there is no gauging or weighing of facts and/or evidence relative to conclusions. That is hard to change and may never change; come what may.

In the end, I have been told that the faith in, and hope for, the Christian heaven is all I get for my sojourn in life. Even with the faith, all I could do is hope for that reward/continuity. Given that I am but a "sinner" before God, for just being born human, with all the attendant consequences, being accepted into heaven is not guaranteed. And having played God throughout my life, going through all I had to just to hold on to and live life because God fell far too short measuring up, the hope of going to heaven gives me no satisfaction for my ordeal in life, which for all I can tell just ends in death. And those for whom just that is satisfactory, I can understand.

Not every reader of this has journeyed life walking in my shoes or through the same path. Therefore not all will see life the way I do, or through my lens. My hope is that the read was enlightening, nonetheless.

References

Resources used and/or recommended

1953 Iranian Coup d'Ètat: http://en.wikipedia.org/wiki/1953_Iranian_coup_d'%C3%A9tat

About the Bible Prophecy on Esau: http://www.aboutbibleprophecy.com/p98.htm

Abraham Maslow: http://aolsearcht5.search.aol.com/aol/search?s_it=topsearchbox.search&q=Abraham+Maslow

Achilles' Heel: http://en.wikipedia.org/wiki/Achilles'_hill

Allegory of the Cave: http://en.wikipedia.org/wiki/Plato%27s_Cave

Apollo: http:www.in2greece.com/English/history/mythology/names/apollo.html

Ask a Scientist; Death by Natural Causes: http://www.newton.dep.anl.gov/askasci/gen01/gen01800.htm

Assassinations Involving Foreign Leaders:

http://www.aarclibrary.org.publib/contents/church_church_reports_ir,htm

A Theory of Everything: http://www.pbs.org/faithandreasons/intro/purpotoe-body.html

A Time to Kill: (http://www.science-spirit/printerfriendly.php?article_id+343

Boston Tea Party: http://en.wikipedia.org/wiki/Boston_Tea_Party

British/Irish Wars: http://wiki.answers.com/Q/What_was_the_conflict_between_the_Catholics_and_Protestants_in_Ireland

Buddha: http://en.wikipedia.org/wiki/Gautama_Buddha

Bunch, Will. (2009). *Tear Down This Myth*. Free Press, New York.

Cardiac Risk in the Young: http://www.c-r-y.org.uk/natural_causes.htm

Carl Jung: http://en.wikipedia.org/wiki/Carl_Jung

Causes of Death: http://www.benbest.com/lifeex/causes.html

Causes of Death: http://www.mereck.com/pubs/mmanual_ha/sec1/ch03/ch03e.html

Cloning: http://www.pbs.org/faithandreasons/intro/genetclon-body.html

Confucius: http://www.hyperhistory.net/apwh/biosb3confucius.htm

Corcoran, Diane: *Advance for LPNs*, April 24, 2006, page 17.

Cosmology: http://en.wikipedia.org/wiki/Cosmology

Creationism: http://www.pbs.org/faithandreasons/intro/evolucrea-body. html

Davidson, Basil. (1993). *The Black Man's Burden*. Ibadan, Nigeria: Spectrum Books Limited.

Death: http://en.wikipedia.org/wiki/Death

Death by Natural Causes: http://en.wikipedia.org/wiki/Natural_causes

Demagogy: http://en.wikipedia.org.wiki/Demagogy

Disappointment: http://en.wikipedia.org/wiki/Disappointment - cite_note-Regret-0

Divine Providence: http://en.wikipedia.org/wiki/Divine_Providence

Don "D. C." Curry: http://www.myspace.com/dccurry

Dr. Jack Kevorkian: http://en.wikipedia.org/wiki/Jack_Kevorkian

Dying of Old Age; An Examination of Death Certificates of Centenarians: http://gateway.nlm.nih.gov/MeetingAbstracts/ma?f=10227304. html

Ethics: Webster's New Ideal Dictionary

Evolution: http://www.pbs.org/faithandreasons/intro/evolu-body.html

Fatwa: http://en.wikipedia.org/wiki/Fatw%C4%81

Franken, Al. (2005). *The Truth*. New York: Dutton, Penguin Group.

Garrett Toren: http://www.meaning-of-life.info/IsThereaGod.html

Genes and "Sin": http://www.pbs.org/faithandreasons/intro/genetsin-body. html

Genetics: http://www.pbs.org/faithandreasons/intro/genet-body.html

Gerry Adams: http://en.wikipedia.org/wiki/Gerry_Adams

Glenn Beck: http://en.wikipedia.org/wiki/Glenn_Beck

Grant, Michael. (1977). *Jesus; an Historian's Review of the Gospel*. New York: Charles Scribner's Sons.

Gravitation: http://encarta.msn.com/enylopedia_761556322/Gravitiation. html

Heaven's Gate: http://www.cnn.com/US9803/25/heavens.gate/

Hibbert, Anthony, A. (1996). *Before the Flames.* New York: Seaburn Publishing.

Hitchens, Christopher. (2007). *God Is Not Great: How Religion Poisons Everything.* New York: Hachette Book Group.

Icarus Paradox: http://en.wikipedia.org/wiki/Icarusl_Paradox

Igbo: http://en.wikipedia.org/wiki/Igbo_people

Immediate Causes of Death: http://newoldage.blogs.nytimes.com/2008/10/23/the-immediate-causes-of-death/?em

Individualism: Webster's New Ideal Dictionary

Iran Hostage Crisis: http://en.wikipedia.org/wiki/Iran-hostage-crisis

Iranian 1953 Coup D'etat: http://en.wikipedia.org/wiki/1953_Iranian_coup_d'%C3%A9tat

Isaac Newton: http://en.wikipedia.org/wiki/Isaac_Newton

Jesus: http://en.wikipedia.org/wiki/Jesus

Jimmy Carter on Energy: http://www.pbs.org/wgbh/amex/carter/fiilmore/ps_energy.html)

Jimmy Cliff: http://www.lyricstime.com/jimmy-cliff-remake-the-world-lyrics.html

JINN, CIA, & Mandela: http://wwwpacificnews.org/jinn/stories/2.23/961101-south-africa

Jonestown: http://www.crimelibrary.com/serial4.jonetown

Joseph Campbell: http://en.wikipedia.org/wiki/Joseph_Campbell

Keller, Timothy. (2008). *The Reason for God.* New York: Dutton, Penguin Group.

Kempe, Frederick "Thinking Global; Africa Emerges as Strategic Battle Ground." *Wall Street Journal,* April 25, 2006Kermit Roosevelt, Jr.; Head of CIA's Operation Ajax: http://en.wikipedia.org/wiki/Kermit_Roosevlt,_Jr.

Leedom, Tim C. (Editor) (2003). *The Book Your Church Doesn't Want You to Read.* San Diego: Truth Seeker Books.

Life: Webster's New World Dictionary of the American Language, Second College Edition, definition 1.

"'Mad Men'; Old Ways Die Hard." *New York Daily News*, September 24, 2009.

Magna Carta: http://en.wikipedia.org/wiki/Magna_Carta

Manifest Destiny: http//en.wikipedia.org/Manifest_Destiny

McCarthyism: http://en.wikipedia.org/wiki/McCarthyism

Maher, Bill: http://en.wikipedia.org/wiki/Bill_ Maher

Martin Luther King, Jr.: http://en.wikipedia.org/wiki/Martin_Luther_King,_Jr.

Matthew J. Murray: http://en.wikipedia.org/wiki/New_Life_Church_shooting

Melting Pot: http://en.wikipedia.org/wiki/Melting_pot

Mohammad: http://en.wikipedia.org/wiki/Muhammad

Morality: Webster's New Ideal Dictionary

Moyers, Bill. (1989). *A World of Ideas*. New York: Doubleday, Bantam Doubleday Dell Publishing Group, New York.

Murphy's Law: http://en.wikipedia.org/wiki/Murphy's_law

Mythology: http://en.wikipedia.org/wiki/Mythology

Narcissism: http://en.wikipedia.org/wiki/Narcissism http://www.referencecenter.com/ref/reference/narcissi/narcissism?invvocationType=arclk

Near Death Experience Research Foundation: http://www.nderf.org/

Nelson Mandela: http://en.wikipedia.org/wiki/Nelson_Mandela

http://www.namebase.org/diamond.html

Ngwa: http://en.wikipedia.org/wiki/Ngwa

Nicaragua: http://www.krysstal.com/display_acts.php?regiocountry=_Nicaragua

Nigeria: http://en.wikipedia.org/wiki/Nigeria

Obasanjo: *U.S. Immigration News*, February 1, 2008, page 15.

Oral Roberts: http://en.wikipedia.org/wiki/Oral_Roberts

Ọfọ-na-Ogu: http://en.wikipedia.org/wiki/Odinani

Ogwugwu Okija: http://en.wikipedia.org/wiki/Okija

Ogwuma, Brown. (2005). *Root That Binds*. New York: African Tree Press, Seaburn Publishing Group.

Old Age Is Not a Cause of Death: http://www.blisstree.com/widowsquest/old-age-is-not-a-cause-of-death/

Oriji, John, N. (1994). *Traditions of Igbo Origins*. (Revised edition). New York: Revised Edition.

——(1998). *Ngwa History* (Revised Edition). New York: Peter Lang.

Ozodi Thomas Osuji: http://.chatafrikarticles.com.articles/257/1/UNDERSTANDING-NUEROSIS/Page1

Paranoia: http://en.wikipedia.org/wiki/Paranoia

Patrick Henry: http://en.wikipedia.org/wiki/Patrick_Henry

Pharaoh: http://www.touregypt.net/kings.htm

Philosophy: http://en.wikipedia.org/wiki/Philosophy

Plato's Cave and the Matrix: http://whatisthematrix.warnersbros.com/rl_cmp/new_phil_patridge.html

Plato's Metaphors: http:www.crytalinks.com/platometapors.html

"Poor Mexico": http://www.huffingtonpost.com/sandy-goodman/poor-mexico-so-far-from-g_b_170899.html

Power: Webster's New Ideal Dictionary.

Prayer: http://www.yourdictionary.com/prayer

Pre-Christ Virgin births of God Figures: http://englishatheist.org/indexd.shtml

Psychic Determinism: Htpp://wilderdom.com/personality/L8-1majorThemesAssumptionsPsychoanlytic.html

Religion: Webster's New Ideal Dictionary; http://en.wikipedia.org/wiki/Religion

Religion; Demographic Distribution: http://www.newworldencyclopedia.org/entry/Religion

Roland Martin: Paul's 9/11 Explanation Deserves to Be Debated: http//www.cnn.com/2007/US/05/18/martin.index.html

Ron Brown Plane Crash—Did Hawks: http://.geocites.com/happy1215us?200922

Salem Witchcraft Trials: http://www.law.umke.edu/faculty/projects/ftrials/salem/SALEM.HTM

Salman Rushdie: http://en.wikipedia.org/wiki/The_Satanic_Verses_controversy - cite_note-3

Sam Panria: http://www.aolhealth.com.health/what-happens-when-we-die/1

Science and Religion: http://www.pbs.org/faithandreasons/intro/histo-body.html

Separation of Science and Religion: http://www.pbs.org/faithandreasons/intro/histosr-body.html

Serenity Prayer: http://en.wikipedia.org/wiki/Serenity_Prayer

Skull: http://en.wikipedia.org/wiki/File:SkullFromStillLifeWithASkull.jpg

Socrates: http://en.wikipedia.org/wiki/Socrates

Stephen Decatur: http://en.wikipedia.org/wiki/Stephen_Decatur

Stephen Hawkins's God: http://www.pbs.org/faithandreasons/intro/cosmohaw-body.html

Stress Statistics: The *New York Daily News* of October 25, 2007, page 8.

Switzerland: http://en.wikipedia.org/wiki/Switzerland

Terri Schiavo: http://en.wikipedia.org/wiki/Government_involvement_in_the_Terri_Schiavo_case

The Militant: http://www.the militant.com/2008/725050.html

Truth and Reconciliations Commission: http://.polity.org.za/polity/govdocs/commissions/1998/trc/2chap1.html

Value: Webster's New Deal Dictionary, 3 and 8 (b)

WASP: http://en.wikipedia.org/wiki/White_Anglo_Saxon-Protestant

Webb, Jeffrey B. (2005). *The Complete Idiot's Guide to Exploring God.* Alpha Books, Penguin Group (New York, USA).

What Are Considered Natural Causes of Death? http://wiki.answers.com/Q/What_are_considered_natural_caus es_of_death

What Really Happens after Death? http://www.gnmagazine.org/afterdeath/?S=2&gclid=CP3WppHy9zkCFRAMDQodOzIAQg

When a Man Dies: http://www.orlandobible.org/dawn/dies.aspx

Who Is Ron Paul? http://www.house.gov/paul/bio.shtml

William James: http://en.wikipedia.org/wiki/William_James

Youth with a Mission (YWAM): http://en.wikipedia.org/wiki/New_Life_Church_shooting